BEYOND GREAT

BEYOND GREAT

Nine Strategies *for* Thriving *in an* Era *of* Social Tension, Economic Nationalism, *and* Technological Revolution

Arindam Bhattacharya
Nikolaus Lang • Jim Hemerling

NICHOLAS BREALEY
PUBLISHING

London • Boston

First published in the United States in 2020 by Public Affairs, an imprint
of Perseus Books, LLC, a subsidiary of Hachette Book Group, Inc.

First published in Great Britain by Nicholas Brealey Publishing in 2020
An imprint of John Murray Press
A division of Hodder & Stoughton Ltd,
An Hachette UK company

1

A CIP catalogue record for this title is available from the British Library

Hardback ISBN 978 1 529 34139 3
eBook ISBN 978 1 529 34141 6

Printed and bound in Great Britain by Clays Ltd, Elcograf S.p.A.

John Murray Press policy is to use papers that are natural, renewable and
recyclable products and made from wood grown in sustainable forests.
The logging and manufacturing processes are expected to conform
to the environmental regulations of the country of origin.

John Murray Press
Carmelite House
50 Victoria Embankment
London EC4Y 0DZ

Nicholas Brealey Publishing
Hachette Book Group
Market Place, Center 53, State Street
Boston, MA 02109, USA

www.nicholasbrealey.com

We dedicate Beyond Great *to our families:*

Arindam: To my wife, Sujata, and our sons, Ishaan and Dhiman
Nikolaus: To my wife, Miriam, and our children, Juliane,
Johanna, and Jakob
Jim: To my wife, Nicola, and our four sons, Nicholas, Christian,
Mitchell, and Alexander

CONTENTS

FOREWORD

How will you navigate these uncertain times? What strategies will you deploy to build an enduring legacy? Throughout its history, Boston Consulting Group (BCG) has helped companies around the world build and retain advantage to achieve top performance. This book continues in that tradition, offering a look ahead at how businesses will thrive in the coming years. As leaders know, the business environment has been changing rapidly for some time, and the mindsets and approaches that have long helped companies become and stay great no longer suffice. The choices facing leaders in setting strategy, deploying capital, building capabilities, optimizing execution, and creating a winning team are dynamic and complex and offer greater risks and returns.

Not surprisingly, against this backdrop, most leaders we speak with are looking for frameworks illustrated with real-life examples that can help guide these choices and shine a light on what will define success for the decade ahead. *Beyond Great* aims to address this need, providing a comprehensive playbook leaders can deploy to help companies thrive in a new, more tumultuous era of social tension, economic nationalism, and technological revolution.

After years of intensive research with leaders across industries and geographies and by leveraging BCG's extensive client work around the world, Arindam Bhattacharya, Nikolaus Lang, and Jim Hemerling have synthesized a set of nine fundamental strategies that leading-edge companies around the world are deploying to become more responsive, sustainable, successful, and resilient amid volatility. I trust you'll be every bit as fascinated as I was to delve into the strategies, spot connections between them, and discover how companies are implementing them in the real world to deliver outstanding value to all stakeholders. You'll be fascinated, too, to find that most of the companies going beyond great are not the large, relatively young digital companies that garner so much attention, but real-world incumbent firms in industries such as manufacturing, agriculture, consumer products, technology, and financial and IT services. Any company in any industry can use the wisdom contained in this book to take themselves *beyond*, enhancing their capacity to thrive and grow in the decade ahead. And as the authors also point out, any leader can cultivate practices that will help drive the transformation skills and mindset required to go *beyond*.

On top of the already rapid changes in recent years, the COVID-19 pandemic and resulting macroeconomic shock add another level of stress and challenge to navigating the years ahead. For most companies, the pressures will be even greater, and degrees of freedom will feel more constrained. But as we face this new reality, there are two essential elements we must remember. First, difficult environments have historically proven to be more fertile periods for innovating and shifting competitive positions. Second, early indications are that the current environment is acting to pull forward the underlying trends of recent years: faster shifts in consumer online behavior and new ways of working, increased emphasis on resilience and scrutiny of business behavior toward all its stakeholders, and heightened societal and geopolitical pressures.

This suggests that the strategies in *Beyond Great* are not nice-to-haves to be deferred for when times get better but more urgent priorities to accelerate. As illustrated throughout the book, companies that have adopted elements of the playbook presented here have pioneered industry-making value propositions, leveraged technology to reengineer their operations, and turned formerly stagnant organizations into powerhouses of dynamism and innovation. In the process, they've accelerated value creation and enhanced their resilience. As daunting as it might be, our current era is no time to behave timidly. It's a time to gain inspiration, forge your own strategies, and lead the way forward. Leaders have long conceived *great* as a worthy ambition. You and your company have it in you to go *beyond*.

I wish you the very best on this exciting journey.

Rich Lesser
CEO, Boston Consulting Group
June 2020

BEYOND GREAT

INTRODUCTION

GREAT IS NO LONGER GOOD ENOUGH

You're an executive at a large manufacturing company, and after enjoying years of growth, you've now got a serious problem on your hands. A global health crisis has broken out, and government authorities overseas have shut down one of your key parts suppliers, preventing its plants from operating. Your supplier won't even pick up the phone. In your highly efficient, just-in-time global supply chain, you lack an alternate source for these parts. Your inventories are running down, and when they're gone, your production lines will stop. If that stoppage lasts for weeks instead of a few days, its financial effects could be catastrophic, wiping out your entire year's profits. What do you do?

Many companies experienced such a scenario in 2020, when the COVID-19 crisis shut down large swaths of the global economy. Although exceedingly rare, such shocks to the system seem to have become more common than they once were—just consider the SARS or H1N1 outbreaks, or economic shocks like the 2008 financial crisis, or political shocks like Brexit. Well before the COVID pandemic, Marc Bitzer, then chief operating officer and now chief executive officer of the durables manufacturer Whirlpool, remarked to us that the global economy had entered a new era, what he called "torn times."[1] Referencing recent political developments around the world, he noted that firms now faced tough strategic questions such as where to locate plants, whether to shift facilities between continents to circumvent uncertainty around border taxes, and whether to abandon global strategies altogether, since doing business in some formerly attractive countries had become too difficult and risky. But, Bitzer said, our more volatile world also presented great opportunity for companies, especially those that excelled at

1

understanding global consumer trends. "Even in our supposedly 'boring' industry," he said, "the growth of digital connectivity has made the pace of consumer convergence just stunning."

More than volatility itself, what these crises seem to highlight is the inadequacy of business strategies that companies have long deployed in order to prosper. During the latter part of the twentieth century, the world's greatest, most admired companies endeavored to deliver outstanding total shareholder returns, or TSR.[2] They did so by selling differentiated products and services, operating at scale and with great efficiency, and optimizing themselves to win within a global system that afforded clear rules and predictable outcomes thanks to trade liberalization and the growth of multilateralism. Today, those customer value propositions and operational and organizational strategies aimed at generating scale and efficiency no longer suffice to produce outstanding TSR, much less sustain them over time. In 1965, the average public company residing on the S&P 500 index stayed parked there for a generation—some thirty-three years. By 2016, the average S&P 500 tenure had shrunk to twenty-four years.[3] Likewise, as Boston Consulting Group (BCG) research has found, the life spans of public companies are shrinking—from about sixty years in 1970 to less than forty in 2010.[4] CEO tenures are shrinking too.[5] The gap separating top- and bottom-performing companies is increasing, and companies that are delivering strong TSR are finding it harder to sustain them.[6]

Peering inside today's increasingly vulnerable companies, local or global, we find an array of challenges that prevent them from delivering sustained, outstanding shareholder returns in a volatile age, much less having a positive impact across society. Leaders are pushing outdated value propositions that customers don't want. They're retaining unwieldy, profit-eroding global footprints, even though local competition and economic nationalism in some high-growth markets pose vexing new challenges. They feel hamstrung by internal processes and culture that prevent them from understanding fast-changing customers and building long-term relationships that deliver on customers' needs. They're struggling with traditional people practices that prevent them from attracting, inspiring, and retaining the best innovators, engineers, data scientists, and digital marketers. On top of it all, leaders face demands from governments, communities, customers, and employees to operate more sustainably and responsibly. As our CEO, Rich Lesser, put it, "COVID-19 has served to dramatically accelerate global trends and pressures and has brought the future forward." Leaders sense the performance bar for companies has transformed and that the legacy business models that worked so well for so long won't suffice in the years ahead. They know they need a new playbook of winning strategies, especially in the post-COVID context, but they aren't sure what exactly it should include.

Going Beyond *Great*

A few companies have begun to forge a new path forward, pioneering strategies designed to help them adapt to this new era and become resilient. As these leading-edge firms realize, it's no longer enough to deliver great performance by selling differentiated products and services. Companies must go *beyond* and offer customized solutions that deliver outcomes and experiences that delight customers. It's also no longer enough for customers to maintain the most cost-efficient network of delivery centers and production plants. They must go *beyond* and develop a network flexible enough to deal with sudden disruptions and changes in the rules (for instance, sudden tariff increases or visa restrictions on movement of people) and to adjust quickly to changing customer needs. Companies have to go beyond the twentieth-century definition of *great* in terms of their growth strategies, operating models, and organizational structures, building new twenty-first-century forms of advantage.

But leading-edge firms are going *beyond great* in a second sense, redefining the very notion of outstanding performance. Shareholder returns remain a core standard for these companies, but they're pursuing these returns with a new sense of purpose, aiming to make a difference not only to shareholders but to *all* stakeholders, including customers, employees, local communities, governments, and the natural environment. These leading-edge companies recognize that the clearest path to long-term, sustained, top-rung TSR amid volatility is to reimagine growth, operations, and the organization in ways that foster resilience and also deliver impact for all stakeholders. And so they're adopting a new playbook of strategies to thrive over the long term, become more resilient in the face of unforeseen challenges and shocks, *and* be more responsive to societal and environmental needs.

You might presume these leading-edge firms are the hot digital companies that dominate the media—the Googles, Netflixes, and Alibabas of this world—and that traditional, big incumbents are uniformly lagging behind. This is actually not the case. No industry is more old-fashioned than agriculture, and yet the venerable company John Deere is reinventing it, pioneering new data-intensive offerings and reconfiguring itself internally to deliver them. Industry leaders such as PepsiCo and Mastercard have likewise adopted new purposes and supportive strategies to win, with PepsiCo transforming itself to thrive sustainably and responsibly and Mastercard positioning itself to compete with nimble fintech companies disrupting the financial services industry. Tata Consultancy Services (TCS), the Indian software services firm, has undertaken a series of wide-ranging transformations to stay ahead of change and become a full-scale strategic partner for its customers. All four of these firms have created and sustained enormous value not just for shareholders but for all stakeholders.

Of these companies, the case of TCS seems especially intriguing given its historical trajectory. Founded in 1968 as part of the Tata Group and having quickly established itself as a global company, TCS grew rapidly during the late twentieth century by competing on the basis of scale, cost advantage, automation, a focus on developing intellectual property, and a lean service factory model the company had pioneered. By 2001, TCS had become a *great* company by the traditional definition, realizing margins of close to 30 percent on $690 million in revenues.[7] TCS should have been hard hit by the global financial crisis and its aftermath, especially given the slowing of economic growth in India and other emerging markets relative to developed ones and the erosion of the company's scale advantage generated by its industrialized model of software service delivery. And yet the company has thrived, not because TCS doubled down on the strategies that had made it great but because its leaders sought out new ones. Over the past two decades, the company has repeatedly transformed itself to keep pace with dramatic changes in the external environment and to render itself more flexible and resilient. The fruits of this effort were particularly visible in 2020, when TCS was able to continue operating with minimal disruptions during the COVID-19 pandemic.

In particular, TCS has redefined its relationships with customers, offering a wide portfolio of services that incorporate the latest technologies, irrespective of where in the world customers are located.[8] It has transformed the offshore, cost-advantaged, large-scale delivery network it pioneered, embracing a new, more flexible global delivery model that includes mid- and high-cost facilities located closer to customers in developed markets, all connected via the cloud. This new delivery network gives customers more cost-related options from which to choose, and it also lowers risk—because if problems arise in one geography, the whole network will still remain intact. TCS has also "servitized" its offerings; instead of providing a single type of service, it delivers customized solutions that involve a complete range of technologies and address specific business outcomes. All along, TCS has aggressively pursued a multistakeholder view of this business, leveraging the company's world-class technological skills to effect change in local communities around the world. Although in this last respect TCS has stayed ahead of the times, it has also returned to its roots. As Tata Group founder Jamsetji N. Tata observed during the mid-nineteenth century, "In a free enterprise, the community is not just another stakeholder in business, but is in fact the very purpose of its existence."[9]

TCS's ongoing and varied transformation efforts, coupled with its overarching determination to contribute positively to society, have allowed the firm to deliver and sustain outstanding value for shareholders. Between 2009 and 2020, the company's market capitalization surged more than tenfold, reaching a peak of over $120 billion. By 2020, TCS had one of the largest market capitalizations of any global IT services firm, in the same league as IBM and Accenture despite much lower revenues.[10] To sustain great performance amid volatility, TCS has pushed beyond traditional strategies to become more resilient and benefit a wider group of stakeholders. "We say growth is the source of all our energy," N. Chandrasekaran (now Tata Group's chairman) has remarked. "Each of the [company's business] units is focused on the right kind of growth: of revenue, profits, knowledge, people, and deeper relationship with customers. For us growth is holistic, not uni-dimensional."[11]

Digital companies may have been early to dispense with strategies that have traditionally benefitted incumbents, but the sustained success of companies like TCS, John Deere, and Mastercard suggests that in this new era of volatility, the playing field between incumbents and digital newcomers is far more level than it once was. Across industries, select incumbents are fighting back, learning from digital firms how to leverage new technologies and innovating strategies that they can layer on top of their existing practices to make the most of their size and create new forms of advantage. Siemens, Philips, Nokia: all are transforming themselves in ways that build more resilience and improve profitability while also allowing them to respond better to social and environmental needs. Diverse companies in the retail, financial services, and consumer sectors have done similarly. How precisely are these firms managing to embrace and increasingly master the challenges of these torn times while so many others haven't? What are their successful strategies? And how can you begin to adapt similar strategies for your own company?

Three Forces That Are Changing the World

In 2016, we came across an article at the World Economic Forum claiming that "globalization is dead" and that global business had "crossed over the edge of the map into *terra incognita*."[12] To us this was a shocking contention, given that in many places around the world business executives were still feeling quite bullish about globalization and global growth. Curious about what had really changed and what hadn't, as well as about whether some leading-edge companies were getting ahead of this shift, we launched a research study of dozens of companies, interviewing executives and probing their growth strategies and the operational measures they were taking.

As we saw then, globalization was neither dead nor dying. When it came to cross-border data flows, the number of international tourists, or even the amount of remittances sent back home by foreign workers, global integration was actually accelerating. But the rules of the game had changed radically, and turbulence had increased, creating threats but also enormous new opportunities. Some global companies were thriving because their leaders were alert to the opportunities and pushing their organizations to adapt and become more resilient. Many others were more passive, clinging to conventional strategies and approaches that weren't as effective as they had once been.

Based on this research, we identified *three fundamental forces* that were (and are) transforming the very nature of global business as we have come to know it over the past 150 years. Each of these forces embodied one or more long-standing historical trends that had unfolded across the domains of technology, society, politics, health, and the environment.

The first force is social tension triggered by two distinct but related shifts: the worsening of the strain on our natural ecosystem and the rising discontent with capitalism and the resulting inequality. A century and a half of industrialization have badly depleted our natural world and its resources, leading to climate change, rampant pollution, the loss of biodiversity, and any number of attendant human health crises. Whereas citizens have long perceived protection of the natural environment as government's role, now they demand that companies take aggressive action. But that's not all they demand. Rising inequality in many countries has fueled widespread skepticism about capitalism among employees, activist shareholders, and others. Calls are mounting from customers and employees for companies to go beyond maximizing shareholder value to deliver clear social benefits.[13]

The second force transforming the global business environment is rising economic nationalism and the ongoing erosion of US hegemony. Although the United States remains singularly powerful in economic, military, and technological terms, China's contribution to global GDP has tripled since 2000. The rise of the intense competition between these two countries impacts not just their economies but the world's. Growing mistrust and retaliatory actions between the United States and China, particularly in the wake of the pandemic, render global geopolitics much more complex and volatile. While in recent decades it appeared that emerging markets would achieve GDP parity with developed markets on the back of quicker growth (what some economists have called the "great convergence"[14]), that hasn't happened. Although COVID-19 has wreaked havoc on developed economies, over the last decade, the growth of developing economies has collectively slowed while that of developed economies has quickened.[15] Asian economies have grown more quickly than the world as a whole, even as growth in countries like Turkey and Brazil, which prior to the global financial crisis boasted rapidly expanding economies, has become more volatile. Within countries, we see inequality increasing and certain industries and segments of the population prospering more than others. For these reasons, companies today must search for industry-specific pockets of growth within individual countries rather than merely seeking to expand writ large in developing countries.

Intensified economic nationalism has also accelerated the decline in the multilateralism that arose in response to World War II. Between 2012 and 2017, the number of protectionist actions undertaken by the United States almost doubled (and is continuing to rise), and most other economies saw increases in such actions.[16] In 2009, about 20 percent of exports from G20 countries were "affected by trade distortions," while in 2017, over 50 percent of them were.[17] Across the world, national identity has taken on new importance and is increasingly influencing consumer behavior—a trend that some commentators refer to as tribalism. In Western societies, rising inequality has likewise spurred on nationalism, with large segments of society feeling themselves victimized by globalization because of stagnating real wages and the loss of classic high-paying manufacturing jobs. As a result, multilateral processes and institutions are waning, and progress in negotiating new multilateral trade agreements has slowed. In one 2018 survey of global supply chains, about one-third cited protectionist policies as, in the words of a journalist, a "major challenge."[18] This challenge will only deepen as COVID-19 further intensifies nationalistic sentiment.

The third and final force rewriting the rules of global business is a technological revolution fueled by the exponential growth of global data and digital technologies. Data flows across countries are doubling every two years, belying any claim of globalization's demise and rendering the online world increasingly borderless.[19] By 2019, the value of global e-commerce, both across borders and within countries, was almost twice that of the trade in physical goods—about $42 trillion as opposed to $24 trillion.[20]

The increasing use of Internet of Things (IoT) technologies in particular is transforming the economics of manufacturing, the nature of work inside plants, and the way companies can deliver value to customers, a transformation accelerated by health-related restrictions on the physical movement of people. Digital connectivity has also led to the emergence of a new global consumer. Reaching customers used to be about delivering goods to them across the geographic divide, but with digital technologies, companies can increasingly deliver services and experiences to customers irrespective of their location—a trend that became more pronounced during the COVID-19 pandemic as a great deal of consumption moved in home. Meanwhile, digital commerce is producing a leveling out of consumer behavior and expectations across borders. Consumers in places like India and China expect quality products and services, timely delivery, an online ordering capability, and responsiveness to their evolving needs, just as consumers in developed economies do.

Nine Strategies for Going Beyond Great

Collectively, these three forces are transforming the global landscape, scrambling the traditional playbook leaders have long used to compete. A new era is indeed upon us—one that over the coming decades will surely evolve further. An abiding feature of this new era is volatility driven by more frequent disruptive shocks to markets and the global economic system. Companies must now contend with an increased number of powerful weather events thanks to climate degradation, faster technological obsolescence and cybersecurity risks due to our reliance on new digital technologies, sudden trade tariffs and nontariff barriers spawning from economic nationalism, and rapidly shifting consumer behavior in response to a tweet or Facebook post from an obscure corner of the world. The three forces are also leaving companies more prone to traditional shocks such as financial or economic collapse, geopolitical conflicts, and health pandemics. Greater global connectedness means that risks are not just more complex but more rapidly spread, as we've seen with the COVID-19 pandemic. As we write this, the Cboe Volatility Index, or VIX—the "fear gauge," as it's known—has reached its peak since the financial crisis,[21] rising on March 18, 2020, to a high of 85.47.[22]

And yet, as volatile and uncertain as the world has become, these three forces have also created enormous opportunities for incumbents to build new forms of advantage. Established firms can deliver strong shareholder returns by leveraging technology to build new, resilient business models, all while generating immense societal benefits. With governments failing to address the enormous threats to society and the natural ecosystem, communities, employees, governments, and, increasingly, shareholders are asking companies to step up and do more. In 2019, the Business Roundtable, an organization representing the CEOs of the largest US companies, released a "statement on the purpose of a corporation" that placed the generation of shareholder value last on a list of five dimensions of purpose, behind "delivering value to our customers," "investing in our employees," "dealing fairly and ethically with our suppliers," and "supporting the communities in which we work."[23] As we documented in our research, leading-edge companies are embracing such concepts of purpose while taking steps to build more responsiveness and resiliency into their growth strategies, operations, and organizations. A good example among many is PepsiCo, which in recent years has aggressively pursued a strategy called Performance with Purpose. PepsiCo isn't abandoning wholesale its old value propositions, supply chains, talent-management strategies, or organizational structures, and neither are other purpose-driven companies. Rather, they're retaining them where appropriate but also building on top of them a new set of strategies that will enable them to wield new forms of advantage, boost resilience, and unleash sustained value for their stakeholders—in other words, that will enable them to go, increasingly, *beyond great.*

Analyzing company actions as well as numerous interviews we've done with leaders and other stakeholders, we've found that executives at these successful leading-edge firms are quietly "liquefying" the organization, as one senior manager told us. That is, they're building fluid, flexible, and nimble organizations capable of adapting to and exploiting shifting consumer needs, regulatory regimes, economic conditions, and technologies. They're delivering incredible new solutions and experiences, in many cases attaching them to physical products. They're rethinking which elements of their global operations they centralize to retain or build scale advantage and which they deepen or build locally to help make the whole system more responsive and resilient. They're building far-flung networks of partners, learning to collaborate remotely. They're developing strong local identities in local markets to conform to public sentiment and government requirements. They're embedding a concern for people, planet, and communities deeply into their growth strategies, rendering their companies more purposeful and mobilizing their organizations' greatest skills and competencies to address pressing societal and environmental problems. At the same time, leaders are keeping many parts of their old strategies, global supply chains, and competencies intact. In effect, the most successful and dynamic global companies out there are becoming dual enterprises capable of doing two things at once—marrying the new and the old, the liquid and the solid, the lowest cost and the highest speed, efficiency and resiliency. The most successful leaders are those who fully embrace this mindset of ambiguity, contradiction, openness, and perpetual change while also keeping one foot firmly planted in the past.

As the features of our new era of volatility became clearer to us; as the emergence of a new, more ambitious standard of performance became undeniable; and as we observed leading-edge companies building new forms of advantage, we redoubled our research efforts. Our aim was to understand and codify the actions and approaches that would enable companies to meet or exceed the performance bar in the decades ahead. Over several years, our team developed dozens of case studies, evaluated extensive BCG quantitative data, performed extensive secondary research, and conducted several hundred additional interviews with senior business leaders.

Perhaps not surprisingly, we concluded that no single silver-bullet strategy existed to help companies go beyond great. Rather, it was a constellation of strategies adopted by companies and tailored to their specific industries and competitive situations that would yield success. Scrutinizing our research findings and drawing insights as well from our extensive BCG client work, we distilled *nine key strategies* and a set of leadership imperatives that would yield the sustained high-performance companies of tomorrow. Collectively, these strategies touched every part of the enterprise, from its value propositions to the global supply chains to the firm's pursuit of its commitments to its people and its stakeholders. A beyond great company has to do the following:

- **Reimagine its core operations to deliver societal impact and hence long-term, sustained TSR rather than regarding social impact as an activity apart from the core.** Firms that can thoughtfully integrate *doing good* into their core strategies and operations will deliver sustained high shareholder returns while positively impacting all stakeholders.
- **Offer compelling digital solutions and experiences, not just physical products or services.** Today's leading-edge companies are taking complete ownership of outcomes and experiences for customers. Leveraging digital technologies, they're going deep into the usage life cycle to fulfill unmet needs, either grafting new solutions onto physical products and services or replacing physical products and services entirely.
- **Grow selectively (that is, where they can claim profitable market share) and in ways suitable for the local environment, not everywhere all at once.** Leading-edge firms are using asset-light, digital, or e-commerce-centric business models to enter into new markets and expand rapidly. They're also becoming more selective about which markets to enter and paradoxically deepening their engagement in their chosen markets.
- **Supplement traditional value chains with dynamic new value webs that can create and deliver solutions, outcomes, and experiences that customers crave.** These value webs or ecosystems have received a great deal

of publicity. But as leading-edge companies are discovering, some ecosystems work better than others.

- **Invest in high-tech, multilocal factories and delivery centers that, combined with low-cost capacities, can deliver customized offerings *fast*.** Today's delivery models must be high speed, responsive, and resilient in the face of disruptions, in addition to low cost.
- **Build a global data architecture and analytical capabilities to underpin the other eight strategies.** Leading-edge companies regard global data as the precious fuel that not only predicts future performance or consumer behavior but also drives winning value propositions.
- **Move away from the traditional matrix organizational model in favor of agile customer-focused teams supported by platform capabilities.** Bureaucracy and distance from the customer are death in an age of volatility—and today's leading-edge firms know it.
- **Acquire, retrain, inspire, and empower a digitally savvy, engaged workforce.** Companies today must attend more closely to what a new generation of employees wants and needs. They must fundamentally shift how they find, inspire, and develop a twenty-first-century workforce.
- **Embrace always-on transformation instead of traditional one-and-done change initiatives.** This strategy is essential for succeeding with the other eight. To compete and win in volatile, rapidly evolving business environments, global companies must become adept at pursuing multiple transformations on an ongoing basis.

No single company we studied was embracing all these strategies. Some were pursuing three or four, and a select few were pursuing five or more. Taken to its logical conclusion, each one of these strategies (facilitated by the leadership imperatives described at the end of the book) entails a profound transformation of the enterprise. Collectively, they lead to the enterprise's wholesale reimagining, making firms more responsive and resilient in the face of much greater volatility and capable of positively impacting a broader set of stakeholders. Ultimately, they comprise the foundation for global success in the twenty-first century, a comprehensive playbook that any firm, local or global, can deploy to grow beyond great.

Beyond Great

Deliver outstanding benefits to all stakeholders (including shareholders)

Build advantage with customized solutions and experiences, resilience, and agility (along with smart scale and efficiency)

Refine Your Global Game

Stream It, Don't Ship It

Let the Data Run Through It

Do Good, Grow Beyond

Flex How You Make It

Embrace Always-On Transformation

Growing Beyond

Engineer an Ecosystem

Thrive with Talent

Operating Beyond

Get Focused, Fast, and Flat

Organizing Beyond

Nine Strategies to Go Beyond

Great

Generate outstanding shareholder value

Build advantage from Scale (via standardized products) and Efficiency

About This Book

As we developed our research, we knew we had something important on our hands: an approach corporate leaders, entrepreneurs, and others interested in global business could adopt to make sense of contemporary markets and chart a sensible path ahead. If your organization is constantly playing catch-up and you personally feel uncertain about how to get ahead of change, this book can help. If your company is thriving, you can use *Beyond Great* to position it for even greater success and resilience in the years ahead. Drawing on BCG quantitative analyses, as well as firsthand stories of transformation from companies like Tata Consultancy Services, Natura, Siemens, Adobe, John Deere, Microsoft, Nike, and many more, we'll lay out our nine strategies, revealing how today's most successful global companies dazzle consumers, attract and engage employees, improve entire communities, sustain and improve our fragile planet, and generate high growth and returns. Recognizing the difficulty of these tasks, we'll round out the book by reflecting on the specific leadership traits and mindsets leaders should cultivate to help them and their companies make the journey beyond great.

Throughout this book, readers will encounter certain themes and related questions that run across the nine strategies. They'll find, for instance, that companies striving to go beyond great are constantly in the position of balancing the local with the global. Which capabilities, processes, and teams should they develop locally and which globally? How should they operate across geographies that might confront them with widely varying and uncertain rules? Likewise, companies moving beyond great no longer regard technology as merely a tool to improve performance or processes but rather as a critical new factor of production. How can they incorporate technology into the enterprise so that it informs every operational activity, just as a company's land, labor, or intellectual property might? Further, how can they make their firms bionic, seamlessly and ubiquitously merging humans and technology? Companies going beyond great seek to engage in balanced ways with all stakeholders. What does this look like in practice? How can companies make sure they really do treat their people well? Finally, and most importantly, what operational and organizational changes can firms make to improve resilience? Such questions usually defy easy answers, but as we'll see, they do serve as a spur to creativity, innovation, and, ultimately, better responses to volatility. In the years ahead, the ability to answer them consistently and well will make up the DNA of the firms that most successfully go beyond.

We understand how challenging the emerging geopolitical shifts, technological transformations, and social tensions are for leaders and managers. But our research has taught us what it takes to master the torrent of change. Millions of businesspeople have long sought to grow their businesses into *great* companies. But in our era of unprecedented disruption and complexity, traditional strategies—which essentially helped leaders to sell more products, wring more efficiencies from global organizations, and reward their shareholders—no longer apply as well as they once did. Ultimately, you must reimagine the global enterprise all over again, but like the forward-thinking leaders described in this book, you must also adopt a new kind of discipline, the ability to show openness, flexibility, and light-footedness—to aggressively deploy new strategies and operational norms without throwing out existing ones entirely. You must become adept at handling ambiguity and contradiction, multiplicity and nuance, and you must master a whole new set of rules about what it takes to be an advantaged and resilient firm.

The really good news is that you don't need to make these changes all at once. Join us in taking the first steps beyond great, imagining new possibilities and beginning to implement some of them in your organization. If you map out a long-term journey and pursue it diligently, you'll find that these torn times, while challenging, also create a set of opportunities—not just for your investors but also for your customers, employees, and the communities in which you operate. Embrace the strategies in this book not just to survive but to thrive, not just to please but to delight and inspire, not just to profit but to heal and improve. In the decades ahead, the old formulas for being a great company will no longer suffice. We must each discover what *beyond great* means for our organization. Hopefully, this book can provide you with a strong foundation for making this journey.

PART I
GROWING BEYOND

CHAPTER 1

DO GOOD, GROW BEYOND

With climate risks and inequality increasing, employees, civil society, and governments are demanding more of companies. Firms that can integrate doing good *into their core operations will not only positively impact these stakeholders but also deliver higher long-term shareholder returns.*

Several years ago, the vice chairman of a US-based global industrial company related to us how governments embracing protectionist policies were now obliging firms like his to invest in their countries if they wanted access to their markets. His firm's existing strategies, which sought to maximize profits by exporting Western products into developing markets, would no longer suffice in an age of economic nationalism. His firm and others like it would have to take their role as corporate citizens in local markets far more seriously than they had in the past, reorienting their strategies to deliver a broader social purpose as well as profits. Otherwise, they would jeopardize their future growth. "There is nothing wrong," he said, "with governments . . . asking us what we are doing to further their countries' development. We have to earn the 'license to operate and grow' in these markets."

Positively impacting *all* stakeholders (including governments, regulators, communities, customers, employees, and the environment) is the right thing to do in a world of growing inequality and climate risk. But pursuing a purpose and delivering societal impact to multiple stakeholders isn't just a matter of altruism or righteousness. In many countries and industries, it's a prerequisite for retaining a license to operate. And, more than that, it's emerging as a powerful core business strategy for companies seeking to sustain high performance in a volatile era. Integrate a concern for societal impact into your core strategies and operations, and you can create new levers of advantage that directly improve long-term profitability. Unfortunately, many global leaders haven't yet internalized these possibilities. As accepting as they might be of multi-stakeholder models, they haven't embraced these models fully to reinvent mindsets, strategies, and operational norms. They continue to limit their firms' involvement to their traditional corporate social responsibility (CSR) efforts, convinced that doing good for all stakeholders would mean sacrificing shareholder returns—something they're loath to do.

> Global leaders are increasingly breaking from this constraining logic, delivering impressive total shareholder returns (TSR) even as they build businesses that positively impact all stakeholders. In updating their mindsets, strategies, and operations, these leaders are attending to total societal impact (TSI), defined by our BCG colleagues as "the total benefit to society from a company's products, services, operations, core capabilities, and activities."[1]

Antonio Luiz Seabra, visionary founder of the Brazilian cosmetic giant Natura, is one such innovative leader. When he started Natura in 1969, he was pursuing a purpose that, as Andrea Álvares, Natura's chief brand, innovation, international, and sustainability officer, told us, transcended a concern for profits.[2] Seabra sought to use cosmetics as a means of promoting healthy connections among individuals, society, and the natural world—what the company calls *bem estar bem*, or "well-being well."[3] This social purpose, derived from Seabra's philosophical belief in the interconnectedness of all things, permeates Natura's business strategies and operations to this day.[4]

Consider, for instance, Natura's distribution strategy. Initially operating out of a small storefront in São Paolo, the company by the mid-1970s developed a direct-sales model similar to what Avon had created in the United States. But for Natura, direct sales wasn't just another distribution option. Rather, it was, as Álvares notes, "born from an understanding that relationships are one of the strongest, most valuable things." Natura's army of female sales consultants formed close bonds with consumers, and the company in turn formed uniquely deep, meaningful bonds with the consultants, energizing them as a salesforce. By 2019, some 1.8 million consultants were selling Natura products (as were hundreds of company and franchisee stores, and online channels).[5]

Natura didn't just throw these consultants into the market and ask them to sell. Recognizing that they tended to hail from low- and middle-income families,[6] the company provided them with extensive skills training in business and personal development. Together with valuable work experience, this training empowered consultants to become entrepreneurs in their communities and more effective advocates on the company's behalf.[7] For many of the consultants, the association with Natura proved transformative, allowing them to pay for shelter, schooling for their children, and more.[8] Consultants in turn became strong brand ambassadors and advocates, helping Natura build strong and lasting relationships with consumers. They also helped make the company more resilient. During the 1980s, when high inflation besieged the Brazilian economy and department stores and other traditional cosmetics distributors closed, Natura's business exploded, experiencing annual growth of more than 40 percent for the decade, thanks to its direct-sales distribution model.[9]

As its company name suggests, protection of the environment was another key expression of Natura's founding purpose. The company began focusing on sustainable development during the early 1980s, long before the practice became fashionable. Today, that focus permeates every part of Natura's operating model. The company has a complete leadership and organizational structure focused on sustainability and publishes an annual environmental profit-and-loss statement alongside its financials.[10] In 2011, it debuted its Amazônia program bent on "promoting new sustainable business based on science, innovation, production chains and local entrepreneurship."[11] The initiative included an innovation center in the Amazon, expansion of sustainable production, and the creation of collaborative sustainable development projects.

Natura's emphasis on sustainability has long extended to its product and brand strategy. In 1983, the company became an early adopter of refill packages, lowering the company's carbon footprint while also enabling lower costs and better customer loyalty. In 1995, Natura launched a line of products whose profits were all donated to help provide quality public education to Brazilians. In 2000, the company launched a line of products, Ekos, that made use of recyclable packaging and biodiverse ingredients. In 2013, Natura launched its Sou line of products, whose value chain was optimized for efficient resource usage and whose brand identity centered on the idea that consumption can be socially conscious so long as products are designed with the environment in mind. The company's products are also completely animal-cruelty-free and, as mentioned, carbon neutral.[12] Further, Natura's branding openly invites consumers to partake of conscious consumption. In 2019, for instance, Natura adopted the positioning slogan "When you care, you create beauty," evoking the importance of diversity, animal welfare, and environmental stewardship.[13]

Natura's production model has supported its broader efforts to build stronger communities and to protect the planet. Sourcing naturally extracted product ingredients from local communities, Natura invests back into those communities, aiming to keep them intact and thriving. By 2019, the company was working with more than five thousand small producers in the Amazon, collaborating on sustainable business models and protecting about 4.5 million acres of rain forest. As part of its production strategy, Natura has invested about $1.8 billion since 2011 into local Amazonian ventures.[14] The company has also helped found the Union for Ethical BioTrade, an organization that seeks to maintain biodiversity and a fair split of benefits with local communities, and since 2010 has spent over $370 million studying cosmetics derived from plants and establishing production capacity, creating, as Natura's cofounder Guilherme Leal put it, "entirely new value chains that simply did not exist before."[15]

In the words of Keyvan Macedo, the company's sustainability manager, Natura believes that "we could use the social and environmental challenges in society and create new business opportunities—not just business, but sustainable business."[16] Incredibly, Natura has been carbon neutral since 2007, and it was only the second company in the world to develop a methodology for monetizing its carbon emissions.[17] "We measure environmental impact along the entire value chain," Álvares explained. "We innovate our products to reduce emissions, reuse materials. For whatever we can't fully offset, we use carbon credits that also have a social impact."[18] One carbon offset program, for instance, removed 3.2 million tons of carbon emissions from the environment while also impacting fifteen thousand families and creating two thousand jobs. For its efforts, the company has received the United Nations Champions of the Earth recognition and the Global Climate Action Award, among many others.

Natura's business success has allowed it to extend its societal impact initiatives far beyond sustainability and women's empowerment. The company has programs in place to address other important social issues, such as access to health care, access to education, and freedom from gender violence. The millions of sales consultants play an important role, partnering with their communities on relevant local causes.[19] "There are a series of things we do to give back," Álvares said, "and we have found ways to monetize that social impact for the society." In fact, as the company has calculated, it has generated 31 Brazilian reals of value for society for every real invested in the Natura Carbon Neutral Program.[20] In 2014, Natura became the first public company to achieve status as a B Corp,[21] a designation awarded to firms "that meet the highest standards of verified social and environmental performance, public transparency, and legal accountability to balance profit and purpose."[22] This was a huge accomplishment for an organization of Natura's size.

Today, as Roberto Marques, Natura &Co chairman and chief executive of the group, told us, total societal impact "permeates the way the company thinks and operates." He added that societal impact has been a "competitive advantage for so many years" and that it remains even more so today given the concern of younger generations for sustainability. The company's purpose and societal concerns have come to define the firm's brand and reputation among communities, governments, consumers, and investors. It has also helped Natura in its aggressive program of global expansion fueled by acquisitions, including Aesop (2016), the Body Shop (2017), and Avon (2020). Since all these firms have missions or purposes consistent with Natura's, integrating them has been that much easier for the company. Natura has also become a magnet for young employees and has built a strong leadership corps, with executives joining Natura to work for a company with similar beliefs in a sustainable business model.[23]

Natura's purpose-driven operational model has benefited shareholders as well as society and the environment. Between May 2004 and September 2019, the company's valuation increased by a factor of approximately fifteen, between two and three times as much as the Brazil 50 index average. The company has also outperformed other large global beauty companies like L'Oréal, Estée Lauder, and Shiseido, its share price increasing by nearly twice as much as Estée Lauder, the second-best performer in this peer group.[24] All told, Natura is an impressive example of a company that has managed to grow beyond great by endeavoring to do good.

Your company has likely taken important steps to address pressing social and environmental problems, but how far have you transformed your core strategies to deliver social impact in addition to profits? As Lord Mark Malloch-Brown, chairman of the Business and Sustainable Development Commission, remarked, "There's . . . a realm of difference [between] those who are trying to make sustainability part of their core business strategy and those who still see it as an 'add-on.'"[25] Leading-edge companies understand this difference and are reshaping strategy and operations to pursue social and environmental goals without sacrificing profits. They're not only becoming more environmentally sustainable, more responsive to local governments and communities, and more supportive of employees and suppliers. Like Natura, they're leveraging these efforts to open new levers of advantage and long-term profitable growth.

Their precise strategies vary. Our analysis of high-performing and socially responsible firms has uncovered three distinct strategic pathways firms are using to benefit the wider society and deliver sustainable benefits for shareholders. Each socially responsible pathway enables firms to gain a distinct business advantage, such as the chance to tap new markets and customer segments, galvanize employees to innovate, or forge more productive and collaborative relationships with local government and communities. Let's examine these different pathways that combine TSI and TSR, focusing on three marquee firms from around the world. But first, let's understand a bit better why societal impact has become such an essential strategy for global firms.

The Push for Total Societal Impact (TSI)

During the late twentieth century, most leaders of global companies felt obliged to serve one master above others: investors. The game, they thought, was to maximize returns to shareholders, and they left it to governments and nongovernmental organizations (NGOs) to solve global warming, poverty, water scarcity, and other abiding societal problems.

The economist Milton Friedman justified this view, writing, "There is one and only one social responsibility of business—to use its resources and engage in activities designed to increase its profits."[26] In line with this philosophy, many companies channeled a portion of their profits to fund CSR initiatives—that charitable action felt good to leaders, and it was good for the brand. Yet CSR was always thought of as "the '*poor cousin*' of the business world," as one CEO has noted, even as the need to address environmental, social, and corporate governance (ESG) goals mounted.[27]

Today, companies and leaders know they can no longer sit on the sidelines when it comes to social and environmental issues. Problems like climate change, inequality, and pandemics are worsening, requiring action beyond what government alone can manage and fueling public demands for business to take responsibility and show leadership. As Roberto Marques told us, "If the world dies, we won't have a business."[28]

Stakeholders also have more power than ever to hold individual firms accountable for taking action. With the democratization of media, the public enjoys unprecedented access to immediate and reliable information about companies, their operations, and their impacts. Standards, metrics, and data relating to ESG issues are becoming more plentiful and reliable. In 2018, 86 percent of the S&P 500 included data about their sustainability performance in their annual reports.[29] Reporting on ESG performance was becoming an industry in itself, estimated to be worth over $400 million by 2020.[30] Even more information about companies will become available in the years ahead. In 2018, investors representing $5 trillion in assets requested that the US government require public companies to disclose standard ESG measures relevant to their businesses.[31] That same year, Chinese regulators announced that, by 2020, listed companies in that country would also have to disclose data on ESG performance.[32]

In our age of transparency and mounting global crises, consumers no longer simply seek a satisfying product, service, or experience from companies with whom they do business. They expect that companies will minimize their negative impacts on society and the environment and even contribute solutions to pressing problems. Research shows that a strong majority of consumers around the world make purchasing decisions based on societal or environmental considerations.[33] Politics play a role, as consumers are becoming increasingly polarized and eager to express themselves via their buying choices. One survey found almost a third of Generation Z consumers globally have refused to do business with a brand they regarded as unsustainable, while in the United States over 90 percent of millennials would leave brands that didn't advocate for a cause for ones that did.[34] Over three-quarters of Americans indicated they would express their displeasure with a brand whose stances clashed with their beliefs by boycotting the brand.[35]

These shifts translate into actual business results. When Indra Nooyi took over as PepsiCo's CEO in 2006, the company and its peers were facing consumer concerns around the health effects of carbonated beverages, rising demands for a "soda tax" by activists, and questions around the sustainability of its production processes (including its water usage). Determined to reinvent the company and deliver positive benefits to all stakeholders, Nooyi in 2006 introduced a new vision for the company called Performance with Purpose (PwP), which integrated sustainability and purpose into the company's core operations. As Nooyi remarked, the strategy reflected a recognition that "our success—and the success of the communities we serve and the wider world—are inextricably bound together."[36]

To bring PwP to life, the company pursued a strategy aimed at delivering top-tier performance for all its stakeholders by focusing on three pillars: "Improving the products we sell, operating responsibly to protect our planet, and empowering people around the world."[37] PepsiCo made its existing products healthier (eliminating excessive sugars, saturated fats, and sodium while removing trans fats entirely) and built a portfolio of healthy products. It hired its first chief scientific officer to help it focus on improving current products and drive its investments in new products. To operate more responsibly, the company launched a sustainable farming program (SFP) designed to make farming more productive and profitable for growers, reduce farming's impact on the planet, and support the rights of farm workers. To empower its people, the company started PepsiCo University, with online courses that helped associates upskill, and it also placed a greater focus on ensuring the diversity of its workforce.[38]

These efforts have yielded tremendous benefits for all stakeholders, including shareholders. By 2016, "good for you" and "better for you" products accounted for about 50 percent of the company's revenues, up from 38 percent a decade earlier.[39] By 2018, PepsiCo sourced over half of its crops directly from farmers in the SFP, and by 2016 its water usage in its legacy operations had become 25 percent more efficient.[40] The company also greatly improved the diversity of its workforce, with women holding 40 percent of its global managerial positions in 2018.[41] All these social benefits have accompanied similarly impressive financial performance. Between 2006 and 2017 (Nooyi's last full year as CEO), PepsiCo's TSR was nearly double that of the S&P 500.[42] Since taking over from Nooyi in 2018, PepsiCo's new CEO, Ramon Laguarta, has built on this strategy, further elevating a sustainability agenda by articulating a vision of Winning with Purpose.[43]

Governments and local communities are also expecting more from companies in exchange for the right to operate. Recognizing that government bodies at all levels can't bring about a more sustainable future on their own, elected leaders, officials, and activists are looking to business to fill in the gap. "Governments must take the lead with decisive steps," former UN secretary-general Ban Ki-moon has said. "At the same time, businesses can provide essential solutions and resources that put our world on a more sustainable path."[44] Governments in emerging markets such as India and China have long run more tightly regulated economies based in part on the belief that businesses must operate on society's behalf. (India, for instance, was the first country to mandate that companies invest in CSR.)[45] Enterprises seeking to grow in these and other markets will have to respond to local governments' concerns and demands, demonstrating their commitment to impact society in positive ways. Doing so makes enterprises more resilient, especially if they operate in industries like mining, oil and gas, and pharmaceuticals, which are heavily regulated or otherwise susceptible to strong government or community pressures.

Employees and investors seek more from companies too. Top talent is gravitating toward firms that share their eagerness to make a difference. In one survey, 92 percent of entry-level employees and students indicated their desire to work for an environmentally conscious company.[46] Investors likewise are clamoring for more sustainable strategies from companies. One survey found that 80 percent of investors make values-based decisions when picking where to channel capital.[47]

Evidence is mounting that companies that pursue sustainable business strategies deliver superior returns. Funds of sustainable companies are less volatile than those of traditional companies, with 20 percent less market-value deviation on the downside.[48] A study spanning the years 2009–2018 found that a company's commitment to social impact seemed to be correlated with higher valuation, lowered volatility, and improved returns.[49] And another review found that in 80 percent of cases, a multistakeholder approach boosted companies' stock prices.[50] Because of investor demand, pursuit of a broader social purpose is increasingly helping companies gain access to capital. In recent years, the CEOs of many leading investment firms have expressed their intentions to pursue sustainable investing strategies. Pressure from investors is poised to become even more intense. "Over time," Blackrock CEO Larry Fink wrote in his much-read 2020 letter to CEOs, "companies and countries that do not respond to stakeholders and address sustainability risks will encounter growing skepticism from the markets, and in turn, a higher cost of capital. Companies and countries that champion transparency and demonstrate their responsiveness to stakeholders, by contrast, will attract investment more effectively, including higher-quality, more patient capital."[51]

Our BCG colleagues estimate that by 2023, $45 trillion will flow into socially responsible assets.[52] The larger private equity firms have created targeted funds related to sustainability and social impact, including KKR's Global Impact Fund, TPG's Rise Fund, and Bain Capital's Double Impact Fund. Other companies are unveiling new ESG investment funds, adding an ESG dimension to existing funds (by refusing to invest in noncomplying companies and becoming more active as investors), and counseling clients on how to integrate ESG into their broader portfolios.

Three Pathways to Delivering TSI and TSR

Leading-edge companies implementing TSI as a strategy are now asking not just how each decision, asset, or business process will help generate profits but also how each will benefit communities and society at large. And yet delivering societal impact can remain disconnected from core operations unless leaders understand it holistically, linking and tracking its effects on the enterprise's operations and performance just as leaders do to maximize TSR. Recognizing this, our BCG colleagues have conceived of TSI as a carefully constructed and evolving set of strategies and

The six dimensions of total societal impact map to the UN's SDGs[1]

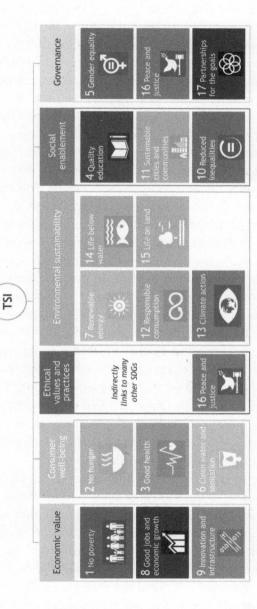

1. Sustainable Development Goals
Source: UN Sustainable Development, BCG analysis

Figure 1. Mapping the six dimensions of TSI to the UN Sustainable Development Goals.

related metrics across six key areas: (1) economic value, (2) consumer well-being, (3) ethical values and principles, (4) environmental sustainability, (5) social enablement, and (6) governance. As the chart on the previous page shows, these six areas map onto the United Nations' key sustainable development goals. Strategies and metrics for these six areas will vary depending on a company's industry and the impact area in question. As our BCG colleagues have pointed out, companies will find it easier to measure TSI in some areas than in others.[53]

Used alongside TSR when formulating corporate strategy, TSI captures the sum total of effects an enterprise's operations and offerings have on the outside world. To connect TSR strategy to TSI, leaders must think through each of the six areas to determine how they can most accurately measure the operational benefits and harms their companies have on society and the environment. Next, leaders should locate the biggest challenges that threaten the firm's future existence and growth, connect these challenges to the firm's core competencies and offerings, and identify tangible and intangible impacts of the firm's strategy. Leaders should also apply a TSI lens when making decisions about strategy, operations, and resource allocation, seeking to maximize the net positive society impact they are having across the six dimensions. As leaders arrive at these TSI strategies, they can also distill from them a defining purpose or reason for being around which the entire organization can rally—not just a mission statement but an animating reason for being. "The most powerful—and most challenging—way to enhance TSI is to leverage the core business, an approach that yields scalable and sustainable initiatives," our BCG colleagues observed. "If well executed, this approach enhances TSR over the long term by reducing the risk of negative events and opening up new opportunities."[54]

The specific models companies will adopt via an evaluation of TSI vary widely across industries and even within them. Nevertheless, our research has revealed three distinct pathways that leading socially responsible companies are following, either singly or in combination, to deliver their net societal impact while also realizing exceptional growth and shareholder value. These pathways are not the only ones that will garner firms a winning business advantage by pursuing TSI, but they are among the most effective and promising approaches we encountered in our research. Let's take a look at each in turn.

*Pathway #1: Build New Business Models That Make Innovative
Products and Services More Widely Available*

Companies can dramatically improve the welfare of local communities or embolden environmental sustainability efforts by endeavoring to make their products and services more readily available
to customers who might otherwise not enjoy access and by using
their innovation engines to support marginalized individuals and
communities.

A great example here is Mastercard. The company had made a significant commitment to delivering social benefits since its initial public
offering in 2006. Upon becoming CEO in 2010, Ajay Singh Banga intensified and scaled these efforts. As a matter of principle, Banga believed
leaders needed to abandon their narrow fixation on shareholders in favor
of a systemic awareness. "Businesses are part of the global ecosystem,"
he has remarked. "And ecosystems, by definition, require balance and
diversity. They also require a point of view larger than oneself and longer
than the immediate future. They require an understanding that we are
stronger as a connected whole than as isolated actors."[55] It is vital that
these efforts be commercially sustainable and scalable, and at Mastercard
there is a focus to make "doing well by doing good" business as usual.

Banga and other leaders wanted to see Mastercard use its core businesses to promote and benefit from social impact, not simply deliver it
peripherally via philanthropic initiatives. And the way to do that was to
broaden Mastercard's presence in developing countries. As leaders saw it,
the company had an opportunity to help underserved populations gain
access to financial services and digital solutions so that they could create
wealth, help build their local economies, and digitally connect to ecosystems and marketplaces. Over time, these marginalized segments of society could potentially spawn new customers for Mastercard, fueling the
company's growth. "Our core business is building the digital infrastructure to give people access to business and commerce," said Tara Nathan,
EVP of humanitarian and development sectors. "We now ask how we
can extend the same core capabilities to the marginalized segments and
population."[56]

The company's new TSI strategy had an even stronger business logic to it. Fintech companies exploded during the 2010s, and their mobile payment solutions threatened to disrupt traditional credit card firms.[57] Additionally, Mastercard was becoming increasingly aware of the economic and social benefits of creating inclusive cashless economies. In response to these realities, Mastercard sought not merely to develop leading-edge digital payment solutions but to pilot and actively market those solutions in new markets, especially developing countries. Banks were often scarce in these markets, leaving consumers bereft of access to financial services and cut off from the digital economy. Like its peers, Mastercard believed these consumers would leapfrog traditional financial products and services and move directly to digital solutions. The company innovated to deliver these new digital solutions, partnering with governments and NGOs to gain access to new consumer pools as they emerged. This would allow the company to build up trust and brand recognition and gain an edge over competitors while delivering significant benefits to these underserved communities.

Mastercard had previously launched its Mastercard Foundation, an independent organization created with a gift of shares in 2006, in hopes of serving as "A Force for Good" and with a special focus on projects in Africa.[58] To realize its new TSI strategy under Banga, Mastercard has gone further and created the Mastercard Strategic Growth division as a vehicle for driving forward commercially sustainable social impact efforts, built around inclusive growth initiatives, novel business models, and innovative partnerships. This division encompasses a range of business units linked to areas such as government engagement, humanitarian and development programs, donation platforms, and enterprise partnerships. As part of these efforts, in 2018 Mastercard established the Center for Inclusive Growth to oversee its corporate sustainability, data for good, and corporate philanthropy activities. The company subsequently committed $500 million to the center (with the first $100 million granted in 2018). As Tara Nathan told us, the emphasis was no longer on simply writing a check, as it had been in the past. "We began to hear more ideas about creating mobile apps or payment technologies—and it piqued our interest . . . It became obvious that we could help design the right solution for the context and desired outcome."[59]

Mastercard has additionally sought to embed sustainable innovation into its core businesses rather than relegating it to a detached philanthropic endeavor. For example, the company committed to "connect 500 million individuals with financial services" and to cutting its greenhouse gas emissions by one-fifth by 2025.[60] Leaders got behind these social impact goals, giving teams across the company permission to experiment with new markets, emerging technologies, and alternate key performance indicators (KPIs), knowing well that the company might not see a return on its investments immediately.

In Uganda, the company partnered with the Ministry of Education and UNICEF to launch a mobile platform called Kupaa. The platform has allowed more than one hundred thousand parents and guardians to make secure tuition payments remotely in small increments instead of as lump sum payments as traditionally required. Beyond rendering it more economically feasible for children to attend school, the platform allows schools to manage payments efficiently and to track teacher attendance and other performance indicators, giving governments more data to use during decision-making.[61]

In East Africa, Mastercard partnered with the Gates Foundation to establish the Mastercard Lab for Financial Inclusion, which focuses on designing, testing, and ultimately scaling new products that support marginalized communities. One of its innovations was a platform called Mastercard Farmers Network, which connects smallholder farmers with buyers. Accessed via smartphone, the app allows farmers more access to market information, empowering them when negotiating and selling their production. By using the platform, farmers can also build a digital financial history, which will help them in the future to secure financing and participate in the formal economy. Farmers can access the platform at no cost, and Mastercard makes this a commercially viable business by charging other actors in the agricultural ecosystem that benefit from improved knowledge and connection to smallholder farmers.[62]

Other innovation projects in recent years have included a technology platform that supported South Africa's Social Security Agency to make disbursements to low-income consumers and a platform that allowed a network of NGOs to distribute aid to needy populations in remote areas that lacked conventional infrastructure.[63] As of early 2020, the company achieved its goal of bringing more than five hundred million hitherto financially excluded individuals into the digital economy. Now, Mastercard is going *beyond*—to extend financial inclusion to a total of one billion people by 2025 and to enable an additional fifty million micro and small merchants to connect to the digital economy.[64]

Mastercard's efforts to help millions of consumers access financial services have enhanced its core business performance, allowing the company to tap into new large high-growth markets and to gain valuable insights into how best to serve emerging consumer groups. It has also helped the company build new partnerships with governments and NGOs and across various industries within the private sector while enhancing brand recognition and reputation. An added benefit: the new markets Mastercard has tapped are often countercyclical, affording the company more resilience in the face of economic downturns elsewhere in the world. As Mastercard's reputation has soared, top talent has flocked to its doors, energized by the company's social purpose (Nathan estimated that about 60 to 70 percent of its new hires chose the company on account of its social impact).[65] In a 2019 Great Place to Work study, 93 percent of Mastercard's employees agreed with the statement "I feel good about the ways we contribute to the community," and an equal percentage agreed with the statement "I'm proud to tell others I work here."[66] Shareholders have benefitted handsomely. Between 2010 and 2019, Mastercard's average total shareholder return rose by 37 percent annually, far outpacing its peers, which delivered only a 14 percent average annual increase, and the S&P 500 (a 9 percent increase).[67] In 2019, *Fortune* ranked Banga among its top ten businesspeople of the year, noting that "Mastercard has emerged as a poster child for how legacy players in financial services can embrace and adapt to a rapidly evolving environment."[68]

Mastercard's externally facing TSI strategy, delivered through its core operations and teams, has set the stage for growth by unlocking future markets and customer segments even as it delivers huge impacts to segments of society that lacked access to banking. But the strategy does require patience and buy-in on the part of senior leadership, in particular a recognition that sustainable initiatives might require more time to mature and yield benefits than traditional businesses would. As Tara Nathan told us, "You have to have the intestinal fortitude to be in it for the long term. You have to have patience. This is very difficult for quarterly earning companies. You have to actually understand the ROI of the investment you are making. ROI is there; you have to be willing to see it."[69]

Pathway #2: Embed Societal Needs into Internal Processes and Functions to Deliver Impact

Some companies are actively embedding societal impact into key internal functions. For example, some companies actively scan for societal challenges as part of their innovation process and then develop new winning products to help meet them.

Consider Omron, the Japanese manufacturing company. Like Natura, Omron was conceived with social purpose, as well as profit, firmly in mind. As founder Kazuma Tateishi remarked, "A company shouldn't be just about pursuing profits . . . it has an obligation to serve society."[70] Today, the company's leadership regards society as the firm's primary customer and societal issues as the primary drivers of revenue and innovation. This philosophy is enshrined as one of the company's core values—"innovation driven by social needs"—and in the company's longtime mission, "to improve lives and contribute to a better society."[71]

But such inspiring formulations aren't mere window dressing at Omron. As leaders told us, societal impact has dramatically influenced its internal innovations processes, from the top of the organization on down. Leaders discuss societal impact at all strategy meetings in the context of growth and new business development. In particular, Omron has defined four areas of social impact where the company might spur innovation: factory automation, health care, social systems, and mechanical components. In each domain, product and innovation teams scan the market for unmet customer needs and underlying social challenges, and then they design products to fill those needs and address the challenges. Using a methodology grounded in an awareness of the connections between science, technology, and society, the company sifts through the social challenges it uncovers, identifying the most relevant ones that Omron can address via its core technical competencies. Further, in its hiring processes, the company seeks out diverse talent that subscribes to its social mission and has the skills required to help it identify and solve societal challenges.

To help Japanese society adapt to an aging population, for instance, Omron pioneered the first-ever automated ticket-gate system for use in rail stations.[72] Such a system has rendered travel easier for older people and minimizes labor inside the stations, which is increasingly in short supply. It also relieved rush-hour crowds, which had been a concern in Japan, and more recently was adapted to help parents keep track of children who were using public transportation.[73] Omron has a long history of delivering socially inspired innovations such as this. Development of various dimensions of the automated train station occurred over a period of decades. Other such innovations include an automated traffic signal (designed during the 1960s to keep roads safer and less congested) and an at-home blood-pressure-monitoring system (designed during the 1970s to help patients spend more time outside hospitals).[74]

Omron's internal approach to realizing its purpose has conferred substantial reputational gains to the company. In 2019, Omron ranked thirtieth on the Best Japan Brands list, up from thirty-ninth the previous year, and was designated a 2019 Health & Productivity Stock Selection, an honor that marked the company's successful entry into that market. Between 2009 and 2019, the company also delivered returns that were twice as high as the Nikkei 225 index. Still, with financial performance lagging behind major international competitors, leaders as of this writing are focusing on better translating its strong TSI performance into higher shareholder returns.

Pathway #3: Partner with Local Governments to Create More Economic Opportunities for Local Communities

Large companies, especially those operating in highly regulated industries and in emerging markets, have long pursued strong CSR programs. They built schools and hospitals, ran nutrition programs, and helped out in times of crisis. Today, stakeholders and local communities are rightly demanding more, and leading-edge companies are stepping up to respond. Bringing their extensive financial and managerial capabilities to bear, they're partnering with communities, governments, NGOs, academic institutions, and other stakeholders to spur economic development in local communities.

The global mining giant Anglo American plc has in recent years embraced such a strategy. In recent decades, the firm had worked closely with governments in South Africa (where it has maintained a presence for over a century) to define its social contract and contributions to local communities. However, like all global mining companies, Anglo American was being asked to do more—by local communities, environmental activists, governments, and investors. Stakeholders wanted the firm to go beyond productivity and financial resilience and deliver on areas such as sustainability and climate change. Anglo American realized it needed to move proactively to sustain its long-term license to operate and grow.

Instead of going on the defensive or just tweaking its CSR strategy, Anglo American chose to radically reimagine itself. Adopting a TSI-driven lens, the company adopted a business model that centered around serving local communities by partnering with them as well as governments, regulators, and other key external stakeholders. The strategy was aimed at delivering not just societal benefits but also business advantage. In 2018, the company adopted a new corporate purpose: "Re-imagine mining to improve people's lives." To deliver on this purpose, the company has adopted a sustainable mining program that includes innovative social, technological, and sustainability elements, or as the company calls it, FutureSmart Mining.

This strategy has two parts. First, by deploying new technologies, the company seeks to reduce the environmental impact it has when extracting natural resources. Second, it wants to build thriving communities by engaging with them in new ways, most notably by creating more economic opportunities independent of its core mining activities. To this end, the company has been collaborating with the government, community representatives, academic institutions, faith groups, businesses, NGOs, and academics to identify opportunities for economic development and to plan future regional growth independent from the company's traditional mining operations. When Anglo American makes local investments as part of its obligations, it does so with a holistic understanding of the community's development needs. When building a road to one of its facilities, for instance, the company might extend it to open up ecotourism opportunities. Or it might look at land use opportunities based on scientific spatial analysis data to help understand what agricultural activities might best allow a local area to flourish. Instead of raising cattle, for instance, land might be used to cultivate crops used in producing biodiesel, which the mine and other users could then purchase.

Anglo American is also investing in upskilling the local workforce to keep pace with new technologies and in the education of young people to ensure that they'll possess the skills they need in the future. Although Anglo American will also benefit from a better-trained workforce, the job training it funds goes beyond the needs of its supply chain. Through its actions, the company seeks to build a local community that is strong and thriving in its own right.[75] Relatedly, the company is fostering ongoing dialogue around commitments and responsibilities at the national and local levels, ironing out disagreements and building new trust-based relationships. As Froydis Cameron-Johansson, group head of international and government relations, told us, "One of the things a twenty-first-century enterprise needs to do is be a partner much more so than a dictate to its ecosystem. TSI, for Anglo American, is a way of thinking that is part of our DNA and something that can only be done through partnership, humility, and listening."[76]

Although it's too soon to understand the full impact that FutureSmart Mining is having, early indications are positive. The company has seen improvements in safety, sustainability, and its ability to foster more diverse social relationships and partnerships. Speaking of FutureSmart Mining, technical director Tony O'Neill noted that investors are "awake to it now. I think it is still in the early stages of the story, but they can see what we are doing and the ambition behind it. Ultimately, it will result in a different investment profile, or more investors because of it."[77] As Froydis Cameron-Johansson suggested, understanding full-impact decision-making would quite obviously benefit the company and its shareholders. "If you're working in an environment and your community is not happy," she said, "that's going to mean production losses for you very, very quickly." On the other hand, collaborating to benefit the broader community environmentally and economically would yield gains for everybody. Speaking of the company's collaborative regional development initiative, she described the potential as follows: "You win; I win; together we superwin, and it becomes 'our win.'"[78] Given the uncertainties inherent in public opinion, the ability to create a "super-our-win" makes the firm more resilient, protecting it against the risks that public dissatisfaction can produce (and that mining companies have often experienced) and strengthening its license to operate.

Advice for Leaders

The imperative to do good and deliver TSI, not as a CSR effort but as a core business imperative, is gaining unprecedented traction among global companies and leaders. "We're seeing a momentum picking up in terms of the private sector taking climate action," former Unilever CEO Paul Polman observed. "This race to make your business models more robust, better fit for the future, is definitely happening."[79] A 2019 YPO Global Leadership Survey of more than 2,200 CEOs from 110 countries found that almost all—93 percent—subscribed to a multi-stakeholder view of the purpose of business.[80] A 2019 ING Research survey of 300 US executives found that 85 percent were taking societal impact and sustainability into account when forging strategies, up from 48 percent the year before.[81]

And yet such positive signs still haven't translated into broad action on the part of most global companies. Companies "publicly communicate [their] commitment to corporate responsibility," a 2017 UN Global Compact Survey found, but many companies still don't set clear targets, track performance against those targets, and assess the impact their operations are actually having.[82]

Has your organization woven TSI into its strategies and operations as fully as it might? If not, that's the first thing you must do—and fast. Pressures on businesses by stakeholders to look beyond shareholder value will intensify dramatically in the years ahead as the climate crisis deepens, demands from countries and communities intensify, and younger generations become more vocal in their desires for sustainable business. Already, entire industries are struggling with rising threats to their license to operate. Big Tech is a case in point: Google, Facebook, Amazon, and other large technology companies have faced loud calls for government regulation in recent years. As an observer noted in the *Atlantic*, "The backlash against Big Tech has accelerated at a dizzying pace."[83] And yet certain companies in the sector are taking strong action in line with an evolved TSI mindset and seeing tremendous benefits. Under CEO

Satya Nadella, Microsoft has embraced the mission "to empower every person and every organization on the planet to achieve more."[84] In line with that, the company has committed itself to become carbon negative by 2030 and to remove all the carbon it has emitted since its founding by 2050.[85] Microsoft is also partnering with governments to solve a variety of social challenges, leveraging the company's financial resources, technologies, and AI capabilities. Thanks to these and other purpose-driven moves, Microsoft has seen a remarkable run of value creation in recent years, as we'll discuss later in this book.

Most companies' slow deployment of strategies that deliver both TSI and bottom-line impact spells opportunity for your enterprise, just as it has for the companies described in this chapter. Execution won't be easy, especially if you operate in a cultural context in which an ethic of shareholder value maximization has been most strongly entrenched (in the United States, for instance, this ethic has historically taken root more deeply than in Japan and other Asian contexts). As you ponder how to imbue your social impact efforts with new focus and energy, consider the following questions:

- Has senior leadership, including the CEO and the executive team, taken responsibility for discovering, articulating, activating, and embedding social purpose deeply throughout the organization?
- Have you constructed a narrative about TSI that aligns with the company's overall business strategy and that internal and external stakeholders (including customers, employees, shareholders, suppliers, and society more broadly) find credible?
- How might you establish partnerships to magnify the impact of your TSI endeavors?
- When operationalizing TSI strategies, what trade-offs will you have to make in order to elevate TSI to traditional drivers of business value? What practices will have to change to drive TSI impact, and at what cost?
- What metrics can your company choose to convey your business's impact while still protecting your reputation?
- How are you aligning your incentives to ensure that everyone in the company is rewarded for delivering TSI?
- How will your company balance its short- and long-term commitments and make the inevitable trade-offs?

It's important you proceed thoughtfully, taking a TSI lens to all elements of your business strategy, including products, supply chains, marketing, and employee engagement, and also using TSI to inform your relationships with governments, regulators, and other external stakeholders. From there, focus on how you can leverage your capabilities—financial, technical, and people—to have the greatest positive societal impact, as that in turn will help build advantage for your business. Passionately engage investors, customers, and the general public by developing a compelling business case as well as an authentic story to tell about your TSI efforts. Explain to internal and external stakeholders what choices you have made and why, backing up your decisions with investments and meaningful metrics. Finally, align compensation internally with achievement of TSI goals, thus ensuring that the new mindset of TSI will penetrate far down into the organization and its operations.[86]

Nineteenth-century American writer Henry David Thoreau once observed that "goodness is the only investment that never fails."[87] That maxim holds just as true for companies as it does for individuals. TSI represents a tremendous business opportunity—precisely because so many companies haven't yet mastered how to do it. More broadly, TSI represents a unique chance to help reimagine capitalism, for the benefit of the world, its peoples, future generations, and shareholders too. At the same time, it is only one of a number of avenues by which large global companies can transform themselves for the twenty-first century and become beyond great. The traditional model of the global enterprise requires an overhaul from top to bottom—strategically, operationally, and organizationally. Let's continue with our analysis of the growth strategies that firms must adopt to win in the years ahead. Once companies have secured their license to operate and positioned themselves well with a variety of stakeholders, their most urgent task is to think hard about customers, making sure their offerings really do speak to current customer needs and desires. As we'll see in the next chapter, the traditional product and service offerings companies developed during the twentieth century to spur profitable growth at scale are increasingly obsolete. Yesterday's companies grew by shipping massive volumes of physical products across vast distances to happy customers. Today's thriving incumbents are streaming innovative digital services on their way to profitable growth.

Key Insights

- To go beyond great, companies today must do good and maximize their TSI, a goal that over the long term will enable them to also grow shareholder returns.
- Your company has likely taken important steps to address pressing social and environmental problems, but how far have you really transformed your core strategies to maximize social impact?
- Our research has revealed three pathways that leading socially responsible companies are mobilizing, either singly or in combination, to maximize their net societal impact while also realizing exceptional growth and shareholder value. These are as follows: (1) expand access to your products and services, (2) let societal needs drive innovation, and (3) partner with local government to create economic opportunity.

CHAPTER 2

STREAM IT, DON'T SHIP IT

*Great companies have traditionally become so by selling superior
physical products and services to customers around the globe.
Today's leading-edge companies are going further, taking complete
ownership of outcomes and experiences for customers. Leveraging
digital technologies, they're going deep into the usage life cycle to fulfill
unmet needs, either grafting new solutions onto physical products and
services or replacing physical products and services entirely.*

Leading-edge global companies are rapidly evolving their value propositions, going *beyond* discrete product-oriented offerings to create
exciting new solutions that deliver outcomes on an ongoing basis across
the usage life cycle. Instead of engaging with customers in a transactional
way, they're becoming full-fledged partners, owning the customer's
experience and often charging for their new offerings based on their performance. They're delivering their new solutions digitally to connected
customers anywhere in the world, from anywhere in the world. Digital
connectivity, ubiquitous broadband availability, and Internet of Things
(IoT) technologies are driving the new offerings, making it technically
and economically feasible to deliver services across borders, either layered onto existing physical products or as purely digital offerings. As one
observer put it, "Technology is making service the new product."[1]

Companies are also developing servitized offerings in order to tap
into the new global customer that digital connectivity has created—a
customer defined not by geography but by membership in cross-border
affinity groups. Further, companies are increasingly personalizing these

offerings, allowing global consumers to download software upgrades and unlock certain features remotely and using data and advanced analytics to tailor experiences to each individual user. A final driver of the new digital or digitally based value propositions is economic nationalism. With tariffs and mounting trade wars making it riskier to build businesses around the cross-border shipment of physical goods, companies are finding it increasingly attractive to drive more profits using cross-border digital services. A country might erect tariffs on new cars, making imports more expensive and favoring domestic manufacturers, but a car manufacturer won't suffer in offering a suite of cross-border customer services delivered digitally based on data uploaded from the car. New-car sales may not grow, but digital services to the old car can— dramatically. In general, servitization makes companies more resilient. During the COVID-19 crisis, businesses built around physical products suffered as governments imposed social distancing. Netflix, Twitch, Peloton, and other digital-services businesses sustained or even increased their revenues.

Throughout most of the twentieth century and on into the twenty-first, companies in many categories staked their claim to global profits on physical products as well as the specific features they contained. Besting the competition meant selling goods that were better, cheaper, and higher quality than other comparable offerings. If you were in the car business, you won by offering more luxury, more reliability, a lower price, or some combination. If you manufactured jet engines, you offered better reliability, better performance, lower operating costs, or some combination. Global companies did sell services attached to these products, such as maintenance contracts, but these were often limited and clearly secondary.

> Today, leading-edge companies are selling a startling array of services layered onto their physical products, and in many cases, they're selling physical products as services.

Consider the durables category. For companies like Whirlpool, a washing machine is increasingly no longer just a washing machine— it's responsive, thoughtful, even "smart," serving as the hub for additional washing-related services companies might sell. Sensors in your cloud-connected Whirlpool washer might allow it to know when you're running low on detergent. Syncing with the app you can already use to control a whole range of appliances, your washer might tell the app to automatically reorder detergent for you. Before you run out, you might open up your front door to find new detergent waiting for you, sold to you and delivered on a subscription basis—*detergent as a service*.

As Whirlpool's former head of strategy Russell Stokes told us, the company is rolling out exciting new digital services delivered through its home appliances. "We've already begun to servitize our products, adding on a software layer," he said. "What if we could repair your dishwasher or download updates to you remotely over Wi-Fi? What if we could download recipes to you and display them on your oven?"[2] This is just the beginning: it's not hard to imagine a future in which appliances in the home or office reorder supplies or speak to one another to complete more complex tasks. In an interview, Whirlpool president and CEO Marc Bitzer reported that enhancing the company's products by layering on digital services was a key strategic imperative.[3] The company was continuing to put the infrastructure and relationships in place to do so, building a global data hub, acquiring some of the basic technologies required, and exploring partnerships with the likes of Google, Amazon, Proctor & Gamble, and others.

If you run a global business, you can't afford to ignore the array of new value propositions bursting onto the market. If you're selling doughnuts, the offering that takes your company beyond might be a new digitally enhanced café experience offered to like-minded doughnut enthusiasts around the world, or perhaps a daily morning delivery of doughnuts and coffee to each of your doughnut club members' cars or offices. If you're a women's fashion brand, maybe you provide a personal shopping experience based on unique styles and preferences via apps and in-store devices. In most categories, these new offerings won't shunt aside conventional products—companies will still need to make and sell delicious doughnuts, high-quality fashion, and, in Whirlpool's case, best-in-class appliances. But increasingly, the ability to deliver exciting and innovative digital offers in conjunction with these physical products will distinguish top players from everyone else. Yesterday's companies shipped their way into customers' hearts and wallets. Tomorrow's will ship *and* stream their way in.

Consuming Services

A number of companies are already shipping and streaming their way in. Total global trade in digital services grew twice as fast as nondigital over the decade starting in 2008.[4] In some categories, servitization has allowed digital upstarts to rapidly expand and take commanding positions on a global scale. Whereas consumers once watched filmed entertainment at home by renting physical DVDs from Blockbuster Video and similar stores, thanks to Netflix's digital service, they can enjoy it 24-7 wherever they live. Netflix launched its streaming service in 2007 and after refining it took the service international,[5] launching it in Canada in 2010 and then over the next two years in South America and Europe. By 2019, consumers in almost two hundred countries could enjoy movies with just a few clicks or taps on their devices, with company revenues topping $15 billion.[6] This breakneck global expansion is remarkable in itself—possibly the quickest in recent history. But equally noteworthy is the company's strategy of no longer targeting local consumers with physical products but rather targeting consumers across borders with a digital service accessible anywhere—a feat matched by competitors such as Hulu and Amazon Prime and, as we'll see later, by music-streaming services like Spotify, Pandora, and Apple Music.

Across consumer categories, we see value streams migrating away from physical products and toward digitally enabled services or solutions as part of the so-called sharing economy. Many consumers today no longer want to buy physical products—they'd rather pay for services on an ongoing basis. They're skipping the grocery store, hopping online to arrange for meal-delivery services from companies like Blue Apron. Rather than purchasing bikes, they're renting wheels by the trip from bike-share services like JUMP (in 2018, consumers took some eighty-four million trips on these services in the United States).[7] Although estimates of the size of the global sharing economy vary, forecasters anticipate massive growth in the sharing economy over the next several years—it could represent a $335 billion opportunity by 2025.[8] Another form of servitization—the offering of products via direct-to-consumer subscriptions—is also expanding. Today, consumers can go online and arrange for regular shipments of many consumer products via Amazon or hundreds of small start-ups, whether it's razors (via brands like Dollar Shave and Harry's), cosmetics (via Birch Box), contact lenses (Hubble), dog food (Chewy), fashion (Stitch Fix), dental supplies (Quip), or even sex toys (Maude). Direct-to-consumer services compete on price as well as convenience, allowing busy consumers to "set it and forget it," as one analyst has put it.[9]

In many consumer categories, servitization is disrupting large incumbents and forcing them to take swift action. The automotive industry, for instance, is rapidly retooling itself, shifting away from its traditional focus on building vehicles to focus on also offering digitally enabled *mobility as a service*, including connected-car offerings (roadside assistance, the ability to pay for items from the car dashboard, the ability to locate nearby parking spots, and so on), autonomous driving, and shared mobility (ride-sharing services like Uber and Lyft). As one news report slyly put it, "carmakers want you to stop buying cars, someday" and imagine a future in which "car payments and parking fees will be replaced by buying transportation by the mile on a subscription service similar to Netflix."[10] A number of structural conditions are contributing to this trend: legacy automakers are suffering from chronic global overcapacity; they're being challenged in key markets by local players like Great Wall Motors and Jiangling Motors in China, the world's largest car market, and Mahindra in India; and they're facing pressure from the new electric-vehicle players and digital companies like Tesla, Google, and Uber. These technology powerhouses, as one news report recently observed, "increasingly [appear] to be the greatest threat to [carmakers'] survival."[11]

In 2017, new-car sales accounted for $79 billion of the global industry's approximately $226 billion in profits, while mobility-services profits contributed less than $1 billion. By 2035, total profits are projected to increase to $380 billion, with connected-car and on-demand mobility accounting for $28 billion and $76 billion, respectively. Margins for data connectivity might be as high as 14 percent, while automakers are expected to lose money on every physical car they sell.[12] Major carmakers will grow and remain profitable, but only if they aggressively offer the digital services consumers crave, either by developing the technology themselves or, as we'll see in Chapter 3, developing successful ecosystems of partners that deliver these services. Carmakers will still have to build high-quality cars and trucks, but they'll have to surround these physical products with a layer of services that will dramatically increase the value they're providing.

Automotive profit pools expected to shift dramatically over next fifteen to twenty years

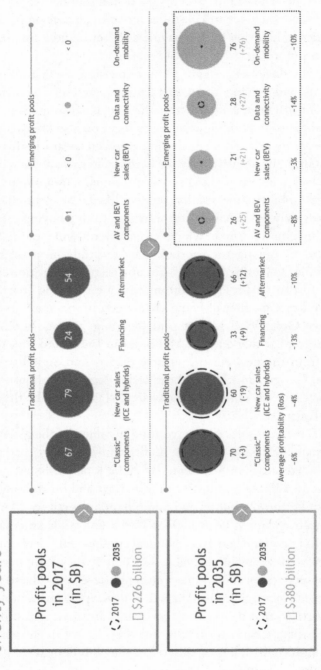

Figure 2. Shifts in automotive profit pools over the next fifteen to twenty years.
Source: "The Great Mobility Tech Race: Winning the Battle for Future Profits," Boston Consulting Group, January 11, 2018.

General Motors is aggressively preparing for the rise of mobility as a service. Under chairman and CEO Mary Barra, the company has been paring down the number of brands and platforms it maintains as well as the number of countries in which it operates, recognizing that, as GM executive Dan Ammann put it, "we can't be all things to all people in all places."[13] In 2018, GM announced its intention to undertake a wide-ranging transformation that would include the closure of eight plants globally, a 25 percent reduction in management head count, and a reconfiguring of the company's portfolio of brands and product platforms.[14] Meanwhile, the company has been investing heavily to develop a network of self-driving vehicles that would function as part of an integrated ride-sharing service. In 2016, it invested $500 million in the ride-sharing service Lyft in addition to acquiring the self-driving-car firm Cruise Automation.[15] In 2017, GM acquired Strobe, a company whose technology could prove critical to automated driving.[16] In 2018–2019, Honda and Softbank announced investments in Cruise totaling $5 billion.[17] Overall, the company seeks to lead in mobility services, where it has envisioned margins as high as 20 to 30 percent,[18] while also streamlining operations to squeeze more profits out of its core car and truck manufacturing operations. "It was once thought that Silicon Valley would devour the auto industry," one observer noted, "but now it appears to be trending toward mutual cooperation,"[19] all in an effort to turn what had been a physical product—a car—into a hub for cutting-edge services and experiences.

Servitization Is for Industrial Companies Too

In 2017, St. Antonius Hospital in the Netherlands became one of the first medical facilities on the planet to deploy Azurion, a state-of-the-art interventional platform manufactured by Philips for performing minimally invasive procedures.[20] The Azurion system looks like something straight out of *Star Trek*—a futuristic white arm moves around a patient lying on a long table while imaging results appear on a large high-definition screen and physicians perform procedures. At St. Antonius, as in other medical facilities around the world, patients were waiting longer than ever for their procedures, which in turn were becoming increasingly complex. The hospital bought Azurion hoping it could improve the functioning of its interventional labs while also keeping costs in check. More precisely, it bought into an ongoing *partnership* with Philips, including services that would allow St. Antonius to optimize its usage of the technology and achieve impressive performance gains.[21]

Upon delivering the new equipment, Philips developed a special curriculum to train team members on how to use Azurion. Once the system became operational, the company collected operational data continuously to see how medical teams might optimize the technology and its usage for this particular facility. For example, Philips combined data about the machine's operations with an analysis of the facility's physical space "to identify opportunities to optimize workflow around the interventional lab."[22] Some clinical space was going largely unused, so Philips and the hospital repurposed it for use by patients (as a waiting area) and physicians (as a work space where they could review documents and report on patient progress).[23]

Thanks in part to this and other collaborative work, the hospital slashed the time it took to prepare patients for procedures by 12 percent, the time it took to conduct the procedures themselves by 17 percent, and the number of patient procedures that ran over the allotted time by 25 percent.[24] As interventional radiologist Marco van Stijen noted, "We were able to change our workflow in such a way that we now can do more patients in a single day, resulting in more patients a week, resulting in more patients per year, with no compromise to patient safety or quality of care."[25] St. Antonius's then CFO Wout J. Adema credited an ongoing collaboration with Philips for his institution's successful introduction of the new equipment. "The success achieved was possible due to the deep and trusted partnership we have with Philips. The Azurion installation provided our interventional team the opportunity to evaluate our existing processes and standardize workflows. This helped us make tangible and significant operational improvements in the short-term, and fostered a continuous improvement culture amongst the team."[26]

Azurion typifies Philips's ongoing transition in recent years from a transactional business to one grounded in relationships and services. Rather than just selling equipment, the company also increasingly seeks to provide its customers with outcomes and solutions—to add value, not merely sell more volume. Philips aims to stay connected in real time to its customers, playing an ongoing role in helping them extract the maximum value from their technology investments. In its Aiming for Zero initiative, for instance, the company collaborates with customers to prevent equipment failures *before* they happen, monitoring data to make repairs and perform needed maintenance proactively. Mobilizing a data infrastructure and advanced analytics, a team of engineers monitors more than twelve thousand imaging systems each day, seeking patterns in the data that suggest that a given system needs preventative maintenance. Each year, this team initiates more than ten thousand maintenance actions to minimize downtime of Philips machinery.[27]

In providing such services, Philips is responding not merely to the broad disruptive forces described earlier but to specific changes in health care. Aging populations, the spread of chronic illness, and the explosion in costs are straining the finances and capabilities of health-care systems. What these systems increasingly need from providers isn't lower costs on individual pieces of equipment but a pricing model that helps systems and providers alike lower costs while improving quality and patient experiences. "Fifteen years ago, we would go into a radiology department to showcase the performance and features of our latest scanner," Philips chief technology officer Henk van Houten said. "These days a head of radiology may ask: how can you help my department become more efficient to meet growing patient demand?"[28] According to media reports, Philips is moving toward a value-based model in which it generates revenues based on performance metrics related to productivity, patient outcomes, caregiver experience, and so on.[29] Under such a model, the provision of ongoing services becomes essential, as it allows Philips to optimize its machines and how medical teams use them, for efficiencies and higher quality for health systems and more revenue for the company.

The transition of health care to a value-based model is still in its early stages. According to one survey, only a third of US hospitals are receiving reimbursements from insurers based on the value they provide.[30] Yet 35 percent of Philips's revenue derives from solutions, and this portion of revenues is growing by double digits.[31] These services and solutions take a number of forms, including the streamlining of how caregivers use patient data, strategic consulting, and the provision of a platform called HealthSuite that collects, compiles, and analyzes clinical data. As of 2019, the company was seeking to continue and broaden its "pivot to consultative customer partnerships and services business models."[32] To that end, Philips is seeking to move away from providing mere products and instead working to collaborate with its customers to create "integrated and connected platform solutions."[33] "We don't invest in anything unless there is clear co-creation with the customer and a clear value model," chief innovation and strategy officer Jeroen Tas said.[34]

> Although servitization in consumer markets gets more coverage in the popular press, industrial companies like Philips that sell to other businesses are increasingly embracing it as well.

Across industries, selling services holds a number of advantages. Notably, it allows firms to avoid being viewed as simply a commodity while saving customers the cost and hassle that come with owning a physical product. As the CEO of a Chinese wind-turbine company told us, customers today care less about a turbine's capacity, performance, and specifications. They want a solution that maximizes their wind farm's profitability based on their local area's specific wind profile. In many sectors, industrial customers today seek a profit solution, not a piece of equipment. Even when they buy a piece of equipment, they want suppliers to mobilize data and IoT technology to help them avoid parts failures before they happen and maximize the time equipment is operational. Servitization is also an attractive strategy because it affords industrial companies sources of recurring revenues—and profits. According to one report, nearly half of companies that are offering services "have seen an increase in their profit margins of over 20%."[35] Servitization also builds more resilient revenue streams. As a leader of an elevator company told us, new-elevator sales may slow depending on the economic cycle, but providing services for the old ones won't. In fact, downturns might prompt an increase in service-related revenues as customers delay replacing old elevators with new ones.

One of the earliest examples of an industrial company embracing a servitization model is Rolls-Royce. In addition to selling engines, Rolls-Royce also sells services to its customers priced on an hourly basis, receiving revenues for each hour the engine is available to run—what the company calls "power by the hour."[36] Although the customer still technically owns the engine, Rolls-Royce assumes all responsibility for its availability and stewardship. Offered as part of its TotalCare servitization program, power by the hour aligns the company's incentives with those of customers. Aviation customers seek reliability from jet engines, and they also hope to prefigure as accurately as possible what their operational costs will be. Under TotalCare, customers pay not for the engine's maintenance but for its uptime. Because they pay only per flying hour, they can know exactly what their operational costs will be—they pay only when the engine is operating and don't have to worry about the costs of unanticipated repairs.[37] Rolls-Royce earns more for itself if it minimizes its engines' downtimes and increases reliability, and it benefits from locking in long-term service contracts with its customers. As of 2020, TotalCare has reduced the time that engines are off-line for repairs by 25 percent, saving customers money while boosting Rolls-Royce's revenues.[38]

Power by the hour sounds simple, but it's by no means easy to deliver. Before TotalCare, customers would wait until problems developed in their engines, and then they'd contact Rolls-Royce and wait for the company's technicians to resolve the issue. Today, Rolls-Royce embeds digital sensors in its engines that monitor performance in real time and send data back across national borders to a centralized analytics facility in Derby, England. At any given moment, engineers at this facility are monitoring the performance of thousands of connected in-service engines worldwide, with the amount of data per flight reaching into the terabytes.[39] A global analytics team uses sophisticated algorithms to proactively plan maintenance or repair activity that minimizes disruption and determines inventory levels of spare parts it needs to maintain at its five regional customer service hubs across the world. Using digital communications platforms, engineers at the data center collaborate in real time with peers at local service hubs across different global airports and maintenance facilities to proactively maintain engines, fixing them before failures can occur. A wealth of cross-border digital technology powers this process, provided by partners that include Microsoft and SAP.[40]

TotalCare is just the beginning of servitization at Rolls-Royce. In 2017, the company launched its R[2] Data Labs, new data hubs at locations around the world.[41] At these facilities, interdisciplinary teams of data experts collaborate with teams across Rolls-Royce's operations to develop new services that help customers maintain their engines, improve operational safety, comply with government regulations, and so on. Teams partner with more than five hundred external technology providers, innovation start-ups, academics, and original equipment manufacturers to identify new ideas for services and rapidly develop them into solutions.[42] R² Data Labs is part of the company's vision for an IntelligentEngine that talks to the customer, other engines, and Rolls-Royce's business partners; that can respond to the external environment without human intervention; and that can learn from its own and peers' experiences to adjust and optimize its performance. As Richard Goodhead, senior vice president of marketing for Rolls-Royce Civil Aerospace, observes, the company is now "taking far more data and doing far more with it," all in the interests of capturing more value from services.[43]

Many other big industrial players are drawing more revenues and profits from innovative services-based business models based on IoT, analytics, and related technologies. Schneider Electric provides a range of services to big utilities that, because of financial pressures, are finding it less attractive to own their own assets and infrastructure. As of 2020, 50 percent of the company's revenues derived from digital systems and services, a category that includes new comprehensive solutions that incorporate physical products as well as value-added services, updates, and applications for products that are themselves sold separately the traditional way. This portion of revenues was growing faster than those derived from the sale of physical assets.[44] Caterpillar's predictive-maintenance offering collects real-time operational data from the construction equipment it sells and uses algorithms to compare the equipment's performance to that of other equipment in the area. The service provides proactive advice on when to service individual pieces of equipment, lowering costs to customers.

These companies represent the vanguard of industrial servitization—there is a long way to go. When it comes to the underlying technology, many manufacturers have been lagging in adoption.

One study of five hundred midlevel personnel in manufacturing across industries found that fewer than 50 percent said that "at least half of their company's manufacturing process is outfitted with industrial IoT technology, and a mere 11% said at least three-quarters of the process are IoT enabled. Only 40% are collecting data through remote sensors."[45] In the years ahead, more companies will have to embrace this technology and develop exciting new services. Otherwise, they'll risk falling behind.

Products, Services, and Experiences Made for *You*

It's a quarter to eight in the morning, and you're leaving your hotel room to head to a client meeting. There's a Starbucks downstairs in the lobby, so as you finish dressing, you click on the Starbucks app and order your go-to morning drink, a grande caffè misto, otherwise known as a café au lait. You're feeling hungry, and you're intrigued to notice as you order that the app has recommended some breakfast sandwiches for you, including a bacon-gouda-and-egg on an artisan roll and a reduced-fat turkey-bacon-and-egg on an organic whole-wheat english muffin. Gouda is your favorite cheese, and the previous week, you'd tried and liked this sandwich. Now, the app offers you an attractive reward: purchase any breakfast sandwich three times, and you receive eighty bonus stars redeemable for free drinks and food. A reward for buying a sandwich you already like! You're pleasantly surprised and choose to purchase the sandwich to go along with your caffè misto. And good thing you did. Fifteen minutes later, as you're finishing your sandwich and heading in a taxi to your meeting, you feel pleasantly full, energized, and ready for your day. The Starbucks app seemed to know what you wanted and needed even before you did, making your day just a little bit better.

That's no accident. While Starbucks has long personalized its in-store offerings, the company has been moving swiftly since 2016 to digitize the personalization of consumers' interaction with its brand, further enhancing consumer experience and driving sales. Personalization has figured prominently in the company's "digital flywheel" strategy, a holistic approach to consumer engagement that also includes its rewards program, ordering, and payment via app.[46] Collecting data about consumers' shopping histories (with their consent) and accounting for other factors such as the time of day, the items a shopper has already placed in his or her shopping cart, the weather, and social media activity, Starbucks personalizes numerous aspects of the customer experience. Deploying multiple machine-learning algorithms, for instance, Starbucks makes real-time personalized recommendations via its smartphone app. The company also determines how engaged a consumer already is, and on that basis it sends rewards offerings. The company might offer occasional visitors who have tried a random sampling of products an opportunity to purchase some of those products more frequently so that the company can meet more of their needs. In the case of loyal customers who always purchase the same product, Starbucks might extend rewards offers via email and recommend products those customers might love. As time passes and consumers become more engaged, the "challenges" required to claim more rewards evolve, creating a fun, gamified experience.

Starbucks's digital personalization efforts have been remarkably successful for the company and engaging for consumers. Within its first year, Starbucks's digital-flywheel program led to an 8 percent growth in spending among active members of Starbucks Rewards, the highest-ever increase on a year-on-year basis.[47] For a company that generated nearly 40 percent of its revenues from its rewards members, this represented a direct and substantial increase in sales.[48] As Starbucks's former chairman Howard Schultz proclaimed, "Our new one-to-one personalized marketing capability . . . will prove to be a retail industry game changer."[49] It certainly seems that way. In 2019, Starbucks's app was one of America's most popular applications for processing payments, with more than twenty-five million members.[50] Starbucks has also synced up the digital flywheel with its point-of-sale software, allowing for an even more personalized in-store experience. The company is also using data and analytics to personalize how it interacts with consumers on social media, in its customer-support center, and across other digital devices.

> In addition to servitized offerings, many companies are weaving personalization into their customer value propositions.

"The future of marketing is bespoke everything," wrote Amanda Mull in the *Atlantic*.[51] The start-up Prose ships personalized hair-care products made to order to customers who fill out a survey beforehand, while Care/of sells personalized nutritional supplements and Curology offers personalized skin-care concoctions.[52] One of the more successful start-ups with a personalized (and servitized) value proposition is the online fashion retailer Stitch Fix, which makes buying fashionable clothes easier and more convenient than it has been up until now. Collecting data via an initial questionnaire and ongoing consumer feedback, the company matches individual consumers with human stylists, who select specific items for each consumer.[53] The company then ships a selection of clothing items to consumers, either as a recurring service or on a one-time basis. Stitch Fix combines "data and machine learning with expert human judgment" to curate clothing recommendations and optimize other aspects of operations, employing dozens of data scientists. In 2019, just eight years after its founding, the company notched nearly $1.6 billion in sales.[54]

One company that has aggressively and impressively pursued personalization as a strategy is the global cosmetics company L'Oréal. For some time now, the company has been personalizing its marketing and communications by leveraging its customer data platform (details in Chapter 6). The company has embraced personalization beyond marketing, however. In 2020, it launched its Perso skin-care system, which uses artificial intelligence to allow consumers to create highly customized cosmetics formulas at home.[55] With consumers' consent, the system collects data about their preferences, skin condition (using an AI-aided analysis of pictures taken on consumers' smartphones), and environmental conditions that can affect the skin. Based on this data, the device creates and dispenses just the right formula of skin-care product for consumers using raw product components in cartridges located inside the device. A similar device for lipstick allows consumers to choose the precise color they want using a panel on their smartphones—a welcome and revolutionary alternative to the common practice of keeping dozens of different shades on hand. In the future, customers will be able to refine their products even more, designing "a lipstick shade to match their outfit or to opt for a color that is trending on social media at that moment."[56]

Personalization is hardly new as a strategy—since the 1970s, the restaurant chain Burger King has promised consumers that they can have their burgers "your way" (i.e., allowing them to choose which toppings were put on their sandwiches).[57] What has changed is the technology, which makes personalization much more economical on a global scale. Under traditional approaches to globalization—what we call the *old globalization*—companies could personalize their offerings for individual consumers, but only by making thousands or even millions of varieties of a physical product. Today companies are making relatively few varieties of the physical product but using software to deliver potentially hundreds of millions of functional variations. Gatorade, for instance, is rolling out a patch that analyzes consumers' sweat, and on that basis it allows them to choose beverage formulations that best serve their bodies' needs (consumed from a bottle that consumers also customize via Gatorade's website).[58] Not to be outdone, Burger King has now deployed digital technology to enhance how consumers can have it their way, feeding them personalized offers as well as customizable sandwiches.[59]

Even a single physical product design can now mean many things to many people across geographies. Tesla offers only four car models (Models 3, S, X, and Y), yet it allows for a highly personalized experience. Postpurchase, drivers can "customize the positioning of their seat, steering wheel, mirrors, suspension, braking, and many other features," creating an individual user profile.[60] This capability, in the words of one reviewer, "creates a unique feeling that the vehicle becomes an extension of a driver."[61] Software updates for the Model S allow the car to learn a driver's daily commute and then provide traffic updates.[62] They also allow the car to download calendar information from a user's smartphone so that the car can automatically generate directions on how to drive to upcoming events.[63] Tesla owners can also name their cars and have those names pop up on the company's mobile app.[64] Tesla seems poised in the years to come to use a camera installed in the cabin to recognize users when they get in the car and immediately reconfigure numerous elements of the car to them—what CEO Elon Musk has called "dynamic personalization."[65]

Tesla's example suggests how global companies might profitably combine servitization and personalization to bring breathtakingly new offerings to market. Tesla's cars are not just physical objects but "connected" vehicles that serve as platforms for the digital delivery of services and the building of an ongoing relationship with consumers. Tesla can make its cars ever more personalized via software updates downloaded from the web. But it also uses downloads to provide many other improvements and optimizations on an ongoing basis. While automakers traditionally spend billions on recalls that can take up to two years to complete, downloading an update costs Tesla hardly anything and takes as little as a month to roll out globally. In 2019, Tesla used connectivity to download updates that allowed it to provide maintenance services to consumers. Tesla cars now self-diagnose problems, book service appointments for consumers, and cause needed parts to be automatically shipped to the nearest service center (owners can cancel their appointments if they deem the servicing unnecessary).[66] Using mobile repair personnel, Tesla can remotely diagnose and repair service issues in 90 percent of cases, keeping consumers on the road and out of the shop.[67] Whatever other challenges Tesla's business has, it is more resilient—and more advantaged operationally—because the company can launch new features and respond to product quality issues more quickly and at much lower cost.

Targeting the Global Consumer

As a number of examples in this chapter suggest, digital technology is allowing both consumer and industrial companies not merely to provide more personalized products, services, and experiences but to do so across national borders for the new global consumer.

Although the music-streaming service Spotify initially offered generic human-curated playlists to listeners around the globe, it is now using algorithms to tweak and personalize playlists to fit individuals' tastes.[68] The company hopes to notch ongoing increases in user engagement, as it did in 2018.[69] Likewise, every element of Netflix's platform is personalized to the user's preferences, which the company gleans by performing experiments during user visits (for example, suggesting certain content to see whether a user clicks on it). By 2019, the company had created over three hundred million user profiles, which Netflix's algorithms used to generate personalized content recommendations.[70] The company uses humans to categorize shows according to themes, enabling the algorithm to then suggest recommendations quite accurately (about 80 percent of the content Netflix's users consume derive from the algorithm recommendations).[71] Instead of segmenting its offerings by nationality or other traditional demographics, the company's algorithms analyze consumers' consumption of content and on this basis allow Netflix to hone in on two thousand global "taste communities."[72] In addition, the company customizes its recommendations on a regional basis, taking into account local preferences and government regulations.

Whether companies personalize their offerings or not, the rise of the global consumer has been so profound that some firms are creating new offerings and promotions to target cross-border groups of consumers defined by affinity, not geography.

In 2019, when music producer and DJ Marshmello put on a virtual live concert for millions of concertgoers within the global video game Fortnite, he was performing for the affinity group of video game consumers located throughout the world.[73] Likewise, when Niantic released its Pokémon Go game in 2016, it targeted the affinity group of gamers across the world simultaneously, racking up almost $1 billion in revenues within a year, according to media reports.[74] The NBA serves a global community of basketball fans, and in the near future it will deploy technology that will allow consumers to personalize their viewing experience no matter where they are physically located.[75]

Other major global companies pursuing digital models are bypassing geography and addressing themselves to consumers with common interests, such as those who remain within a common brand ecosystem (like Apple, Android, or Tencent) when seeking out products and services. The rise of seamless global digital connectivity at decreasing cost (described in the introduction) means that companies will define consumers not just by their country of location but by their digital identities. All users of the rapidly expanding transportation network company Gojek (think Uber for motorbikes) access the service using apps on their phones, and the service is identical or at least similar across national borders, subject to legal or regulatory limitations. To Gojek, these consumers aren't defined by their identity as Indonesian or Thai or Vietnamese (the company currently operates across Southeast Asia). They're global consumers, and the company's value proposition is designed to serve them seamlessly everywhere.

Implications for Leaders

In the years ahead, value propositions that merge the physical with the digital and that leverage data to deliver personalized offerings to global customers will flourish across industries. Many companies will no longer sell products or services per se but rather deliver outcomes and shape experiences. One large technology company told us that the servitized solutions it offered for its line of computer servers will soon account for 50 percent of its revenues, up from 10 percent in 2019. Among industrial companies, digital services attached to physical products are the fastest-growing part of the business. For car companies, as we've seen, the future lies in connected-car and mobility offerings. Companies that become adept at building and evolving these capabilities will thrive. Those that don't will either become suppliers to those who do or go out of business.

How do you build and deliver these new value propositions? Based on our work with clients, we recommend that you start by pondering the following core questions:

What key pain points are you already solving for your customers? Do you really understand these in sufficient depth? You might assume that your customers might rely on you for their fuel purchases, but what they're really solving for is being able to go from point A to point B. How else might your company help customers solve this more fundamental problem via a digital servitized offering?

Is the opportunity attractive enough? In addressing customer problems, does a servitized value proposition you might deliver create a large-enough market opportunity? What kinds of costs (related to capital investments, retraining, realignment of incentives, etc.) would you accrue in the process of bringing this solution to market? Which companies would be competing with you? How will this new value proposition affect your existing businesses?

Do you have the right resources in place to develop a winning solution? Have you assembled a team capable of offering experiences and not just services? Do team members have the agility, collaborative mindset, and sense of the zeitgeist required to fully address the customer pain points that you set out to solve? What other infrastructure (manufacturing capability, data architecture, etc.) must you put in place?

Are you prepared organizationally? If you're a large global company, will your entrenched bureaucracy prevent you from pioneering new value propositions and getting them off the ground? How might you better position your teams to function like start-ups? Are your senior leaders focused enough on these projects in order to ensure their success? If you have traditionally been a product-focused company, what internal adjustments will you have to make to successfully deliver a service or solution?

Ultimately, creating new digital value propositions requires a mindset shift on the part of leaders, a new form of customer centricity. No matter what kind of product or service you currently offer, you must be willing to fundamentally reimagine it so as to maximize the value customers derive over the lifetime of that product or service. If you have long sold washing machines to local consumers, should you still do that? Or should you sell a clothes-washing *solution* to global consumers that, say, allows your consumers to operate remotely, change the cycle, and compare notes with other washing-machine owners on what settings and detergents work best for certain kinds of dirty clothes? If you currently sell a hair-care product to local consumers, should you still do that? Or should you sell a hair-care solution that allows customers anywhere to receive a personalized product, perhaps delivered as a service on a subscription basis?

To answer such questions, you must develop a much deeper, more rigorous, and more empathetic view of customers and their needs than the one you currently possess. Traditionally, companies developing new offerings have sought out the voice of the customer, but they've generally limited their research to fielding surveys and conducting focus groups, involving only marketing and R & D teams. Succeeding with digital-physical business models means bringing together customers, business unit teams, technology teams, customer-behavior experts, and outside partners to take what we call a *customer journey*; mapping out how customers use and derive value from your product or service throughout its entire life cycle; and then exploring how you might increase that value with digital and other means. When undergoing such journeys with clients, we at BCG determine what customers *really* want, what they don't care so much about, how we might deliver more of what they want, and how we might best charge for it. When buying wind turbines, what power companies really want is a solution that maximizes their profit. Digital twin technology allows a provider to optimize the wind turbine's operations in real time, thus maximizing profit. Instead of simply selling a wind turbine, a company might sell a solution that generates revenue based on its ability to maximize the power company's profits.

A successful customer journey analyzes the entire customer experience from a deep ethnographic standpoint, identifying pain points and developing solutions that layer digitally enabled services on top of physical products. The process unfolds in four phases:

1. We set up the project and conduct intensive research into customers and the industry.
2. Next, we ideate around the digital business model, prototyping it and iterating with a client's customers to refine it.
3. We conduct a series of sprints to define, build, and pilot the minimal viable product. What technology solutions will we require? What kind of data infrastructure? How exactly will we structure the service and interactions with the customer (what we call an *engagement model*)? What regulatory hurdles will we have to surmount?
4. We create a long-term business model and a road map for rolling it out.

Just because you've isolated a customer pain point and developed an innovative digital solution doesn't mean you should necessarily go ahead and roll out a new offering at scale. It's important to consider whether customers will actually pay enough for your new offering so that you can deliver it profitably, or, failing that, if other partners might share enough of the value with you to ensure economic viability. If you're a refrigerator maker like Whirlpool, you might think of outfitting your products with Wi-Fi and sensors inside the box that can track consumer usage of perishables like milk, eggs, juice, and cheese. You could offer a service that automatically alerts consumers when they're running out of these goods, orders milk deliveries from Amazon, and charges consumers' credit cards. But would customers be willing to pay enough for this service to make it worthwhile for Whirlpool? Would Amazon or another provider help subsidize the service by giving Whirlpool a cut of the purchase price? How will your proposed digitally enabled service impact your existing business? If you can't make this idea work, you might still want to develop it because a competitor is doing so. But failing that, you might be better off scouting about for another idea to pursue.

Companies that win with new business models think globally instead of limiting their view to one or a few markets, since the underlying data infrastructure enables quick entry across national boundaries. These companies also dedicate themselves to refining their innovative digital-physical offerings on an ongoing basis and to creating new ones. Once Netflix had set up its global offering, it could use the massive amounts of data generated to further optimize new elements of its service, including the original content it was creating. Further, it was only after analyzing this data that Netflix developed a new way of segmenting consumers, discovering that consumer behavior broke down across global taste communities as opposed to national boundaries. Similarly, the explosives maker Orica amassed extensive global data about the mining companies that were its customers, including the geography of their mines and the performance of explosives in those mines. Using this data, the company could create a new branded offering that optimized how customers were using the explosives to maximize productivity and profits. As your data comes in, what new offerings might it enable? What deeper insights into customers might you glean?

It's one thing to devise an exciting new value proposition—quite another to execute it well. Doing so will require that you mobilize many of the other strategies described in this book. Depending on your industry and the nature of your offering, you might need to develop an ecosystem of partners to help you deliver (Chapter 3), new flex manufacturing plants to produce custom-designed goods (Chapter 4), and a global data architecture to collect and process data (Chapter 5). You'll almost certainly want to reorganize yourself around customers and make other internal moves designed to make you more agile and able to compete in a digital world, as described later in this book. In this way, going *beyond* physical products and services can set you on a path to totally reimagine your global enterprise, adding a comprehensive new layer onto your current strategy and operations.

Your next logical step in reimagining your global enterprise might well be questioning your traditional assumptions about which new markets to enter and how fast. The ability to provide and sell digital solutions and experiences is profoundly changing how leading-edge companies think about geographical expansion. If GM wants to sell its cars in major markets like India and China, it has to set up plants in those markets—a relatively slow, capital-intensive process. Players like Uber, Google, and

Netflix can expand inexpensively and with lightning speed; they don't need data and analytics centers in every market to deliver their digitally based solutions and experiences. Such companies might just need to put in place an app downloaded from an app store and a payment solution, and they're in business across many borders all at once. As we'll see in the next chapter, digitally based business models can contribute to new asset-light strategies for expansion, allowing companies a whole new path to success in a competitive arena that in recent years has grown far more challenging.

Key Insights

- Global companies are rapidly evolving their value propositions, going beyond traditional, product-oriented offerings to create exciting new solutions and experiences.
- Mobilizing digital connectivity and IoT technologies, companies are layering new digital services onto existing physical products (servitization). Yesterday's companies shipped their way into customers' hearts and wallets. Tomorrow's will ship and stream their way in.
- Consumer companies like Whirlpool are embracing servitization, but so are industrial companies such as Philips, Rolls-Royce, and Caterpillar. Firms like Netflix, Apple, and Pandora offer purely digital forms of servitization.
- Companies are customizing their offerings at scale (personalization) and developing solutions that combine servitization and customization.
- Companies like Niantic, Netflix, and Alibaba are increasingly targeting global consumers irrespective of their locations.

CHAPTER 3

REFINE YOUR GLOBAL GAME

Although global growth continues to create huge value, companies today are taking a more sophisticated approach to expansion than they did during the late twentieth century. They're using asset-light, digital, or e-commerce-centric business models to enter into new markets and expand rapidly. They're also becoming more selective about which markets to enter and paradoxically deepening their engagement in their chosen markets.

In recent years, leaders at many large incumbent organizations have begun to regard their companies' global footprints more critically—ironically enough, at a time when successful start-ups are globalizing more quickly than ever. Global expansion still remains a viable and attractive path to profitable growth. Maintaining a portfolio of markets at different stages of development and levels of country-related risk also makes sense because it renders global firms much more resilient to unforeseen shocks. At the same time, certain underlying beliefs that have driven globalization in the last century no longer hold. To take full advantage of today's opportunities, leaders have to refine and optimize their global presence, adopting a seemingly contradictory playbook for profitable global expansion that goes *beyond* traditional scale and asset-heavy growth strategies.

On the one hand, leaders have to go *asset light*, pursuing swift, wide-scale global expansions without building expensive new infrastructure or mobilizing large teams (a feat made possible by relying on digital and local partners). Such a strategy allows firms to minimize risk in turbulent times. On the other hand, leaders running businesses with existing global footprints have to become more selective about the markets in which they maintain an asset-heavy physical presence while also going all in and becoming highly local players in a smaller number of high-priority, profitable markets. Ultimately, companies have to become smarter and scrappier in how they expand, bobbing and weaving to generate the maximum amount of value from their globalization initiatives while capping the country-related risks they are willing to assume amid increased volatility.

To understand the first of these strategies (swift, asset-light, more resilient global expansion), consider the experience of Chinese electronics giant Xiaomi. Founded in 2010, the company was soon selling more of its value-for-the-money smartphones in China than Samsung, snagging a 14 percent market share by 2014.[1] Over the next few years, the firm would take its business global. Conventional thinking would have led them to try to drive growth, scale advantage, and profitability by slowly building a broad-based global footprint. It would have had them invest heavily in each market to establish a strong local presence and customize products to local tastes.

Any number of successful companies pursued such an approach during the late twentieth century. If you were McDonald's, your long-term performance hinged on getting as many people in as many countries as possible eating Big Macs (or whatever you called that sandwich in a given locale), especially consumers in rapidly developing markets like China and India. Ditto if you were a carmaker like Toyota or GM, or an industrial company like Caterpillar, General Electric, or Siemens. The greater your presence in individual overseas markets, the more you sold. Your profit margin increased as well: with increased volume, scale economies made it cheaper for you to produce each unit. Of course, given the significant investments in infrastructure required, global expansion usually took decades to achieve. McDonald's had to buy or lease real estate and build physical restaurants to achieve cross-border growth. As a result, it took the company thirty-three years to enter 47 countries and forty-two years to enter 100 (by 2018, it counted 37,855 restaurants in 120 countries).[2]

Xiaomi wasn't about to wait around, and by calling upon digital technology and partnerships (both local and technology based), it didn't have to. Unlike other big mobile phone makers, the company opted from its earliest days to pursue a three-part growth strategy, relying on its software, the internet, *and* its hardware to expand. Xiaomi wouldn't have to invest heavily in each market to reach consumers or continuously upgrade its products. Rather, it could sell new and exciting services inexpensively via its online store.

To pilot this unique strategy, Xiaomi opened its first overseas office in Singapore.[3] It imported its phones and began marketing them online, allowing consumers to upgrade software for their phones online. The company hit gold, selling out its initial inventory during the first day.[4] Realizing that they had hit upon a successful strategy for entering new markets, leaders set their sights on a much bigger prize: India. Players like Nokia and Samsung were already entrenched in the country; having played by the book, they had invested heavily to customize their products to fit local tastes, build large production facilities and physical distribution networks, and unroll big brand advertising. No matter: Xiaomi dispatched a small team to India and formed a partnership with Flipkart, a leading online e-commerce marketplace.[5] Once again, Xiaomi sold its imported phones entirely online, positioning select models as high-quality, feature-rich, value-for-the-money phones. Forgoing expensive traditional advertising, the company relied on Flipkart, social media fan clubs, and flash sales to get the word out. The response was once again overwhelming, with Xiaomi's first models selling out in seconds and Flipkart's website crashing because of intense consumer interest.[6] By the third quarter of 2018, Xiaomi had become India's largest smartphone company, scoring 27 percent of the market.[7] And after tasting success in India, Xiaomi rapidly expanded into new markets using its new asset-light playbook. Within a decade of its founding, Xiaomi was selling smartphones into some eighty countries.[8]

From Xiaomi's earliest days, founder Lei Jun didn't question whether the company should be global. He took it for granted that Xiaomi had been born as a global company—a mindset embraced by many Chinese entrepreneurs. But he also understood that global markets were changing in fundamental ways, and that to succeed he would need to create his own playbook for expanding into new markets, one that overturned the belief that companies can achieve profitable global growth only by investing massively to establish significant global and local scale.

Leaders at other leading-edge companies—both incumbents and start-ups—are arriving at similar conclusions. When it comes to managing large existing physical footprints rather than rolling out a new business model, incumbent companies are rethinking whether it still makes sense to play in every market.

This holds especially true for firms that drew on their global brand and scale economies to enter and grow in formerly hot emerging markets. With many of these markets now cooling and growth becoming more volatile,[9] and with trade policies in both developed and developing countries influencing economic conditions more than long-term global trends, companies are now making more nuanced, risk-adjusted judgments about which individual countries to enter and which to exit. Historically high-growth nations might adopt inhospitable policies and protectionist regulatory regimes and feature fiercely competitive local players empowered by digital and intelligent technologies, while low-growth economies might have huge underserved markets that companies can capture with the right strategies. As the CEO of a global consumer products company told us in a 2018 interview, "We were used to chasing growth in a world that seemed stable and experiencing secular expansion. Since the financial crisis, we've had to adjust to a new era in which we had to 'shape' growth amidst uneven and shifting growth rates in countries."

Companies also have to engage more deeply in those countries where they do choose to compete. In a world with common rules of the game spelled out in multilateral trade agreements, global firms could drive a common global business model and a cost-optimized supply chain from a centralized corporate headquarters—doing so was both economic and efficient. In the twenty-first century, with economic and geopolitical fragmentation on the rise and nationalists resisting the extraction of economic value from their local economies, leading-edge companies have realized that it no longer makes sense to apply a standard operational template across countries in an attempt to drive efficiency. Instead, companies must develop a country-first mindset, as the vice chairman of a large industrial conglomerate told us, thinking of themselves as a collection of local businesses inside a global enterprise. Further, they must turn to technology to connect these local businesses (Chapter 5) and provide global-scale capabilities and processes (Chapter 6). "We have been highly successful [growing in new markets] driving growth through efficient deployment of technology and products," a leader at a Chinese technology company told us in 2019. "The countries now want global companies like us to think how best to meet different local needs."

Growth remains a top agenda item for CEOs of global companies, despite the global instability and complexity that mark our present era. But the path to growth is markedly altered. A favorite question from a Wall Street analyst in the 1990s and 2000s was "What is your emerging-markets growth strategy?" That question is now hopelessly out of date. To win, leaders must abandon their former preoccupation with expanding into as many markets as quickly as possible, deploying a new playbook that is smarter, scrappier, and more resilient, if somewhat contradictory on its face. At chapter's end, we'll present some questions that we pose to our clients to help shake up how they think about global growth so that they can reduce risk and make the most of the opportunities now available to them.

The Many Flavors of Asset Light

The new asset-light models don't come in just one flavor—they come in many. First, and perhaps most obviously, digital platforms and data-led business models are allowing companies to enter and establish market share without physical products and the costly infrastructure required to deliver them. In 2006, when Nintendo launched its revolutionary Wii console, video game enthusiasts in the United States got their hands on the device first, followed by those in the United Kingdom the next month.[10] It took two long years before the device hit stores in India, South Korea, and Taiwan, three before it launched in Hong Kong.[11] Today, this rollout seems anachronistic and incredibly slow. In 2016, a San Francisco–based start-up called Niantic, originally incubated within Google and helmed by John Hanke, the former head of Google Maps, launched another revolutionary video game product, the augmented reality game Pokémon Go. Although Niantic made no claim to be a global company, Pokémon Go almost instantly became the top-selling video game in 55 countries. By 2017, consumers in 129 countries had downloaded the Pokémon Go app, putting almost $1 billion into Niantic's coffers.[12]

Netflix, as we've seen, needed just seven years to take its business to almost 200 countries, a feat that in the context of the old globalization would have taken media-content companies decades to accomplish.[13] Likewise, within a decade of its founding in 2008, Airbnb had amassed more than five million listings covering almost every country, dwarfing the Marriott group and its 1.3 million hotel rooms (a portfolio of assets that had taken decades to build).[14] Airbnb's model is asset light par excellence. The company doesn't own any accommodations but books revenue by earning fees from guests and the local property owners who host them and list their properties on Airbnb's platform. Digital models in general amount to asset-light strategies for global growth, with digital companies requiring much less in the way of foreign assets to generate a comparable amount of foreign sales.

Like Xiaomi, companies that sell physical products can also enter markets more quickly, intelligently, and economically, forgoing large investment in infrastructure and instead either leveraging partnerships with established local players or connecting with consumers directly via e-commerce and logistics platforms. Since launching its first product, Fitbit Tracker, in 2009 (followed by its Ionic Smartwatch in October 2017),[15] the US wearables maker Fitbit has deployed a global asset-light model and sold more than seventy-six million units in eight-six countries.[16] Fitbit initially entered markets using a direct-to-consumer distribution model that required relatively little investment. Realizing it needed a stronger retail presence, the company formed partnerships in countries around the world rather than building and operating its own stores and distribution networks.[17] In the United States alone, it enlisted dozens of partners to carry its products, from Bed Bath & Beyond to Costco to Sak's Fifth Avenue.[18] In December 2018, Fitbit continued to strengthen its asset-light global business model with the launch of its new operating system Fitbit OS 3.0, which allows it to offer fitness-related apps on platforms like iPhone and from its partners through its own Fitbit App Gallery.[19] In late 2019, Google announced that it would purchase Fitbit for $2.1 billion.[20]

Indian motorcycle manufacturer Bajaj Auto is also going asset light, albeit in a different way. The company is not only one of the world's largest purveyors of motorcycles and a leader in three-wheel vehicles; it has been one of the fastest growing, thanks to its high-growth international business. In 2005, when the company began focusing on this business,[21] it sought to avoid the bureaucratic challenges of administering a large number of subsidiaries, and it also wanted to focus on its strengths in product and brand management. So, very much like Xiaomi, Bajaj deployed an asset-light franchise-based business model and leveraged its technical knowledge and manufacturing excellence to support its channel partners. Under this strategy, distributors in foreign markets handled logistics and helped to localize the products, while Bajaj's international offices closely supported the distributors, and its corporate team retained control over brand, product, pricing, and so on.

A decade later, the company had executed a highly successful global expansion using this model.[22] As Rakesh Sharma, executive director, told us, its leadership wondered at this point whether the company was now ready to invest massively to build assets in different markets, as automotive companies traditionally have done to increase profits. Leaders concluded there was no reason to change Bajaj's approach, as it had allowed them to gain share in nearly all its markets and achieve more resilience as the company competed with larger global peers. Instead, Bajaj doubled down on asset light, leveraging digital technologies and platforms to better support its local partners and build stronger customer relationships.

Today, the company uses digital platforms to provide training, diagnostics, and best practices to local teams and to respond better to customers even without an army of customer-service reps on the ground. If a customer in a small Nigerian town has trouble with a rickshaw's engine and the local service technician can't diagnose the underlying issue, the technician can photograph the engine smoke and file a failure report online. The company's global team of customer-support experts in Pune, India, diagnoses the problem and provides a solution virtually, often in under six hours. As of 2019, Bajaj operates in seventy-nine countries, is the number one or two player in twenty-one of them, and continues to enter new markets.[23] International business, which accounts for 40 percent of its revenues, grew by 20 percent over 2018–2019, reaching $1.64 billion.[24]

The massive growth of third-party e-commerce, logistics, and last-mile delivery networks has rendered it far easier for companies to reach consumers in emerging markets with reduced investments through many transient and fit-for-purpose partnerships, a far cry from traditional one-on-one joint ventures and long-term partnerships. One successful platform company that created many of these global networks is the Alibaba Group. In 2019, the group's B2B online marketplace, Alibaba. com, enabled US-based small and medium businesses to join its global B2B e-commerce network, enabling these sellers to instantly onboard themselves; access CRM, communications, and digital marketing tools; and reach ten million active business buyers in over 190 countries and regions.[25] As an Alibaba Group executive put it, "You get to compete and act like a multinational company in a way you've never had the tools or technology to be able to do so."[26] Unlike large incumbents, whose arrangements with existing bilateral partners might preclude forming new relationships, start-ups today are free to build up networks of partners quickly to expand across borders (a theme we'll develop in Chapter 4). They can use services like Tmall Global, Alibaba's cross-border e-commerce platform that allows international brands and SMEs to test the China market and engage with more than seven hundred million Chinese consumers without having to set up operations in China. To date, more than twenty-five thousand brands and retailers from ninety-two countries and regions have joined the platform, with more than 80 percent of these entering the Chinese market for the first time.[27]

Alibaba itself exemplifies asset-light global expansion with a strategy built on local partnerships and investments. By 2036, Alibaba aims to serve two billion consumers globally, helping ten million small and medium enterprises operate profitably and creating one hundred million job opportunities. Unlike its competitor Amazon, which often purchases large assets and deploys large management teams in foreign markets, Alibaba has expanded by building up a vibrant digital economy of local partners. Already, Alibaba's logistics network, Cainiao, works with one hundred partners worldwide on cross-border logistics services, covering 224 countries and regions. Meanwhile, Alibaba has invested in local platforms such as Paytm and Lazada to expand its presence in India and Southeast Asia, respectively, rather than build its own infrastructure from scratch. In the course of investing, Alibaba shares technologies with these partners, allowing them to upgrade their infrastructure, operate more transparently and efficiently, and improve their financial performance. The strategy allows Alibaba to maintain a small physical

footprint, with just fourteen principal offices around the world. Our
BCG colleagues François Candelon, Fangqi Yang, and Daniel Wu have
described such investments as an "enabler" strategy, noting that other
leading Chinese technology companies such as Tencent are following it
as well.[28]

In addition to helping companies enter new markets, asset-light strategies deployed across country borders are enabling industrial companies
to unlock more value from their existing asset-heavy global infrastructure and its global customer base. The explosives manufacturer Orica's
servitization offering called BlastIQ takes data from customers' mining
operations around the world and draws insights to improve the safety,
productivity, and efficiency of mines. Orica delivers this offering with
very limited additional investments in these individual markets. Orica
can offer BlastIQ as a stand-alone service or layer it on its explosives
sales to distinguish itself from low-cost competitors in local markets and
increase its margins. Manufacturers such as Siemens Gamesa and Caterpillar have unrolled similar cross-border asset-light digital solutions
for wind turbines and tractors, respectively, to unlock new value globally
from their existing physical footprints, with only incremental additional
local investments. In many cases, such strategies actually reduce investments in local assets (warehouse and inventory, for instance) and local
maintenance teams, lowering cost and increasing margins. In general,
services-based value offerings amount to asset-light global expansion
strategies, as they yield more value for every dollar of investment. The
greater percentage of revenue a company gleans from its services business, the greater its total gross margin tends to be.

As the profusion of asset-light models suggests, globalization
remains an attractive option for many companies, allowing for
rapid expansion and the extraction of greater value from a bigger
country footprint. But as you enter new markets, you must be willing to open up your thinking and consider how best to mobilize the
new tools and capabilities that digital technology affords. Likewise,
if you already possess a sizable global footprint, you must show
open-mindedness and sophistication in determining whether and
how to adjust its size—a topic to which we now turn.

From Growth Everywhere to *Smart* Growth

The shape and scope of global footprints are changing as companies adapt to the conditions of our new, more volatile era. We saw this happening in entire industries like automotive and banking. Consider banking. For large global banks, the pathway to profitable global growth used to involve construction of physical branches—thousands of them—in dozens of countries around the world. Today, banking has gone digital and mobile, especially among younger consumers. In the United States, fintech lenders now originate close to 40 percent of all new personal loans, while in China the mobile payment app WeChat Pay claims almost a billion monthly active users.[29] Amid this disruption by asset-light digital models, traditional brick-and-mortar banking is becoming a local or, at best, regional play, with banks focused on serving established customer bases in their most hospitable markets and contracting their brick-and-mortar footprints in emerging markets. Whereas Citibank once operated retail branches in fifty countries, by 2018 it was present in just nineteen (although the bank maintains a geographical presence in almost one hundred markets).[30] Over a seven-year period ending in 2016, HSBC shrunk its global footprint from eighty-eight countries and territories to seventy, parting ways with about 20 percent of its workforce.[31] As former Citigroup CEO Vikram Pandit has remarked, "Banks are figuring out that providing every product and every service to every client in every country was just wrong."[32]

In lightening their footprints, global banks have responded to a range of factors. Many institutions cut back operations in the wake of the global financial crisis of 2008–2009 in order to sustain profitability and growth. More recently, regulatory requirements in individual markets (concerning money laundering, for instance, or bank secrecy) have determined which products and services banks might viably sell, as have variations in interest-rate structure and the extent of globalization. Local markets have also become more turbulent, with regional banks such as Qatar National Bank and Grupo Aval threatening the big global players in specific countries. To remain competitive, banks are now, as an article in the *Financial Times* noted, "more focused on the earning power of each country rather than simply accepting weaker outposts that 'plant the flag' to support the brand."[33] Citibank has withdrawn from Japan on account of regulations, even though the business was highly profitable.[34]

As traditional banks slim down their bricks-and-mortar presence, some are expanding across borders by deploying digitally based asset-light strategies in markets or among demographics that remain under-served. Some banks are digitizing existing offerings, while others are launching entirely new branded services to compete with fintech and big digital firms. In 2019, the Singapore-based United Overseas Bank (UOB) launched TMRW, a digital bank targeting millennials in South-east Asia.[35] To build an offering that would attract young consumers, UOB mobilized an internal team focused on using technology and con-sumer insight to enhance customer engagement, and it also partnered with outsiders, including a cognitive banking firm.[36] The result was a site that offers an in-app chatbot, AI capabilities, and a fun gamified experi-ence to help consumers build savings.[37] Rolled out in 2019 in Thailand, TMRW will expand to other key markets in the region, including Indo-nesia, Singapore, Malaysia, and Vietnam. Given the relative youthfulness of the region's population, UOB hopes to gain a strong foothold and build a user base of up to five million people within five years.[38]

> Across industries, companies are more willing than ever to depart from a conventional *everywhere* approach when deciding where to compete.

In recent decades, falling tariffs and trade barriers combined with fast growth in emerging markets led companies to amass large global foot-prints. Now companies are confronted not just with new value pools tar-geted by highly competitive asset-light players but with new challenges. Companies used to think about expanding in regional terms—they'd pursue an *Asia strategy* or look to *enter South America*. But leaders can no longer assume that investment in developing markets will yield growth, as the overall growth rate of these markets slows and huge disparities among them emerge. Asking whether "investing in emerging markets still [makes] sense," a 2019 *Financial Times* article noted that "high com-modity prices are a fading memory. Trade is stuttering and global supply chains are being disrupted. Far from catching up with the developed world, many supposedly emerging markets are growing more slowly."[39]

Greater economic variation and volatility within regions is also push-ing companies to take a more refined and realistic view of their pros-pects in individual countries. In South America, Brazil's economy has been among the most volatile, most recently lagging in growth, while other economies, like those of Peru, Chile, and Colombia, have posted above-average growth rates.[40] Within countries, growth has also occurred unevenly. In Mexico, three industries—soaps and cleaners, electrical appliances and housewares, and household audio and video—have consistently outpaced the nation's GDP growth rates over the past decade.[41] Thailand had two such industries, household audio and video equipment and health services.[42] In plotting their global footprints, companies need to analyze local economic conditions on an industry-by-industry basis to determine whether selling into that country makes sense given the nature of their product or service.

Rising tariffs and other protectionist policies are also making individual countries less desirable—just ask American and Chinese companies struggling with the trade war between those two countries, or Europeans and British companies contemplating Brexit's impact. Stronger threats from local competitors are also changing the calculus of many companies as they frame growth plans. During the late twentieth century, when competition centered primarily around product offerings, large global companies enjoyed a cost advantage over smaller local firms because of their bigger scale. As more industries migrate toward digitally based services, and as partners like Alibaba grant small start-ups access to world-class capabilities, that advantage is dwindling. Meanwhile, local competitors can better navigate local policies and work them to their advantage. Chinese-based Megvii, known for its facial recognition, AI, and machine vision, has more access to personal data for use in its systems and R & D activities than its Western competitors do.[43] In particular, Megvii can access official photos from government identification cards when developing their solutions, while Western competitors cannot.[44] Local competitors like Megvii also benefit from their ability to respond more quickly to changing customer needs, as they aren't encumbered by long, drawn-out innovation and global decision-making processes, as Western multinational companies are.

Physical scale still helps global businesses to absorb general and administrative costs and to fund innovation. Nevertheless, a number of global companies are doing what the big banks have done—pulling out of some markets and entering or concentrating in others selectively. In 2007, Mexican concrete giant Cemex was operating in fifty countries, with revenues of $21.7 billion.[45] More recently, the company has been shedding assets and geographic reach, even as its revenues have continued to grow. In 2016, it announced the sale of plants in the United States, while in 2018 it announced that it would shed up to $2 billion in assets so as to focus on markets that offered the greatest long-term growth prospects.[46]

During the 1990s and 2000s, when globalization was at its height, the Indian steelmaker Tata Steel expanded internationally through a series of acquisitions starting with NatSteel in Singapore in 2004 and continuing with Thailand's Millennium Steel in 2005 and Corus in 2007.[47] Tata Steel's expansion strategy was to build a steel company that was global in scale and also integrated across geographies. With the Corus acquisition, Tata Steel moved from the global steel industry's fifty-sixth largest player to its sixth largest.[48] But in 2008, as the global economic crisis slowed growth and hit the steel market hard, the foundation for global-scale-based competitive advantage changed dramatically. It was no longer the extent of your global footprint that conferred advantage but how competitive your supply chain was in a particular market as price and demand fell.

Such considerations led Tata Steel to alter its expansion strategy, focusing only on markets where it had scale and where it could compete. The company began to exit countries in which it couldn't lead the competition, and it doubled down on its market-leading India presence.[49] It shrunk its footprint in the United Kingdom, entered into an agreement with Chinese steelmaker HBIS Group to sell its operations in Singapore and Thailand, and entered into a joint venture with thyssenkrupp's steel business for the rest of its European operations.[50] Unfortunately, the HBIS and thyssenkrupp deals have fallen apart because of lack of regulatory approval.[51] As of this writing, Tata Steel continues to think globally but is highly local in its country strategy. It focuses on core market profitability, pursues selective closures, and makes only targeted investments in its international operations.[52]

As Cemex and Tata Steel both learned, building global scale and a large country footprint isn't enough to ensure profitability in each market, and it won't protect firms from sudden economic downturns. We found something similar when we performed a country-by-country analysis for one of our large clients in the consumer durables business to determine whether its scale approach still worked. Much to our client's surprise, the company stood to improve its profitability by 3 to 5 percent by shaping and refining its footprint, without losing competitiveness or increasing risk. The move would also better position the company to invest in emerging profit pools. As we found in this case, a company's scale and market share in *individual* markets was the biggest driver of profitability, not global scale. Carefully assembling a portfolio of individual countries in which you can achieve profitable growth at scale yields the greatest risk-adjusted growth overall.

Another strategy that companies are deploying to deal with more complexity, variability, and risk in global markets is deploying flexible business models that enable them to shift resources quickly into and out of countries as economic growth waxes and wanes. Instead of launching a product extensively—and expensively—in an entire region or large country market, candymaker Mars tests it in smaller emerging markets that require relatively modest initial investments, such as Chile in South America and the Baltic countries in Europe. Once Mars establishes demand for the product, it pours in more investment. Mars typically sources its new product launches globally from existing suppliers, allowing it to move more quickly to market and grab share from rivals like Hershey in the competitive confectionary space.

Mars recently took this more flexible, lower-risk approach when launching its Maltesers candy in the United States.[53] The company used its existing manufacturing base in Europe (consumers there had long enjoyed the candy) to supply the market, allowing it to test the product without having to invest tens of millions of dollars in a new US-based production facility. Rolling out Maltesers online and at movie theaters, the company could achieve a decent profit margin right away while providing for only a limited supply of the candy. Only once Mars had demonstrated that Americans did in fact have a hankering for Maltesers did Mars manufacture the candy in North America (as of 2019, it did so out of its Newmarket, Ontario, Canada, facility).[54]

Go Deeply Local to Win Globally

As companies become more selective when framing their global footprint, they're also increasingly taking steps to *go deep* in the markets they choose to enter and operate in, localizing their operations and outlook far more than they previously had and building more cultural understanding and relationships with local talent. Going deep also helps them build greater resiliency into their network to deal with economic turbulence.

This strategy to go deeply local to win in these markets starts at the top of the global organization. Global companies historically ran their empires from headquarters, typically with an executive leadership team that reflected the company's origin and country's culture. This approach no longer works in a world shaped by economic nationalism and a multicultural, digitally connected global consumer. As Masaaki Tsuya, CEO and chairman of the world's largest tire company, Bridgestone, told us, the vast majority of senior leaders at his firm were of Japanese origin a decade ago. With customer needs and government expectations in local markets changing, Bridgestone found it needed to render its thinking and strategies more diverse and culturally sensitive. So, the company began appointing non-Japanese executives to its business units, a move that has led to drastic leadership changes. Subcommittees led by non-Japanese leaders were created for business functions such as digital, R & D, manufacturing, and logistics and supply chain. Top executives at each business unit and function were required to attend their quarterly leadership meetings each year in addition to biweekly CEO calls to ensure coherent alignment and adjustment of both strategy and operations. Today, communication among the business units has increased drastically, and the company's global executive council includes members from six different nationalities. "It's been a journey of trial and error," Tsuya reflected, "but we've managed to build a mindset that is truly multicultural and global, and this helps our local business."[55]

Operationally, companies are moving beyond the standardized global approach they used to take when entering new markets, thinking and acting like local players—what we might term a *local for global* strategy. Siemens has built a tightly integrated and highly successful presence across the globe for more than 150 years, operating in industries such as power generation, industrial automation, and medical technology. All along, Siemens has honored its German heritage of engineering excellence and product innovation, maintaining tight control on technology and quality in its plants around the world, and exporting a large percentage of its global sales from its German factories via tightly integrated global supply chains. No one in the company doubted that executives in the firm's Munich headquarters called the shots.

Lately, this strategy has chafed against the fragmentation of global markets. As chief strategy officer Dr. Horst Kayser outlined for us in a 2019 interview, possible global trade restrictions require that companies adhere to different technical standards when designing products—a trend that promises to intensify in the years to come.[56] Local communities are also demanding that companies serve as good corporate citizens, helping to build up their economies and create jobs locally. "Anything valuable or high value always generates geopolitical interest in making sure the local communities [are] served and [the] local economy is built," Kayser said. As a result, it was important for Siemens to think and behave like a local company, deeply invested in each country's own economic development.[57]

Siemens's operations in China exemplify the strong local-for-global strategy the company has adopted to win. As of 2019, Siemens had more than thirty-three thousand employees in this important market and had tailored its products to fit local needs. It used the Chinese e-commerce giant Alibaba for its cloud services instead of Microsoft's Azure or Amazon Web Services, which it used elsewhere.[58] The company had entered into many joint ventures with Chinese companies, having signed an agreement with the Chinese government that allows for wide-scale commercial cooperation with Chinese industry. Siemens had set up twenty-one R & D hubs in China employing nearly five thousand staff, had partnered with more than ninety universities, and had almost thirteen thousand active patents and patent applications.[59] It had participated in more than seven hundred advanced-technology projects with Chinese organizations and had also sponsored PhD research by international students. "We play a social role in the regions where we operate," Kayser explained to us, "especially in emerging markets. In particular, there is a need for local proximity given the nature of our businesses and government expectations."[60]

Operating like a committed local firm within a global company in a large market has unlocked new value for Siemens. Revenues from the company's Chinese operations grew to approximately $9 billion, an annualized growth rate of almost 10 percent since 2005.[61] Even if business in Europe or other parts of the world were to slow, the company's deeply local operations in China would remain relatively unscathed, making the company as a whole more resilient. Although government policies favoring local businesses might have partially influenced Siemens to go deep into China, the strategy nevertheless represents a template on how companies can win in today's fragmented world when competing in large markets against strong competitors.

Alibaba has approached this deeply-local-to-win-globally strategy differently, as a glance at its Malaysian business suggests.[62] As of this writing, Alibaba is partnering with the Malaysian government to establish an "electronic world trade platform" hub, the eWTP, in Kuala Lumpur. The hub will help Malaysian small and medium-sized enterprises sell their products on e-commerce platforms overseas and build infrastructure for marketing, logistics, cloud computing, and mobile payments. Meanwhile, Alibaba affiliate Ant Financial will help local Malaysian banks provide small loans to these companies. To facilitate trade in the region, Alibaba's logistics division, the Cainiao logistics smart network, is working with local partners to establish an "e-hub" that provides smart logistics services. Alibaba Cloud has established two data centers in Kuala Lumpur and has also collaborated with Sena Traffic Systems to create the infrastructure for a smart traffic management system in Malaysia. In addition, building on Alibaba's twenty years of experience, the group has established Alibaba Business School to train Malaysian digital entrepreneurs so that they can create similar growth opportunities in their home markets.

The strategy of going deeply local to win globally represents a significant mindset shift for leaders. Incumbents have traditionally regarded their global business as a pyramid, with headquarters at the top and local countries at the bottom. Corporate leaders issue directives from on high, and local businesses execute them to conform with the global template. To succeed in our increasingly volatile and fragmented global economy, with new players targeting new profit pools, and strong local players responding far more speedily and flexibly to customer and regulatory shifts, leaders must reverse this mental model, much as Bridgestone has done. They must regard countries with their local business models at the top of the pyramid and headquarters at the bottom as enablers of the country teams. This is not an easy transition to make, but as we'll see in Chapter 6, a number of leading-edge companies are putting in place a very different organizational model to make their new global strategies work.

Advice for Leaders

The imperative to refine global growth strategies is not a passing fad. Given the deep economic and social divides that have arisen in developed countries, it seems unlikely that protectionist policies will fade anytime soon and that the global economy will return to the more open trading of decades past. In fact, crises like the COVID-19 pandemic could potentially exacerbate economic and social differences. More fundamentally, the prominence of asset-light strategies will grow as industries move irrevocably toward value pools deriving from digitally based services. Technologies now on the horizon should lighten global footprints even further. Augmented reality will soon allow low-level employees to receive guidance on maintenance and repair issues in real time from global experts located elsewhere in the world. Instead of retaining large teams of skilled maintenance workers at local plants, companies will keep smaller teams on hand at each location, supporting them with global experts spread across the world and connected digitally. In this way, companies will maintain the same or superior maintenance and repair capacity at a lower cost. This is just one of many emerging technologies that companies will deploy to cut the costs of cross-border growth.[63]

Given how rapidly and profoundly global conditions are changing, the time to rethink your traditional approach to selecting and entering markets is *now*. Begin by posing some general questions that might inform your new global operating model:

1. Why have companies in your industry globalized over the past few decades, and how are the economic drivers behind such growth evolving? Are historical assumptions about globalization still relevant given changes in the competitive landscape? Which markets should you enter, defend heavily, or exit, and why?
2. What confers scale, competitive advantage, and profitability across your value chain today? Does the path to scale vary depending on the product or service you offer?
3. How might you compute local- and global-scale effects across the value chain per product type and within each product for each step of the value chain?
4. What investments are required to execute today's emerging operating models, and what risks accrue to them? Model the impact they might have on revenue and compound annual growth rate, profit, up-front investment and risk, and potential valuation.

As you reflect on these questions, look to the leading-edge companies discussed in this chapter for inspiration and practical guidance. When deciding which markets to target, select your bets carefully, and seek out countries, regions, segments, and customer subsegments where you can compete against local players to capture profitable market share. Don't allow yourself to become enthralled with the overall GDP growth numbers and the penetration of your products and services in a given country. Pay special attention to asset-light strategies that leverage third parties, resource-light teams, or both, as Xiaomi and Bajaj Auto have done. Consider, too, how you might reorganize the supply chain regionally to move resources quickly into and out of markets as needed, like Mars did. And shift your mindset about whose perspective prevails operationally inside your company, putting countries and their unique needs at the top of the pyramid, so to speak, rather than at the bottom. Together, these strategies will help you to build a more resilient growth path for your company.

Rethinking your organization's global growth path isn't easy. Given the dynamics of global commerce today, you might have to take the unpleasant move of scaling back or completely exiting markets that had formerly proven lucrative, alienating some within your organization who might not love the idea of evaluating the attractiveness of markets in new ways. Further, partnering with others in implementing asset-light entry strategies means that you will lose end-to-end control over your brand and product delivery, and your resource-light teams might find it harder to operate and prove more difficult to control. Still, as difficult as such challenges are, rethinking growth doesn't require you to completely jettison your existing global footprint and relegate yourself to your home market, and it doesn't mean abandoning every facet of your current market-entry strategies. It entails making changes where they make sense, layering on new practices and operating models over the old. As we'll see in part 2 of the book, going beyond great involves a similar evolution when it comes to executing operationally on your strategy and delivering new value propositions to your customers. In the next chapter, we'll explore how some companies have looked beyond their traditional supply chains, complementing them with new value networks that allow them to move quickly and build the breathtaking digital solutions and experiences of tomorrow.

Key Insights

- Certain underlying beliefs that drove globalization in the last century no longer hold. Companies are refining and optimizing their global presence, adopting a seemingly contradictory playbook for profitable global expansion that goes beyond traditional scale and asset-heavy growth strategies.
- Firms as diverse as Xiaomi, Alibaba, and Bajaj Auto are going asset light, pursuing swift, wide-scale global expansions without building expensive new infrastructure or mobilizing large teams (a feat made possible by relying on digital and local partners).
- When it comes to managing large existing physical footprints rather than rolling out a new business model, incumbent companies like Tata Steel and Cemex are rethinking whether it still makes sense to play in every major market. Others are adopting strategies that allow them to move into and out of markets quickly as economic conditions change. It's about smart growth, not growth everywhere.
- Where companies do engage, they are doing so more deeply. With economic and geopolitical fragmentation on the rise, it no longer makes sense to apply a standard operational template across countries in an attempt to drive efficiency. Instead, companies like Bridgestone, Siemens, and Alibaba are adopting a country-first mindset and local-for-global strategies.

PART II
OPERATING BEYOND

CHAPTER 4

ENGINEER AN ECOSYSTEM

*In addition to conventional supply chains, many global companies
are forming digital ecosystems as new-age value networks to create
and deliver solutions, outcomes, and experiences customers crave.
But as leading-edge companies are discovering, some ecosystems
work better than others.*

To deliver the pathbreaking digital services and experiences and the global growth strategies we just discussed, companies are going beyond traditional supply chains to create dynamic delivery networks, or *ecosystems*, of cross-industry partners. Formerly, large global companies conceived of their supply chains as a collection of long-term, highly structured, bilateral partnerships with suppliers. Although those partnerships remain essential for many companies, others are supplementing them by building and managing intricate new ecosystems, or *value webs*. These arrangements can be quite large (thirty or more partners across eleven or more industries and fourteen or more countries), and they enable companies to compete in ways that they never could have managed on their own.[1]

The most successful ecosystems are already disrupting industries and, indeed, transforming entire societies. One key example is Ant Financial (the operator of Alipay), an affiliate of the tech giant Alibaba. As of 2019, Ant was comprised of a number of successful businesses, including the consumer loan product Huabei and the world's largest money-market fund, Yu'e Bao. But the company's core business remained Alipay, China's biggest online payments platform, with a market share in 2018 of almost 54 percent.[2] Ant Financial in particular has grown globally by building a powerful ecosystem rather than trying to do everything itself.

Since 2004, the company has built a massive network of partners and has continued to add new global partners since spinning out from Alibaba in 2014.[3] To gain traction outside its home market, Ant has forged alliances with overseas retailers, airlines, hotels, and banks, among other partners (to tap into their local merchant relationships) while also partnering with local e-wallets in nine overseas markets (e.g., Paytm in India, KakaoPay in South Korea, and bKash in Bangladesh) to tap into their digital payments infrastructure. In 2016–2017, for instance, as part of its expansion in Asia, Ant forged merchant alliances with Starbucks, arranging for the latter to accept Alipay in its Malaysian locations, and with Cathay Pacific, arranging for the airline to accept Alipay for in-flight transactions.

In Europe, its alliances with acquirers and bank partners such as Barclays, BNP Paribas, and UniCredit allowed it to arrange for local merchants in the United Kingdom, France, and Italy, respectively, to accept Alipay. Meanwhile, Ant Financial was forming partnerships with hospitals, arranging for them to use its platform to accept payments, and with various apps and services. All told, the company had 16,000 hospital partnerships, 380 financial partners, and approximately 40 million merchant partnerships around the globe, all part of a massive network.[4]

In composing this network, Ant Financial has relied on different forms of strategic partnerships that support its mission of providing financial inclusion to underserved small businesses and individuals around the world. To expand into India, Ant made a strategic investment in the local e-wallet service Paytm, purchasing a minority stake in the leading fintech operator in that market. The company has made similar strategic investments in local e-wallets in Thailand, Pakistan, the Philippines, and elsewhere.[5] When Ant takes equity stakes in companies, it considers them core partners and provides them with monetary and technological support. As one observer described the strategy, the idea was to "pick the right partner in every market that looks ripe for an Ant Financial-style approach, buy a minority stake, benefit from the licenses and branding that partner already has, inject Ant's own tech in the back end and watch the money roll in."[6] Meanwhile, so-called alliance relationships pursued by Ant to enhance and expand the customer experience are considered noncore and are nonequity commercial partnerships. The partnerships with the European banks named previously were alliances, as were the deals with Starbucks and Cathay. Aside from equity stakes and alliances, Ant has at times forged other kinds of deals, including joint ventures. It has also implemented a standardized application process to handle applications from merchants to participate in its ecosystem.[7]

Ant Financial's exhaustive and ongoing efforts at ecosystem building have reaped immense dividends. Ant Financial's Alipay in 2019 exceeded 230 million daily active users and 1.2 billion distinct users (together with its global e-wallet partners).[8] Ant Financial was operating in over fifty markets and was expanding rapidly, building on its two-pronged strategy of partnering with local e-wallets and connecting local merchants with the global spending power of Chinese Alipay users.[9] As of 2019, Ant Financial had become the most valuable fintech firm globally, with a value that exceeded that of financial giants like Citibank, Goldman Sachs, and Blackrock.[10] More broadly, Ant Financial was a driving force behind a far-reaching societal change—namely, the rise of a cashless economy in China.[11] By 2017, the vast majority of consumers there (over 75 percent) were already using digital means to complete transactions, having leapfrogged from cash to mobile payments.[12] A news report proclaimed that "China is showing the rest of the world how to build a cashless society."[13]

The success of ecosystems like Ant Financial's will not come as news to global business leaders. One 2018 survey of leaders found that a majority identified ecosystems as a means of disrupting their industry, and almost 50 percent reported having responded to disruption in their industry by constructing an ecosystem.[14] And yet much of the attention that experts and advisers have paid to ecosystems has been superficial, leaving business leaders unsure how best—or even whether—to pursue them. As alluring as ecosystems are as a basis for disruption, they remain maddeningly difficult to execute. A few highly successful networks make headlines, but many more fail to deliver.

Leaders can't let the struggles of many ecosystem-building efforts scare them away. As industries move toward servitized offerings and digitally enabled business models, flexible networks of partners—value webs—are poised to unlock trillions of dollars in value while also helping firms become more resilient (in a loose partnership of independent companies, risk is shared instead of passed on, as it is with contractually integrated companies in a supply chain). Companies in virtually every industry—from banking to health care, consumer electronics to industrial equipment—will participate in ecosystems capable of delivering highly complex and integrated digital solutions. The time has come to learn and master an entirely new game, what we have termed "the emerging art of ecosystem management."[15] In this chapter, we'll sketch out this new art form, drawing on a rigorous study of dozens of leading ecosystems to explore how some companies have succeeded with ecosystems where others have so far failed.

Five Fundamentals of Ecosystems

Amid all the hype about ecosystems, it remains unclear to many precisely what these collaborative arrangements are and how they differ from traditional supply chains. Observers have noted that these new collaborative arrangements are designed for much more speed, innovation, and adaptability than supply chains can muster, as well as for a capacity to deliver integrated solutions. But few have methodically reviewed existing ecosystems to observe their distinguishing characteristics.

We define an ecosystem as a group of firms that collaborate to deliver a digitally enabled, integrated customer value proposition. Applying this definition, we analyzed more than forty of these networks from a range of industries and included both incumbent and digital players. Our analysis allowed us to document five key defining features of ecosystems. First, these networks are made of *multilateral relationships between participants*. In a traditional supply chain, relationships between companies tend to be bilateral. A given company might serve as a supplier to another one, which in turn supplies a third company, up the chain until it reaches the original equipment manufacturer (OEM), who assembles the supplied parts into a finished product. Lower-tier suppliers never deal with the final customer, only the OEM. The OEM closely manages and monitors the performance of suppliers in this vertical chain, laying down rules that cover pricing, design specifications, delivery criteria, and so on. Such rigidity allows for the optimization of cost, quality, and delivery up and down the chain.

By contrast, digital ecosystems are much more fluid structures, comprising multilateral partnerships that span across industries and that evolve and expand over time. Let's look at the automobile industry. You can picture a digital mobility ecosystem as a web with the OEM at its center and providers in other industries clustered around it. Such an ecosystem, which evolves alongside technology and market demand, has partners who provide the software and operating system, the IoT and cloud-platform capability, specific services offered to drivers via the car platform, hardware technology, applications, telecommunications connectivity, and so on—all coming together to create a connected car that offers a range of exciting services to consumers layered onto the automobile itself.

In its Together 2025+ strategy, Volkswagen proclaimed its intention to "not only stand for the best vehicles, but also for exciting and superior digital products and services."[16] To bring that vision to life, Volkswagen has moved to deliver a digital mobility platform that is now called We Connect and that includes an expanding and interconnected array of digital services, including security services, advanced navigation, preventive service and maintenance, and the ability to control your car remotely—all offered under the We Connect brand.[17] Yet the company couldn't have done it on its own—it lacked digital skills and the agile mindset that would enable a quick rollout of offerings to consumers. So Volkswagen built an ecosystem of partners to supplement its traditional supply chain. Seeking access to software capabilities (operating system, AI, and so on), the company formed alliances with several firms, including Microsoft (United States), Argo (United States), Nvidia (United States), Pivotal (United States), Cymotive Technologies (Israel), WirelessCar (Sweden), and Mobvoi (China), all of whom derive value from the totality of Volkswagen's network. To electrify and digitize its drivetrain, Volkswagen formed alliances with Northvolt (Sweden), QuantumScape (United States), SK Innovation (South Korea), and CATL (China). Seeking access to IoT and cloud capabilities, Volkswagen forged alliances with the likes of Microsoft (United States), Amazon (United States), and SAP (Germany). To build scale for its state-of-the-art product platforms (which in turn enable the digital mobility platforms), Volkswagen forged alliances with the likes of Ford (United States) and JAC (China).[18]

In total, the company by 2019 had built an interconnected network composed of roughly sixty partners spanning at least eleven countries and six industries—all to add a digital mobility layer onto its existing automotive products and thereby keep pace with competitors like Daimler, BMW, and GM. Unlike in traditional supply chains, Volkswagen's

The collaboration model in the automotive industry has evolved significantly

Traditional bilateral auto partnership

Digital mobility ecosystem

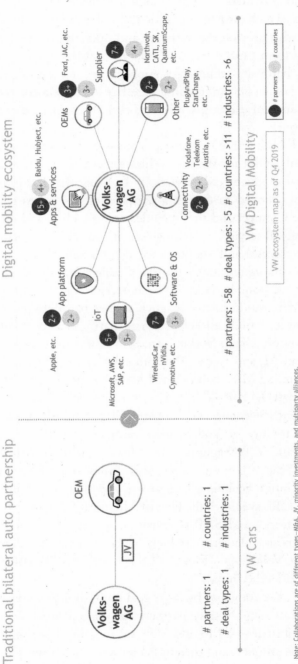

VW Cars

partners: 1   # countries: 1
deal types: 1   # industries: 1

VW Digital Mobility

VW ecosystem map as of Q4 2019

partners: >58   # deal types: >5   # countries: >11   # industries: >6

- # partners
- # countries

Figure 3. How Volkswagen is building a digital mobility ecosystem via multilateral, multicountry, multi-industry partnerships.

ecosystem generated revenue streams for various participants that existed independently of the consumer's actual car purchase (as when, for instance, consumers paid for ongoing digital services). As orchestrator of the ecosystem, Volkswagen works to "organize and manage the ecosystem, define the strategy, and identify potential participants."[19]

A second common feature of the ecosystems we studied was their *geographic reach*. Virtually all the ecosystems we studied (90 percent) counted participants in at least five countries, and most spanned both developed and developing countries. Samsung's SmartThings smart-home platform counts more than one hundred partners in over a dozen countries.[20] Xiaomi's platform counts partners in China, the United States, India, the United Kingdom, and elsewhere—at least seventy. Such geographical expansiveness means that companies must bridge cultural barriers and also take steps to protect their intellectual property, even though laws might vary widely across the ecosystem's geographies. Such steps might include limiting access to intellectual property (IP), seeking to retain expert employees, educating employees about the importance of protecting IP, building a local IP organization, systematically strengthening IP protections in local countries (by applying for patents, etc.), monitoring for violations and litigating if necessary, and acquiring *favored company* status from local governments (which can provide for strong IP protections).

Ecosystems also tend to *cross industry lines*—a third core feature we documented. In more than half of our sample, ecosystems brought together players in at least five industries, and almost all (83 percent) spanned at least three industries. Vacuum maker Dyson assembled a relatively small ecosystem to build its vacuum robot offering—just six partners. Yet these players spanned five industries. Dyson partnered with Amazon Alexa to offer smart-home solutions.[21] It called on the digital agency AKQA, based in San Francisco, to develop a smartphone app to run the vacuum and partnered with Imperial College, London, for help with general R & D tasks.[22]

A fourth important characteristic of digital ecosystems is their *malleable deal structures*. Whereas conventional bilateral supply chain relationships tend to be long-term joint ventures, companies can implement a range of potential deal structures to bring the relevant players together. Structuring deals as minority investments, platform partnerships, or shorter-term contracts allows ecosystem orchestrators to move nimbly to take advantage of opportunities and protect against threats as they arise. To build its industrial robot ecosystem, the Swiss pioneering technology leader ABB convened an ecosystem of forty-four players hailing primarily from developed markets and China. To obtain robotics hardware, ABB made both large and small acquisitions (for instance, of the Swedish firm SVIA and the Spanish start-up NUB3D) as well as minority investments (for instance, the US firm Grabit). To build strong cloud capabilities, ABB has performed acquisitions and made investments and alliances (for instance, with the Chinese firm Huawei, to provide industrial cloud solutions to its Chinese customers). Additionally, ABB has partnered with Microsoft, leveraging the tech giant's Azure cloud services to build its Industrial IoT platform and ABB Ability digital offering. ABB has also deployed a variety of deal types to acquire training, connectivity, and various other capabilities for its ecosystem, such as AI solutions by the preferred partner IBM.

Critically, companies tend to construct ecosystems *that ensure everyone benefits as the network generates value*—the fifth dominant characteristic we observed. Conventional supply chains can sometimes give rise to a zero-sum logic, with companies seeking to extract the maximum amount of value for themselves at the expense of their vendors. Although squeezing suppliers isn't best practice, it does happen. As networks, digital ecosystems tend to become more valuable as the number of participants increases and the capabilities they bring expand, leading to a bigger pie from which everyone shares. A classic example of this is Apple and its App Store, which since its launch in 2008 has grown to encompass approximately five million apps.[23] As the number and variety of apps increase, Apple's ecosystem becomes more valuable to consumers, attracting more of them and increasing the value entering the system—which in turn leads to the development of more and better apps. Apple's revenue share plan makes app development an attractive proposition. Developers working in Apple's operating system iOS receive up to 85 percent of revenues generated by their apps. Revenues earned by developers were up 30 percent in 2017, 28 percent in 2018, and 22 percent in 2019.[24]

We see a similar willingness to share the bounty in health-care platforms, which thanks to the COVID-19 pandemic have become more relevant than ever. In its Good Doctor health-care platform, Chinese insurer Ping An allows partner hospitals to keep all the patient registration fees they originate. Participating doctors keep 70 percent of fees for patients they see virtually, while Ping An gets the remainder (a similar revenue split holds for in-person medical visits to specialized medical facilities). Ping An gets a small commission of about 5 to 10 percent on pharmaceutical sales, giving the rest to pharmacies and pharmaceutical companies.[25] Similarly, the popular European online medical booking platform Doctolib allows doctors on the platform to keep their full fees, charging them a monthly fee. As the platform grows, attracting more patients (who don't pay a user fee), it becomes even more valuable for the doctors as a revenue source.[26] And as the number of doctors on the network grows, it becomes more attractive to patients, creating a virtuous cycle of growth.

Three Types of Ecosystems

In addition to the five key defining features, there are three distinct types of ecosystems: digitizer networks, platforms, and superplatforms.

Digitizer networks are ecosystems designed to provide a digital layer onto an existing physical product without adding much managerial complexity—Dyson's described previously is a good example. In general, digitizer networks contain partners outside the orchestrator's industry that allow it to access technology or intellectual property or to add new services. *Platforms* are more advanced and complex, connecting large numbers of consumers or smart devices into a single network. With standardized relationships between the orchestrator and contributors, platforms ensure high levels of service across the network and limit the occurrence of inconveniences, or friction. Orchestrators of these platforms can develop them as revenue sources and can also use the data these platforms generate to fuel adjacent businesses. Smart-home offerings such as Samsung's SmartThings are a good example of platform ecosystems, as are industrial ecosystems like Cisco's Connected Mine and Maersk's digital trade documentation platform as well as digital companies like eBay or Airbnb. The most complex ecosystems, *superplatforms*, aggregate other platforms into a single user interface. Orchestrators collect the data generated by the platforms, monetizing it by using it to fuel adjacent businesses. Amazon's Alexa is a superplatform composed of platforms such as Sonos, Uber, and Philips Hue, which themselves count millions of diverse partners and either are strategic partners or provide specific skills integrated into Alexa.[27]

Three major types of digital ecosystems—each with distinct characteristics

Ecosystems

	Traditional Product	Digitizer	Platform	Superplatform
Objective	• Engineer and manufacture a high-quality product while minimizing costs	• Digitize an existing product with the help of partners while keeping managerial complexity low	• Seamlessly connect smart things / connected users on a platform while ensuring high service levels and limiting friction	• Integrate several platforms into one fully integrated service offering while capturing user data from the integrated superplatform
Opportunity	• Premium product • Capture consumer premium	• New functionality • Capture consumer premium • Digital service revenues	• Revenue streams from platform usage • Adjacent business and/or service models using data	• Broad set of user data • Data monetization via adjacent business models
Characteristics				
Openness to new partners	🔒 1	🔒 1	🔓 1	🔓 1
Number of partners	At least 2	20–100	5–10 million	>10 million[1]
Number of industries	~1	~5	<5	>10

1. Includes direct platform partners and associated contributors. In the case of superplatforms that integrate smaller platform ecosystems, the number of partners may be significantly lower.
Note: Numbers of partners and industries are illustrative only.
Source: BCG Proprietary analysis of more than forty global ecosystems

Figure 4. Three types of digital ecosystems and their characteristics.

Ecosystems can serve multiple functions at once. Aside from functioning as a superplatform, Alexa also is a digitizer, adding digital capabilities to physical stereo speakers, and a platform that convenes partners who add specific capabilities, such as the ability to order pizza via Alexa or call for help in emergencies. Caterpillar's smart mining ecosystem, developed as part of its strategy called "the Age of Smart Iron," functions as a platform for servitizing CAT equipment and providing analytics. It is a closed platform built around CAT products and incorporating about thirty partners chosen by CAT in the areas of analytics, software, robotics, and smart devices. At the same time, CAT's ecosystem functions as a digitizer, as the company uses its network to operate autonomous mining trucks that can operate remotely in dangerous situations (including, potentially, on the moon) and without humans at the wheel.[28]

In all types of ecosystems, companies can operate as either orchestrators or participants. Companies need not choose one role or operate in only one ecosystem. Sonos has its own platform ecosystem, yet as we've seen, it also participates in the Alexa superplatform. The Chinese delivery-service company SF Express likewise serves as both an orchestrator of its own ecosystem and a participant in multiple others. As an executive at the company told us, SF Express spreads out its participation so as not to become too dependent on a specific ecosystem orchestrator such as Alibaba, Tencent, or Baidu.

The Secrets of Successful Ecosystems

Because ecosystems differ so profoundly from traditional supply chains, leaders can't manage them in the same way and hope to succeed. A rigorous science arose around supply chains over the past century as they became part of companies' global operating models. By contrast, designing and managing ecosystems remains an art, and one that industrial incumbents find especially difficult to master. To bring more structure to this art form,[29] we tracked the financial performance of each ecosystem as well as its popularity among users and the number of patents it received relative to its size. We also interviewed experts in their respective industries. What emerged were five factors that mark successful ecosystems.

First, *strategy matters over speed.* You might think that the first company in an industry to assemble an ecosystem wins the prize, but that's not necessarily true. Customer needs evolve, and the first company with an ecosystem might lack a value proposition capable of luring customers and partners. Apple CarPlay and Android Auto didn't launch their digital automobile platforms until 2014, years after GM (2007), BMW (2008), and Volkswagen (2011) had launched services of their own. Yet Apple and Android rapidly added partners to their platforms, and by 2019 Apple had sixty-three partners, the most of any service. Speed helps when it comes to setting up an ecosystem, but a winning strategy matters far more, and it can more than compensate for a late start.

Two other characteristics that tend to set successful ecosystems apart from the rest are *a significant global footprint* and *depth of partnership expertise.* As we've seen, all digital ecosystems are global and span across industries, but the best of them are especially expansive, with forty or more partners spread out across at least ten countries. Xiaomi's sprawling digital ecosystem counts dozens of partners across Asia, Europe, the United States, and South America. In Samsung's SmartThings ecosystem, more than one hundred partners in a dozen countries enable consumers to connect their dishwashers, refrigerators, televisions, and other household appliances. More expansive ecosystems tend to adapt to market conditions more readily than their peers while also scaling up offerings across borders more effectively. This is not to say that smaller, more local ecosystems can't work (Dyson's example suggests they can) or that larger ecosystems aren't more difficult to manage—they are. But from a financial and competitive standpoint, bigger really is better when it comes to ecosystems.

A fourth quality that successful ecosystems share is a *strong existing business with large numbers of customers.* Most successful ecosystems that we studied enjoy a built-in advantage as they were crafted by orchestrators that already occupied commanding positions in their industries. The search engine firm Baidu, known popularly as the "Chinese Google," was already the world's second-largest search engine when it announced in 2017 that it would create Apollo, an open-source platform for self-driving cars that includes hardware, software, and cloud data services.[30] Baidu proceeded with the support of the Chinese government, having been selected as one of the country's "champions for artificial intelligence,"[31] and the company also benefited from its ability to implement its existing AI-based virtual-assistant technology into the driving system.[32] By July 2018, Baidu had amassed an ecosystem with more than 130 partners, including automakers, suppliers, government departments, and technology companies.[33] By 2019, Baidu's autonomous driving system was estimated to have logged more than one million miles in Chinese urban areas,[34] and the company was slated to operate a fleet of autonomous taxis in the city of Changsha later that year.[35] If you're an incumbent operator in an industry, you hold a distinct edge in constituting a thriving ecosystem by virtue of your established size and resources. This is just one more reason not to attempt to undertake a digital play yourself or to simply buy up pathbreaking technology but to develop a more open and free-flowing collaboration with others.

A final success factor we've uncovered concerns companies' *ability to manage the more complex web of relationships that make up digital ecosystems.* The great profusion of deal types, geographies, and industries that exist in most ecosystems can prove challenging to navigate. To succeed, companies must choose and manage partners wisely and strategically. Technology companies tend to do better here, developing clear strategies from the outset and dedicating teams to the tasks of onboarding and managing ecosystem participants. When Amazon developed its Alexa personal assistant, dedicated teams worked together with developers to help them create apps for the system. An Alexa Skills Kit made it easier for developers to build and publish skills for Alexa, while a $100 million Alexa Fund supported new start-ups that promised to create alluring new skills.[36] App stores like Google Play and Apple's App Store have deployed similar tactics to collaborate with developers. By contrast, incumbent companies tend to develop ecosystems almost by happenstance, learning about what works and what doesn't as they go. The more deliberate and organized companies can be in developing and managing ecosystem partners, the better.

Advice for Leaders

If you haven't explored whether to take part in one or more ecosystems, either as an orchestrator or partner, don't delay. As companies rely ever more on digital interfaces to add product features, they'll need to establish partnerships and even entire networks in a matter of months rather than years. As Stephen Elop, the former CEO of Nokia, remarked in an internal memo to his employees, "The battle of devices has now become a war of ecosystems. . . . Our competitors aren't taking our market share with devices; they are taking our market share with an entire ecosystem. This means we're going to have to decide how we either build, catalyze or join an ecosystem."[37] That memo was circulated way back in 2011. The "war of ecosystems" is being even more intensely waged today.

To understand whether to develop a digital ecosystem for an existing or new business, consider the following questions:

- Do important gaps exist between the digital offerings you wish to bring to market and your in-house competencies?
- Are collaborations in your industry now increasingly oriented toward providing integrated solutions for a seamless customer journey as opposed to delivering a single product?
- Can you spot innovative ways of collaborating in the industry, such as minority investment in ecosystem partners, open collaboration, and multilateral partnerships?
- Are outside players entering your industry, and are your competitors entering theirs via digital means?
- Are IP and nonmonetary assets (e.g., partnership networks) becoming the key winning assets in your industry?
- Can you spot movement toward agile and flexible partnerships, given the need to constantly attract new partners and adapt offerings faster?
- Do innovation and speed to market now function as key competitive differentiators in your business?

As you contemplate whether to pursue a digital ecosystem, you'll want to think about which kind of ecosystem to pursue and how to participate. The three types of ecosystems are appropriate for fulfilling specific goals. If you seek to digitally enhance your existing products, a digitizer platform might be best. Platform ecosystems can help you to generate revenue streams from usage of the platform or to generate data that could feed other businesses. Explore setting up a superplatform if you seek to amass vast amounts of data that you can monetize via other complementary businesses. Of course, these three options require varying degrees of openness on your part vis-à-vis collaborators. If you find openness difficult, a superplatform probably isn't for you. Because they're smaller and less complicated, digitizer platforms afford orchestrators the greatest amount of control.

Whichever platform fits your strategic needs, think about whether to assemble a new ecosystem or contribute to someone else's existing one. In the years ahead, every company will have to grapple with this question as a fundamental strategic issue. The deciding factor is whether you interface with the end customer or whether another player does. If you do, then you should attempt to orchestrate the ecosystem, as you'll likely possess an understanding of customers and their needs that is deeper than those of other players. Otherwise, you should consider a role as a participant. Bear in mind that it isn't always the largest companies that get to orchestrate the ecosystem. Automobile manufacturers are partners in Baidu's autonomous-driving ecosystem, even though they are larger players. Your goal should be to deeply understand customers' needs and behaviors and to occupy the position in the ecosystem that maximizes your ability to create and capture value for the end customer.

If you're thinking of orchestrating your own ecosystem, it also pays at the outset to consider how you might structure it. Here, you'll want to think through the following executional questions:[38]

- What rules or processes will you establish to govern participation in the ecosystem, and what specific metrics will you put in place to gauge their performance?
- How will the ecosystem create value, and how will you apportion this value to attract and maintain partners?
- How will you attract the partners most likely to help you maximize the ecosystem's value?
- How might you structure partner relationships to maximize the ecosystem's flexibility and adaptability and make it more resilient?
- How might you protect partners' IP up front to ease their concerns and ensure their enthusiastic participation?
- How might you nurture bonds among ecosystem members and foster regular, ongoing collaboration and experimentation?

Once you answer these questions, consider how your ecosystem will operate in relation to your existing businesses. It's difficult to succeed with ecosystems if you operate them as just another part of your legacy business. Digital start-ups can make decisions quickly across their business functions, enabling rapid execution, and a legacy company's ecosystem must be similarly nimble. For this reason, leading-edge global

companies put different internal rules and processes in place to govern
their ecosystems, they allow for different reporting structures, and they
often physically separate administrators of their digital ecosystem from
their legacy businesses. The accommodations companies must make to
succeed with ecosystems extend also to areas like culture and talent management, which we'll cover later in this book.

As valuable as they are now becoming, digital ecosystems are not
replacements for conventional supply chains but rather vital supplements to them. Ultimately, it is the *combination* of the two that enables
a company to deliver pathbreaking offerings. Companies must venture
beyond the more rigid and closed mindset associated with traditional
supply chains and embrace fluid, flexible, and dynamic ways of collaborating. But supply chains, for both products and service delivery, still
matter, and companies must retain the capacity to manage those well
too. As we'll see in the next chapter, the supply chains of tomorrow
won't be identical to those that fueled the success of so many global
companies in recent decades. Leading-edge companies are beginning to
redeploy their productive assets (people, factories, service-delivery centers) in ways that enable them to respond better to shifting markets, to
navigate tariffs and other protectionist measures, and to make the most
of the technologies now transforming industrial production and service
delivery. These companies are going *beyond* low-cost delivery models
focused on efficiency and embracing instead what we might call *flex*
delivery. Let's take a look.

Key Insights

- To deliver the pathbreaking digital services and experiences
described in Chapter 1, and the global growth strategies evoked in
Chapter 2, companies are going beyond traditional supply chains to
create dynamic delivery networks, or ecosystems, of cross-industry
partners.
- Much of the attention previously paid to ecosystems has been
superficial, leaving business leaders unsure how best—or even
whether—to pursue them. As alluring as ecosystems are as a basis
for disruption, they remain maddeningly difficult to execute.

- We closely analyzed more than forty of these networks from a range of industries and included both incumbent and digital players. Our analysis allowed us to document five key defining features of ecosystems.
- In addition to the five key defining features, our study led us to discover more complexity in the ecosystem phenomenon than observers had previously assumed. In particular, we found that three distinct types of ecosystem exist: digitizer networks, platforms, and superplatforms.
- The secrets of successful ecosystems include the following: the existence of a strong strategy, creation of a significant global footprint, the existence of sufficient depth of partnership expertise, possession of a strong existing business with large numbers of customers, and the ability to manage the more complex web of relationships that make up digital ecosystems.

CHAPTER 5

FLEX HOW YOU MAKE IT

*Companies have set up globally optimized delivery models to
minimize total costs when producing goods and delivering services.
Cost still matters, but delivery models now must also be high speed,
responsive, and resilient in the face of disruptions.*

Although the new digital services and experiences companies are
developing have generated a fair amount of publicity, a quieter but
no less exciting revolution is emerging in how firms make and deliver
what they sell. During the 1980s and 1990s, the internet's growth enabled
global companies to control production from afar and to track goods over
long distances. Companies mobilized these capabilities to fundamentally
redesign their manufacturing footprints. Seeking to minimize costs, they
built huge plants (or subcontracted for them with local companies) in
China and other countries with low labor costs. Using materials supplied
by local companies, they shipped the output of these plants to markets
worldwide. Nike, Walmart, IBM—they all did it, as did countless others. Customers benefited from lower prices, while shareholders reaped
higher profits. In 1990, only around 7 percent of global manufacturing
took place in low-cost (top twenty exporting) countries. By 2010, that
number had risen to over 33 percent. In some labor-intensive industries
like textiles, leather, clothing, and apparel, low-cost countries accounted
for an even greater share of global production.[1]

Today, this so-called low-cost global delivery model, or globally integrated supply chain, is becoming increasingly obsolete.

Managing production and delivery networks is no longer just about minimizing costs but about also achieving more flexibility, speed, and resilience for the enterprise.

Leading-edge companies are looking beyond big global manufacturing plants in locations with low labor costs, setting up bespoke factories that are higher tech, smaller, more numerous, more local, closer to customers, more flexible, and thus more capable of quickly producing and shipping personalized goods that reflect ever-shifting consumer needs. In addition, companies are looking beyond cost when deciding how to source parts and raw materials and where to locate production, taking steps to make their companies both more flexible in meeting customer needs and more resilient to shocks from tariffs, extreme climate events, and even pandemics. Finally, as products become more intelligent and their customers seek better performance, companies are building new software capabilities in their supply chains to offer product upgrades far more quickly (in months or weeks rather than years), delivering them digitally via software embedded in products rather than physically.

We call this the new *flex* approach, and it doesn't just apply to products. Companies that sell services and experiences are implementing it too. Let's return to the example of TCS and the IT services industry, which we developed in the introduction. TCS's then COO N. Chandrasekaran (now Tata Group's chairman) decided during the 2000s to implement a new set of strategies that would help the company achieve higher growth and deliver higher value while retaining the company's cost advantage (which was then eroding) and thus protect its high margins.[2] One such strategy was to pioneer a new, more flexible global delivery model, serving customers not merely out of the company's low-cost, high-scale facilities in India but also out of mid- and high-cost facilities located closer to customers in developed markets, all connected via the cloud. The idea was to layer new capabilities onto the existing low-cost offshore delivery capacity, allowing TCS to offer the same value propositions to customers in the United States and Europe as his global peers did while still maintaining comparatively high margins. Instead of sourcing all the software coding and other technical work out of its Indian software plants, TCS would set up delivery centers around the world closer to its customers that used a combination of local (and higher-cost) teams and teams stationed in India and other low-cost countries. Flex delivery would enable more system-wide resilience, mitigating risks related to geopolitics and the concentration of delivery capacities in just one geography. Critically, TCS would also be in a better position to offer higher-value, higher-skill, and customized offerings such as IP creation, services related to emerging technologies, the setting up of digital centers of excellence, and so on.

During the early 2000s, TCS introduced what it called its Global Network Delivery Model, transforming the way that companies delivered IT services globally. The model was comprehensive, including the creation of verticalized business units that became repositories of domain knowledge, the unleashing of entrepreneurial energy across the company, a focus on IP creation, early investments in digital technology, and an increased focus on R & D. But flex delivery was also a key element. By 2019, TCS had built a network of about two hundred delivery centers in more than fifteen countries covering both its biggest markets in United States and Europe and low-cost or talent-rich countries like Hungary, China, Argentina, and Chile, with the largest capacity continuing to be in India.[3] These centers operated as a globally integrated delivery network with capacities and skills distributed across three levels: (1) large, highly automated low-cost facilities with a large array of standard skills (SAP services, for example) at scale; (2) regional delivery centers in locales like Hungary, Brazil, and Uruguay that could serve regional customers with certain specialized skills and capacities but that had language and cultural requirements; and (3) local or near-shore delivery centers in places like New Jersey, Arizona, and Peterborough (United Kingdom) that offered customers high-touch, high-skill, but smaller-scale service.[4]

Because these facilities were all linked by a global technology infrastructure with state-of-the-art collaboration tools, the company could source its services seamlessly and flexibly from desirable locations in the global delivery network, giving it a huge competitive advantage. It could customize its delivery team and capacity across its global centers. And the company used the highest-quality software-engineering processes for consistent quality. The network delivered cost, talent, speed, customization, and resiliency. Over the past decade, it has proven wildly successful, underpinning impressive growth at TCS. As of 2020 the company was one of the most valued global IT services firms.[5] While competitors reap margins in the low teens, TCS's run above 25 percent.[6]

As TCS's story suggests, the centerpiece of late twentieth-century production and service delivery—large-scale offshore production and delivery centers in low-cost countries—isn't suddenly obsolete. Global companies are continuing to leverage manufacturing and delivery capabilities in low-cost countries, but they're layering on additional multicountry capacities in major high-cost markets and regional centers, seeking speed, flexibility, and responsiveness, not just the lowest possible cost. Such flex delivery networks, which have gone beyond traditional supply chains, are more adaptive and resilient to challenges posed by increasing and uncertain tariffs and growing nontariff barriers. By adding a layer of new software capabilities, they also deliver more intelligent products that meet customers' demands for better performance and enhanced product experiences. At the end of the chapter, we'll suggest how you can begin to approach building such a flex delivery capability to establish an advantage for your firm, putting the same kind of creativity and innovation into this area that you are into creating exciting, attention-grabbing new value propositions.

Coming Soon, from a Flex Factory Near You

To better understand why companies are now seeking more from their production and delivery arrangements (highly flexible production and delivery as well as the lowest delivered cost), let's reflect for a moment on the evolution of manufacturing in the sneaker industry. If you were a nineteenth-century English lord and you wanted a new pair of dancing shoes for the upcoming London ball, you'd call the local shoemaker to your manor house and explain what style and color you had in mind. He'd measure your feet and then go back to his workshop to cut, size, and stitch according to your preferred design. Some days or weeks later, he'd return with an initial version of the shoes for you to try on. If you loved them, great. If not, he'd go back to his workshop and make the required adjustments just as you wanted before delivering the finished product to your door and taking his payment.

The Industrial Revolution changed how dancing shoes—and most other consumer goods—were made. Large factories and steam engines displaced local craftspeople, mass-producing cheap goods for wider markets. As shipping improved and the advent of containers slashed costs, these large plants began exporting mass-produced goods around the world. Later still, with the internet's emergence and the further lowering of freight costs, companies began relocating these plants to emerging countries, taking advantage of their drastically lower labor costs. By the mid-2000s, Asia produced over 80 percent of the world's shoes in large-scale plants and across product categories.[7] China in particular became known as the "world's factory" because of the numerous large-scale plants serving global markets that had been established there. For most consumers, goods became much cheaper and more accessible, although companies didn't make them to their personal specifications as skilled craftspeople once did for our aristocratic forebears.

This picture is now poised to change once more, for four reasons. First, consumer expectations are increasing. Accustomed to personalizing even the smallest dimensions of their digital lives, the new global consumers described earlier in this book now expect to do that off-line as well. According to one BCG study, "When the shopping experience was highly personalized, customers indicated that they were 110% more likely to add additional items to their baskets and 40% more likely to spend more than they had planned."[8] Consumers are also seeking the latest shoe designs, experiences, and outcomes, and companies such as adidas and Nike are providing this, as well as personalization, via their websites.

Second, the rise of IoT and Industry 4.0 technology promises to make it possible for shoe companies to fulfill consumer expectations and still make a profit. These technologies are transforming the old trade-off that favored production in low-labor-cost countries despite the higher shipping costs that producing there entailed. The steep cost curve that had led companies to source production from large labor-intensive plants to begin with became flattened. Highly automated plants in high-cost markets are becoming more viable, as is more flexibility, smaller production lots (enabling custom orders), and quicker production times. As the cost of IoT technologies continues to fall (3-D printers, for instance, that used to cost $300,000 in the 1980s can now cost less than $200, with much improved speed and performance), automated plants in high-cost markets will only become more attractive.[9]

Third, an increasingly larger portion of companies' delivery of customer solutions or experiences is taking place electronically via downloaded software. Thanks to the rise of digital technology, electronics and software are becoming more important as a component of products. Nike, for instance, has introduced an entire digital ecosystem to help consumers gain more health benefits from their shoes, while cars are rapidly becoming computers on wheels. In fact, a sophisticated vehicle like the BMW 7 Series can contain up to 150 electronic control units (electronic hardware mechanisms that operate systems such as windows, seats, and the car's sophisticated engines), which in turn requires more than one hundred million lines of software code to operate (in comparison, Facebook utilizes approximately sixty million lines of code).[10] The machines and plants that make everyday products like cars are also increasingly controlled by electronics and their software. Customers of these products, both consumer and industrial, expect their suppliers to improve performance and functionality by upgrading products frequently via software updates (think of what people expect from their smartphones, for example). That in turn means that companies must acquire more high-skill, high-cost technical staff to help them design and deliver these upgrades quickly (often weekly or monthly, unlike the physical products that could have a life cycle of years), as the old delivery model cannot do it. (It also means that physical goods are accounting for a lower percentage of global trade than in the past and digitally enabled services a higher percentage.)

Finally, the growth of economic nationalism and the weakening of multilateralism have led to a growth in average and specific (between-countries) tariffs. This is providing an additional incentive for companies to produce goods locally rather than import them into markets from global supply centers subjected to higher import tariffs. "It used to be that companies could replicate the same business model in different markets, with leaders assuming that high tariffs were relics of the past," Emmanuel Lagarrigue, chief innovation officer at the French energy and automation company Schneider Electric, told us. "Today, the world is fragmented, and tariffs are back."[11]

Responding to these forces, players in the shoe industry have begun to rethink their manufacturing networks and to pilot new plant concepts. At locations in Germany and the United States, adidas has tested revolutionary SpeedFactories, fully automated plants that use robotics,

3-D printing, and other Industry 4.0 technologies to enhance production and hasten delivery of custom-designed products to local consumers. Whereas traditional shoe factories employ thousands of workers and can take up to eighteen months to get shoes to markets across the world, adidas's experimental plant concept employs fewer than two hundred workers and could potentially get the latest high-end fashion designs into nearby stores in just four months.[12] As adidas's former CEO Herbert Hainer observed upon the launch of these pilot facilities, "SPEEDFACTORY combines the design and development of sporting goods with an automated, decentralised and flexible manufacturing process. This flexibility opens doors for us to be much closer to the market and to where our consumer is."[13]

If the company were to roll out SpeedFactories at scale, millions of consumers would enjoy the kind of high-touch shoe-manufacturing service that had once been reserved for the wealthy. adidas would leverage the new technologies' full capabilities and allow consumers to design their own one-of-a-kind shoes online, which the nearest SpeedFactories would then make. One might even imagine that drones would one day pick up these shoes from SpeedFactories and deliver them to consumers' homes. Instead of sourcing from a smaller number of large-scale plants in low-cost countries, the company's manufacturing network would be multicountry, composed of both large-scale plants in countries with low labor costs and a number of smaller high-tech plants located closer to consumers in major markets.

In late 2019, adidas announced that it was closing its SpeedFactories and transferring the concept to facilities in Vietnam and China.[14] The company had struggled to make manufacturing located in or near major markets economically viable and scalable given the cost of today's technologies. The company had drawn many lessons from these pilots. The company wouldn't shift the bulk of its production to Western countries over the next five to ten years, not just because of the technology or economic scaling challenges but also because the ecosystem of suppliers in Western countries had eroded. Still, adidas would build elements of the SpeedFactory technologies into its existing supply network in countries like China, Indonesia, Vietnam, and India to both improve cost and increase flexibility. The company's highest growth markets were in Asia, so flex manufacturing there allowed it to serve these markets most quickly. The manufacturing of shoes still requires significant manual labor compared to industries like automobiles and pharmaceuticals. One solution to mitigate costs was to introduce more automation in these large mass production plants and make them more efficient and flexible.

SpeedFactory in its original guise was perhaps ahead of its time. Improvements in automation and falling costs of automation would allow adidas to further refine manufacturing technology to make it cheaper and more efficient. Over the next decade and beyond, these improvements could render SpeedFactory-type flex production increasingly cost-effective for premium and custom-designed products, finally enabling shoe companies to deploy it at scale in many markets. More broadly, flex manufacturing is set to become ubiquitous within global delivery models over the next two decades, especially as technologies such as 3-D printing become less costly.

Reimagining Closed Supply Chains

As much as multicountry networks are helping companies make "delivery" more flexible, responsive, and resilient in addition to low cost, they aren't enough. Companies are also dramatically rethinking their broader approach to the traditional model of "closed" supply chains.

Companies have always been very clear on two important points as they set up their global supply chains. First, they mark out what is core to them—the steps of the design and manufacturing and delivery processes that they will keep in-house. When it comes to these steps, they want to retain total control over quality and the IP involved because they believe this affords them a competitive advantage and differentiates their products. Second, they specify the role of suppliers for noncore activities, managing them tightly to enable the OEM to develop and supply the product or service at the lowest cost and highest quality. Supply chains are a closed system with fairly strict rules.

But this reality is fast changing. To respond quickly to changing customer needs, companies must upgrade their manufacturing and delivery process, quickly bringing online new capabilities (especially digital) they don't already possess. Because these capabilities often require time to develop internally, companies are taking a more open approach than they have in the past, approaching supply chains in ways similar to the digital ecosystems described in the last chapter. With trade uncertainties flaring up around the world and other disruptions becoming more frequent, companies are also increasingly forced to rethink their closed, highly controlled supply-chain strategies to make supply chains more resilient, reduce risk, and optimize both tariffs and total costs.

Two strands of new thinking on integrated supply chains are coming together here. First, companies are embracing new forms of partnerships that leverage suppliers' skills and capabilities. Second, they're doing this even when it comes to manufacturing processes formerly thought of as core to the business. As Peter Rosenfeld, a senior adviser to BCG and former head of global procurement at Ford, told us, companies are increasingly turning to their supply chains to help them provide more value to their end customers. Instead of assuming that they must retain total control over their core manufacturing, "they're asking: how can we leverage our supply base while bringing in our own expertise?" Rosenfeld explained that companies are now opting to "design the product while surrounding themselves with an extended enterprise that can deliver the best product to win."[15] They no longer feel that they have to be the biggest manufacturer in a market—it's far more important to be the best in delivering it overall.

Rosenfeld points to the automobile industry, where vertical integration was once paramount. Now, companies are turning to horizontal partners to make formerly sacred parts of their final product, like the engine or powertrain. According to Rosenfeld, companies are discovering "that there is a continuum of possible relationships with suppliers."[16] In some cases, they're colocating teams with clients and cocreating solutions. In other cases, they're embarking on partnerships with suppliers as opposed to managing them in what had been a relationship of unequals.

In the health-care space, Johnson & Johnson has established innovative partnerships to develop innovative surgical tools and devices using 3-D printing. In one collaboration with researchers at Trinity College Dublin, the company has established a new material sciences lab focused initially on orthopedic research.[17] Johnson & Johnson is also developing 3-D-printed knee tissue in a partnership with Aspect Biosystems.[18] As Rajesh Gopinathan, CEO and managing director of TCS, told us, TCS has increasingly become a nontraditional supply-chain partner in the knee-replacement space because of its world-class design and data-processing capabilities. A surgeon in a US hospital, the customer of a US medical-implant supplier, might upload a 3-D scan of a knee about to be replaced and send it to TCS. TCS designs the mold for the knee's manufacture and detailed software instructions for the 3-D printer that will make the mold and the knee. TCS sends the software instructions to its customer, the knee manufacturer in the United States, who prints the knee and sends it to the hospital's surgeon. By taking over this data-intensive part of the manufacturing process that had been core to the knee manufacturers in the old delivery model, and building capabilities and scale to deliver at speed detailed designs of molds for different types and complexities to customers around the world, TCS makes the supply chain nimbler and more responsive while contributing best-in-class skills from around the world. The growth of such unorthodox supplier partnerships led one Johnson & Johnson supply-chain executive to remark that "we see an increasing degree of integration with external partners, because they can help their customers become more agile, more flexible, and more responsive to meet customers' needs and improve the end-to-end supply chain."[19]

If the new supply chains enable more flexibility and responsiveness, companies are also redesigning them to make them more resilient in the face of tariffs and other geopolitical risks. In particular, companies are embedding more optionality into supply chains, maintaining a pecking order of sourcing and toggling between suppliers depending on developments in the trade wars. The chief strategy officer of a global aluminum company told us that it has become critical for its "complex matrix value chain of multicountry operations and sales around the world to have a dynamic model that can map source plants with markets against a set of assumptions on trade policy [i.e., tariff and nontariff barriers]." On the basis of this analysis, this executive said, "I should be able to compare my costs against competitors under various scenarios and arrive at the best possible plant-sales country pairing under the current tariffs."

In response to tariffs, one US-based tool manufacturer planned to build a new production facility in Mexico after performing a detailed analysis and considering a number of other locations, including Indonesia, India, and Vietnam. The manufacturer might have realized lower absolute costs in other locations, but risk-adjusted cost was higher. adidas has likewise focused intensively on building flexibility into its supply chain, diversifying its sourcing countries in recent years (as have other shoe manufacturers) in a bid to reduce country risk.[20] As of 2019, most of its footwear production (43 percent) came from Vietnam, its largest sourcing country, while China accounted for 16 percent.[21]

Companies like Samsung are shifting production in response to trade tensions between the United States and China. They have closed some manufacturing facilities in China and are expanding or establishing new factories in its major markets. As of 2020, Samsung has unveiled plans to invest $500 million in a new smartphone-display manufacturing facility in India, on top of a $700 million investment it made in a separate Indian plant in 2018.[22] In addition, it has opened a $380 million facility in South Carolina to manufacture home appliances.[23] Such a strategy for reimagining supply chains strengthens the multicountry model discussed earlier while minimizing the risk of sudden changes in the cost of goods due to tariffs and other impediments. As the CEO of a Nordic industrial company told us, his firm had built a new multicountry supply chain with plants and suppliers located in all its major markets, an arrangement that insulated the company from any sudden tariffs between these countries.

Shifting production from high- to low-tariff locations and building more optionality into supply chains aren't the only strategies companies are using to render them more resilient. They're also embracing short-term measures on an ongoing basis to deal with the "new normal" of volatile tariffs. Such measures can include taking a hit on margins, sharing the hit with suppliers, or exploiting regulatory loopholes (arguing, for instance, that a product wasn't primarily made in a country hit by tariffs, or reclassifying products so that they don't fall into categories covered by tariffs). A client of ours in the home-improvement space was about to see $1 billion in cost increases due to tariff measures and other protectionist actions. In response, we set up a control room that would perform detailed analysis of tariffs' impact across product categories and develop comprehensive strategies for countering the immediate tariff threat and reducing the company's long-term vulnerability. In the short term, the control room developed a plan that included adjusting prices, renegotiating terms with suppliers, and looking for loopholes in trade policies. In the longer term, this company will possibly make design changes to their products, using lower-cost components sourced from lower-tariff locations.

Software Centers: The New Hardware in Supply Chains

Increasingly, all physical products and services are becoming digital value propositions in some form or shape. To deliver them and improve the performance of the flex delivery model itself, companies are moving software centers from the periphery of the supply chain, where they had formerly been, and making them primary.

During the late twentieth century, most large companies in sectors like industrials, consumer products, and retail didn't do much software development—it was regarded as, at best, an exotic capability on the fringes of the organization. These firms would tuck away their developers in obscure parts of the world, housing them alongside their IT teams. Today, these same firms are bringing online highly sophisticated, centralized digital capabilities staffed with thousands of people as part of their supply chains. That's because value propositions are much different today than they used to be. Products have gone digital to an extent never before seen, a phenomenon we discussed in Chapter 2. Using software updates, makers of physical products can respond quickly not just to service issues but to create solutions that target new value pools. Digital centers containing various kinds of software capacities are becoming as integral to the delivery of products and services in the twenty-first century as physical plants alone used to be for industrial companies.

As we found in our research, a global fashion retailer developed a software development / digital center as an integral part of its flex global delivery model, using its capabilities to help it optimize pricing and promotions across its stores worldwide in real time. Legacy retail companies collect a huge amount of data across their stores and supply chains, but they've long lacked the ability to analyze that data on a daily or even hourly basis to drive pricing and promotions. As a result, retailers have lost untold millions unnecessarily marking down products to clear stock or promoting new fashion designs in unhelpful ways. At this particular retailer, the data center collects vast amounts of data from online and off-line channels and deploys powerful algorithms to analyze it. As a result, this company can put the right items on sale at the right times and at the right prices to maximize revenue. The company can also enhance consumers' shopping experience—for instance, by personalizing their promotions to make them more relevant.

This fashion retailer built their digital center within the confines of the flex delivery model, intending primarily to help lower the cost of internal operations and improve their speed and flexibility. Schneider Electric has gone further, extending the delivery chain by setting up design labs that enable it to cocreate new digital products and solutions with customers and external partners. Traditional product development took years, but these new design labs allow Schneider Electric to roll out new offerings in weeks or months. As of 2019, the company was designing more than 150 products each year at eight of these labs in the United States, Europe, and Asia, and those numbers were poised to increase.[24] Similarly, Siemens has opened dozens of MindSphere Application Centers around the world tasked with developing "new business models, digital solutions and services" for customers. Staffed with data scientists and software developers, these facilities are designed to be "close to where customers operate" so that team members can "learn about customer headaches and work on solving them."[25]

Leading-edge companies are taking different routes in building a global software and digital capability into their flex delivery model. In some cases, they're creating these assets from scratch. Other times, they're reorganizing existing assets that had been previously fragmented, creating one or a few digital hubs located in talent-rich locations like Silicon Valley, Berlin, Tel Aviv, and Bangalore. At these hubs, companies are making the digital features and functionalities required to deliver new, digitally integrated products and services, mobilizing powerful collaborations across features thanks to the concentration of talent in these locations. As we'll see in more detail later in the book, companies are also mobilizing these hubs to change how their teams work, promoting more agile and responsive development of products and services.

New software capabilities aren't just revolutionizing the development, delivery, and management of products for end users. In the future, they will also control the machines and plants making these products, fundamentally changing how companies set up and manage plants or delivery centers. So-called digital-twin technology will figure prominently here. A digital twin is a virtual model of a plant, product, or process created by design and software engineers. With such a model in hand, engineers can simulate the performance of the real (physical) plant, product, or process, using data about past operations to improve future performance. Today, local teams managing a plant or product are usually the ones using digital twins to monitor performance. In theory, digital-twin technology should eventually allow global companies to set up, monitor, and drive improvement in their performance remotely and in real time. Companies will build virtual software models of all their machines and plants, linking them together and monitoring and controlling the entire network from one or a few centralized locations. The next evolution of the resilient flex delivery model will be upon us.

In fact, it already is. When General Electric builds wind farms for power companies, it first creates digital twins of them, modeling the wind farm in the precise location where it is to be located in real life. Engineers custom-design turbines, optimizing them to perform where they will be constructed. After the real turbines go into operation, software monitors their performance remotely, making adjustments. The technology increases energy production by 20 percent, boosting the lifetime value extracted from a 100-megawatt wind farm by $100 million.[26] Because of such potential for added value, the global market for digital-twin technology is projected to expand exponentially, reaching $35.8 billion by 2025.[27] According to one estimate, digital-twin technology will be adopted by half of the large industrial companies by 2021, significantly enhancing operations.[28]

Advice for Leaders

As we've seen in this chapter, the twenty-first-century global enterprise will mobilize a very different approach to manufacturing and service delivery than its forebears did. Eventually, companies will have their own networks of multicountry, automated, and flexible plants, each with its own local supply network and each linked together and controlled remotely using digital-twin technology. These networks won't crop up overnight. Given the large investments global companies have made in their existing plants and service-delivery centers, as well as technical challenges relevant to scaling, these companies will require decades to build the next-generation global manufacturing and delivery models we've described in this chapter. On the one hand, these highly resilient models will include high-technology, multicountry local plants and delivery centers that afford speed, customization, and access to new talent. On the other, they'll include traditional low-cost mass production, albeit integrated with technology to improve cost and flexibility.

To prepare for this new reality, leaders must dedicate themselves to doing two things at once: (1) moving toward a highly flexible, high-speed network while (2) retaining low-cost existing facilities where appropriate. Leaders must consider how to become more responsive, speedy, and resilient while also optimizing how efficiently they deliver products and services. Further, leaders should begin to modify their supplier strategies so that they are more flexible and open. As products and services become increasingly intelligent, leaders should look to build digital hubs with software capabilities integrated with the physical product-delivery network. And as they build out a more flexible capacity for making and delivering what they sell, leaders should consider how they can make supply chains not merely more cost-effective and faster but also more resilient in the face of sudden economic and geopolitical shifts.

As they begin to redesign manufacturing and service delivery for their companies, leaders should focus in on the following four areas of strategic inquiry:

1. To what extent do your customers require speed and customization? If some of them regard it as important and are willing to pay a premium for it, how might you adjust your manufacturing-and-delivery network to deliver products and services to these customers more quickly?

2. How fast is the intelligence quotient of your products and services growing, and how big are these new value pools? What kind of software talent do you need to tap into these value pools, and how might you attract, hire, and retain that talent (more on this later in the book)? What kinds of partnership might you form with external suppliers to complement your internal software and digital skills? What kind of centralized digital capability do you need to make the most of the trove of data you might already have but that has until now been underutilized?

3. As customer expectations change, what core activities still comprise the basis of your competitive advantage? What noncore activities can you hand off to others via partnerships? More generally, how will your supplier relationships need to change as value chains become increasingly disintermediated, with the customer-facing firm no longer owning many parts of the value chain?

4. As trade regimes become more uncertain, which strategy or combination of strategies should you deploy to build resilience while also balancing trade-offs between cost and risk? For example, how many plants and delivery centers should you build close to markets to remain insulated against supply-chain shocks? To what extent should your plan sacrifice cost to allow you to seamlessly shift capacity between plants so as to mitigate risk?

Many organizations might resist holding discussions around these questions. For some leaders, it will seem foolhardy to propose making changes to a historically global supply and manufacturing structure that has proven its usefulness. Further, localizing or regionalizing manufacturing and supply requires significant planning and can prove damaging if executed poorly. Investing in digital technologies, both in manufacturing and in product capabilities, is costly and time-consuming. Also, adjusting production and service delivery so that it deploys more digital talent to produce the software components of products might leave existing talent feeling less important, causing them to resist. Finally, any supply strategies you deploy to deal with market uncertainty carries trade-offs and risks for the organization that are not always easy to understand or quantify. These strategies might also sow confusion within your existing manufacturing-and-supply network if not executed properly.

As daunting as these challenges might seem, leaders can surmount them by treading carefully. Craft a vision for your organization and its offerings, soliciting input from employees, partners, and customers. A cocreated vision will ensure that your stakeholders buy in as the plan begins to materialize and your supply chain changes in turn. Don't rush the creation of this strategy. Take your time to fully assess the trade-offs posed by specific changes you might make to your manufacturing-and-service-delivery functions, remembering that none of the tactics we've highlighted will work in every circumstance or for every company. To ready your supply chain for turbulence and volatility, evaluate your organization's tolerance of risk, and model possible scenarios to better understand which tactics your leaders can plausibly agree to implement.

The five key strategies we've examined thus far in this book—delivering benefits to all stakeholders and not just maximizing returns to shareholders, embracing new digital value propositions, expanding globally in smarter ways, engineering a digital ecosystem, and embracing flex manufacturing and delivery—all share an important trait: *they depend on data flows*. The new services and experiences that companies are offering mobilize global data and digital platforms. The new profit pools created by these digital offerings put pressure on companies' existing geographic expansion strategies, leading some to back away from a broad-based global footprint. Global data sharing, the low cost of connectivity, and the existence of virtually connected customers make ecosystems possible and desirable. And the flex factories that will revolutionize manufacturing require a global data highway knitting them together and connecting them with a centralized control facility. Data really is at the center of these and all the strategies we highlight in this book. As we'll argue in the next chapter, the twenty-first-century enterprise must go beyond traditionally fragmented data collection to build a sophisticated and strategic global data architecture. In the years ahead, data will serve as the new and irreplaceable fuel global companies need to grow. If your organization isn't moving yet to obtain and mobilize that fuel, you had better get started.

Key Insights

- The so-called global delivery model, or low-labor cost-driven global supply chain, is becoming increasingly obsolete. Managing production is no longer just about minimizing costs but about also achieving more speed, flexibility, and resilience for the enterprise.

- Looking beyond the shoe industry, we find a similar movement toward more flex manufacturing beginning to take place among large industrial companies.

- As much as multicountry networks are helping companies make delivery more flexible and responsive in addition to low cost, they aren't enough. Companies are also dramatically rethinking their broader supply chains.

- To meet the growing needs for digitized products and services, global companies are rapidly adding an entirely new dimension to their delivery models: digital and software development.

CHAPTER 6

LET THE DATA RUN THROUGH IT

Companies have long treated data as if it were an exhaust emitted by their operations, making use of it only after the fact to measure and improve. Today, leading-edge companies are going beyond this traditional approach, regarding data—and, specifically, information that is globally collected, stored, and analyzed—as pivotal, the fuel that not only predicts future performance or consumer behavior but also drives winning value propositions for global customers.

Global product and services companies have long sought to glean competitive advantage from physical supply chains and access to raw materials, but this is fast changing. Physical supply chains and raw materials still matter, but data is now a new, equally critical raw material for many global companies. The responsive, personalized, dynamic solutions that companies are providing to their digitally connected global customers depend on the constant generation, flow, and analysis of massive amounts of data. It follows that global companies don't merely require new software-development capabilities, a global network of high-speed flex manufacturing plants or delivery centers, and ecosystems of external partners across industries and geographies. They also need a new global digital architecture for the handling of massive data flows across geographies.

Leading-edge firms are going beyond by building powerful global data architectures capable of turning the fuel of digital information into more efficient processes, better pricing, and more valuable products, services, and experiences. Connecting users seamlessly to platforms and partners around the world, these data architectures comprise a new kind of supply chain for the twenty-first-century enterprise, designed strategically to drive growth and unlock massive amounts of value.

Traditionally, global product and services companies kept their data fragmented and localized, using it to make only incremental improvements to their products, supply chains, or collaborations with partners. Data was the exhaust of commercial activity, studied long after it was collected and used to enhance performance in the product or service supply chain. Global industrial companies, for instance, made money not from their data but by designing, manufacturing, selling, and servicing physical products like cars or steam turbines. Companies often retained large amounts of performance data about their products, but these were scattered in service centers around the world and were rarely made available to teams within the company in real time. A car designer might have seen some fragmented data related to a car model's performance in summary form weeks or months after it was first generated.

In the old era, global service companies made money by designing and selling service offerings primarily on a local basis. Global banks would sell mortgages, say, out of local retail branches. Any data generated during the process of designing, making, selling, and using these mortgages was captured locally and then (perhaps) summarized in monthly reports for employees or managers to see. It wasn't compiled and analyzed globally in real time to inform pricing and other decisions or to deliver services to customers.

If companies didn't make more of their data back then, it was because they couldn't—they lacked the technical ability. But in recent years, a slew of social and technological developments has finally enabled firms to globalize their data and use it to fuel their businesses. As we've seen, consumers around the world are increasingly connected and spending more time online, generating massive amounts of data. The cost of storing that data on the cloud and processing it has declined dramatically over the past decade. Firms like Amazon Web Services that sell digital infrastructure as a service (IaaS) have enabled global companies to rent the infrastructure they need without building it themselves. Of course, some companies are investing in expansive centers of their own to house global data. As of 2017, Facebook's data center space extended to almost fifteen million square feet.[1] New start-ups have arisen to provide sophisticated data science and data analytics, while Oracle and other existing IT companies have built up their data-analysis capabilities. Finally, advances in technologies such as machine learning and AI have opened the way to entirely new ways of using global data both operationally and commercially.

The Data Revolution at a Glance

- In 2020, global data flows will exceed sixty thousand gigabytes per second, over triple that of 2015. Cross-border data flows are expected to double every two years through at least 2025.[2]
- Between 2013 and 2020, the number of connected devices increased by 400 percent.[3]
- By 2020, two-thirds of the world population was actively using the internet.[4]
- Over the past decade, the cost of a fixed broadband basket decreased by over 40 percent.[5]
- Over the past decade, the average cost of sensors has fallen by over 50 percent. By 2022, there will be an estimated twenty-nine billion connected devices creating data.[6]
- The cost of cloud infrastructure has declined by 66 percent over the past decade.[7]
- The volume of data created worldwide has doubled every three years since 2011 and will amount to 175 trillion gigabytes by 2025.[8]
- In 2018, over $9.3 billion in funding flowed into AI companies—a record high.[9]

As globalized data has become easier to amass and disseminate, it has begun to transform companies from the inside out. Internally, global data flows enable employees, contract workers, and partners to easily collaborate across geographies. Companies can monitor their global operations in real time and respond quickly to any challenges, thus rendering them more resilient in the face of volatility. They can also optimize how they deploy assets so as to reduce cost, improve productivity, and reduce environmental burdens. Collecting data about workforces, they can proactively engage employees, improve talent retention, and enhance performance. Commercially, global data allows companies to create unique footprints for individual customers, allowing for personalized marketing and product strategies. Companies can also build experiences and solutions that change continuously, using feedback data from millions of customers around the world, through social media activity, product reviews, customer-satisfaction surveys, and so on.

One of the best-known examples of such experiences is Epic Games' popular video game *Fortnite*, which evolves dynamically based on data flows from millions of users around the world.[10] *Fortnite* allows for a gaming experience in which up to one hundred players can compete against one another or in teams to be the last one standing. Advances in computing and internet speed have made all of this possible, as has Epic Games' Unreal Engine, a programming environment that software developers can use to create new games. The technology in Unreal Engine allows games to run across gaming platforms, lowering the barrier to entry (users can play *Fortnite* using mobile, handheld, PC, and Mac devices). Unreal Engine also allows games to use user feedback about the games they play to further upgrade the engine and the gaming experience. By 2018, one of *Fortnite*'s two games—*Battle Royale*—had more than two hundred million users worldwide and earned an estimated $3 billion in profits.

Epic Games is just one example of many companies that were born digital and have been among the first to gain competitive advantage by collecting and analyzing data on a worldwide basis. But incumbent product and services companies in many other sectors are beginning to do so, hoping to grasp the unique opportunities that data represents for their businesses. While digital companies have built strategies and operating models around data flows from day one, incumbents who have treated data as exhaust face a more difficult challenge. In addition to the task of upskilling their people, which we'll cover later in this book, they must clarify their strategic goals in mobilizing global data, whether it's to protect their market position from rivals, target new profit pools, drive new efficiencies, or something else. They must also design a digital architecture or supply chain capable of delivering on these goals as part of a digital operating model. Both tasks are challenging but essential. Before addressing how to handle them, let's delve a bit deeper into how one incumbent global firm has made the leap to global data, achieving advantage by treating data not as exhaust but as fuel.

Farming, Reimagined

Agriculture is among the oldest of all human industries. It is also one of the most complex, with a farmer's success or failure hinging on the vagaries of weather and soil conditions as well as numerous operational decisions. In modern times, the latter includes how much fertilizer to apply, how deep to plant seeds, how much to water, which pesticides to apply, and so on. Fortunately, data can help with many of these decisions, and today, it frequently does, enabling farmers to optimize their profits per acre of land tilled. "Today's farm is powered by data," one observer has written, "along with a variety of devices and technologies, including sensors, GPS satellites, drones, and robots."[11] And the role of data is only expanding. According to some estimates, the market for analytics in the agriculture sector will reach $1.2 billion by 2023, up from $585 million just five years earlier.[12] The potential impact is immense, with some observers predicting that analytics and artificial intelligence would bring about $250 billion in annual cost savings and new revenue opportunities for the global agriculture sector.[13]

Given this vast potential, vendors in the agriculture sector and beyond have designed solutions that use data to help farmers make better decisions and optimize profits. Through simple apps on their phones, farmers can track weather patterns, soil conditions, and much more, acting to reduce risks to crops and improve productivity. If you sell farm equipment, seeds, or other products or services helpful to farmers, you will no longer beat the competition by simply providing the best products or services. Rather, you need to win the fight to become the farmer's primary and ongoing source of productivity-related solutions. And that means building the best data-advantaged operating model to deliver the best profit-per-hectare solution to the farmers.

One of the first industry players to understand these shifting dynamics was John Deere, the world's largest farm equipment maker. In 2012, the company rolled out MyJohnDeere, a digital platform that farmers could use to oversee their fleets of equipment and operate more efficiently.[14] MyJohnDeere, updated, enhanced, and renamed the John Deere Operations Center, allows farmers to view all operations taking place in each acre of the farm and manage operational metrics via smartphones and other digital devices. The system makes use of data flowing from sensors embedded in John Deere's equipment as well as third-party "historical data on everything from weather and soil conditions to crop features."[15] As Alejandro Sayago, the company's head of strategy, told us, "Our goal is to provide growers with tools and value added solutions that help implement precision agriculture." Mobilizing a full technology stack (including connected machines and digital solutions) to deliver these solutions, John Deere hopes to enable farmers to manage fields at the level of individual plants, thus maximizing farm profitability while allowing the company to claim more value.[16]

In line with this strategy, the data-generating digital layer built into John Deere's farming equipment has become increasingly pronounced. Today the company's S-Series combine harvesters come equipped with ActiveVision cameras that make use of seven automation technologies; these allow the operator to monitor the processed grain coming out of the combine and analyze it for real-time grain quality, foreign material, and other performance factors.[17] The combine sends data to the John Deere Operations Center, an online farm-management system that allows farmers to see data about their fields; share it with advisers, vendors, and others; and make decisions that allow them to increase crop yields and reduce costs.[18] Combining software tools that enable better planning with advanced electrical drives and mechanical components on its machines that enable precise execution of these plans, John Deere allows customers to farm more acres in less time.[19]

Meanwhile, sensors in the machinery optimize its functioning, alerting farmers and their equipment dealers to problems as they arise.[20] The company was on the forefront of deploying computer vision and other advanced technologies to help farmers make operational decisions. For example, a computer vision / AI system could identify weeds and apply the right amount of herbicide to each one individually (traditionally, farmers made such decisions on a field-by-field basis).[21] John Deere was "very much pushing into artificial intelligence, computer vision, and machine learning," John Stone, SVP of John Deere's Intelligent Solutions Group (ISG), said. "What's amazing is how all of this technology is such a hand-in-glove fit for agriculture."[22]

To deliver this added value to farmers, John Deere established a distinct Intelligent Solutions Group, a digital division that looks and functions like a new-age tech start-up within the traditional business. In addition to separate facilities at its headquarters in Illinois, John Deere established a presence in the Silicon Valley, starting John Deere Labs and acquiring a start-up, Blue River Technology, to access digital talent and stay connected to the latest innovations. The combination allowed the company to arrive at breakthrough insights and applications.[23] But John Deere went much further, mobilizing a data architecture that has kept its information both global and in line with the European Union's Global Data Protection Regulation, a law that covers the handling of data to ensure consumer privacy and protection. The company allows customers to compile their data on the platform, add external data if they wish through interfaces John Deere has built, and use that platform to work to create customized plans for their farms with the help of trusted advisers. These plans then yield prescriptions for a specific set of tasks that are then sent to individual pieces of farm equipment to execute with great precision. In this way, John Deere has been able to become a fully integrated partner to farmers globally, helping them create and execute their plans as precisely and efficiently as possible in areas such as planting, spraying, and the like.[24]

Using Amazon Web Services as the platform for its digital architecture, John Deere has created a uniform user experience on a global scale, making its machines simple to connect and operate and easy to scale across regions.[25] The company has also created interfaces that allow customers (if they so wish) to share data with a select number of third parties that meet its data-security and governance standards. In this way, customers can access technology related to soil sensors, drones, weather data analytics, and so on to provide integrated solutions to customers.[26] In 2019, the company reached a deal with other equipment manufacturers to enable equipment from different companies to communicate with one another in real time.[27] This enables farmers to track and operate all their machinery together using John Deere's operations center or portals operated by competing brands.[28]

Thanks to its digital solutions strategy and efforts to build a new operating model, John Deere is becoming a preferred partner to farmers worldwide and laying the foundation for future growth. The company's brand loyalty among customers is intensifying, allowing the company to increase market share in smaller markets and fortify its leadership in key markets like North America, and driving higher profitability. Rather than selling machines and digital solutions separately, the company's sales force and network of dealers are selling integrated solutions. Inside the company, the profile of digital technology among the leadership ranks has increased. John May, the company's new CEO as of 2019, previously served as chief information officer and also as president of the division responsible for software-based intelligent solutions.[29]

John Deere is hardly alone in mobilizing global data to its advantage. Caterpillar now collects data to run predictive maintenance on its large industrial machinery. Starbucks collects it to personalize the customer experience and to offer unique drink suggestions and promotional offers based on the local weather and prior drink purchases. And many players in the automobile industry—already one of the world's most globalized industries—are creating the data supply chains they need to drive innovative digital products and services.

> Your firm can mobilize data as a springboard for leaping ahead of the competition, even if your existing strategies and IT systems are out of date and your legacy data is local and fragmented. The first step is to build the right data-advantaged operating model for your business.

Build Your Data-Advantaged Operating Model

Forging a strategy for layering digital and data onto your existing operating model might seem daunting. As an incumbent, where do you start?

> In the course of our research and client work, we uncovered four distinct platform pathways you can pursue when turning data into fuel. Understanding these pathways can help you orient your company and shape its efforts to build a powerful digital supply chain of its own.

Your company already has a unique set of assets and capabilities related to your customers, your position in the value chain, and so on. Choose one of these pathways, and you can proceed to build value propositions, operational strategies, and partnerships that maximize the global data advantage available to your company. Before you can turn data into fuel, your firm must first understand in general terms how it might burn that fuel to its own and customers' benefit.

Platform Pathway #1: Reimagine Your Business Processes and Internal Operations

Of the four pathways, the most common mobilizes global data to improve, optimize, or reimagine one or more parts of a business's operations. The opportunities here are practically endless, limited only by leaders' creativity and the kind of data at their disposal. Incumbents have used global data to transform virtually everything about their operations, from how they design and develop products and services to how they source materials, from how and where they make products to how they transport, store, promote, price, and sell them. Every part of a company's value chain might yield hundreds of improvement opportunities that use global data while also providing opportunities to make the firm more adaptable to new conditions as they arise.

L'Oréal, the world's largest cosmetics company, has built a customer data platform (CDP) that organizes consumer data (obtained with consumers' consent) from multiple local touch points and partnerships into a global data platform across its brands, creating a comprehensive view of customers on an individual basis.[30] This platform also aggregates information from multiple data sources, again obtained with consumers' consent. This includes partner data (from vendors such as Amazon and Sephora or partners such as Google and Facebook); media data (interactions and responses of anonymized consumers to targeted ads and messages); first-party data (from the company's own CRM, e-commerce websites, and apps); and a content hub (a repository of highly customized and branded digital content). Segmenting this data by demographics and spending habits across each of its brands, the company can precisely identify, predict, and meet each shopper's needs. For example, L'Oréal's CDP allows the company to identify whether customers of its Nyx brand, who tend to skew younger, use any of its other products. The company can then use this insight to target the marketing of these other brands, engage with highly interested customers, and drive sales effectively.[31]

The company also leverages internal data to help shape product innovation and refinement. To imagine and create new products, L'Oréal and its data integration partner, Talend, compile data related to L'Oréal's product formulas and raw materials, combining it with data about consumers' perceptions of product performance.[32] The amount of information handled is huge: some fifty million data points run through the system each day.[33] To date, L'Oréal has used the system to help its finance department track KPIs and to help its researchers study a range of subjects related to skin care. Thanks to such big data applications, L'Oréal's ecommerce sales rose by 49 percent in 2019, contributing over 10 percent of the company's total global revenues.[34]

In the retail apparel industry, digital leaders like H&M have unleashed hundreds of operational improvements using global data, maximizing sales and minimizing costs by transforming how they assemble their collections and how they stock them in stores. Investing heavily in data analytics, they're also increasing sales by adopting personalized marketing on a mass scale. Digital companies like Uber and Amazon are deploying global data to revolutionize pricing and promotions in their respective industries. Again, none of these improvements would have been possible even a decade ago, since companies lacked global data capabilities and didn't fathom how global data could serve as fuel for their business.

In some industries, all or most major players are leveraging global data to improve operations, and they're doing so not just to improve internal processes but to reimagine them across company boundaries. Take pharmaceuticals. Large pharma companies have traditionally developed new drugs using in-house resources, conducting biomedical research, building product-development pipelines, and then introducing new medications. More recently, many big pharma companies have modified their R & D processes, building new research partnerships with startups and academic labs, taking R & D virtual, outsourcing it to other companies, restructuring R & D organizations to make them smaller and nimbler, adopting crowdsourcing, and more. Whereas internal R & D labs at pharma companies traditionally accounted for as much as 62 percent of all new drugs, today start-ups in pharma and biotech produce the vast majority of new drugs launched (78 percent).[35] As part of opening up R & D, companies are creating and maintaining open data lakes that outside researchers can access to collaborate on research. With immense amounts of data flowing back and forth, companies and outside actors can work together to bring to market commercially viable solutions and experiences that companies never could have conceived and developed on their own.

Big pharma companies haven't replaced their traditional R & D model so much as supplemented it with an open model. Outside start-ups benefit from the enhanced collaboration, since they often lack the means to conduct costly clinical trials of their drugs as well as the marketing and sales expertise to get these drugs into the hands of doctors and patients. Big pharma companies benefit, since collaboration with outsiders allows them to expand their expertise, access more promising new ideas, and bring them to market more quickly, all while reducing R & D costs. Of course, patients benefit from having more pathbreaking drugs available for their use. As one 2019 report found, external firms (start-ups and small ventures) produced almost two-thirds of new medications that had recently won government approval.[36] Open innovation models also allow pharma companies to become more resilient in the face of shocks. During the COVID-19 crisis, pharmaceutical companies deployed common data platforms and an open R & D model to develop vaccines and treatments, enabling far more rapid progress than would have previously been possible.

To better position themselves to turn data into fuel, big pharma companies are moving R & D labs closer to major biotech hubs so as to facilitate collaboration. They're developing internal venture programs to encourage employees to pursue small-scale drug-development projects and creating open innovation forums to collaborate with external researchers. Further, companies are establishing centers of excellence designed to break down internal hierarchies, creating new ways of incenting scientists to make discoveries and establishing R & D partnerships with other firms who have developed useful data sets.

The pharma giant GlaxoSmithKline (GSK) has formed multiple external R & D partnerships in a drive to strengthen their pipeline of products.[37] To gain access to new data, GSK inked a collaboration with 23andMe, the world's largest consumer genetics and research company, to jointly develop new therapies. As part of the agreement, GSK researchers would use data from millions of anonymous customers in 23andMe's genetic database as well as its data analytics.[38] Previously, GSK had joined other big pharma companies in partnering in the Open Targets consortium, whose web platform helps researchers find promising new drug targets for diseases by giving them access to large amounts of publicly available data.[39] The company had also collaborated with the UK Biobank, a health-care resource containing an array of data compiled from five hundred thousand participants.[40]

As powerful as this first pathway is, it only scratches the surface of what is possible using big data. To thrive in the twenty-first century, companies must go further and consider how they might generate completely new sources of competitive advantage and unlock new, highly protected value streams. The next three pathways allow companies to do exactly that.

Platform Pathway #2: Leveraging Expertise at Scale

Most incumbents possess deep technical expertise in their areas of operation. Some companies are now mobilizing global data to codify that expertise, combine it with their intimate knowledge of customers' global operations, and create new solutions that solve real business problems for their customers at scale. Take the German engineering conglomerate Siemens. By the end of the twentieth century, the company had emerged as an industrial giant, making everything from cell phones to hearing aids, telecommunications networks to mass transit systems.[41] For all its technical expertise, however, Siemens had not always been at the forefront of new technology. During the early 2000s, the company had missed the emergence of mobile phones as a general consumer product (formerly, companies had designed and marketed the technology primarily for business users). In 2005, the company sold off its unprofitable handset unit at a loss of some $450 million.[42]

Determined to stay ahead of technology, the company in 2014 unveiled its Vision 2020 strategy, which identified digitalization, electrification, and automation as Siemens's core business priorities. Yet in one of these areas—digitalization—Siemens faced a difficult challenge. Although it possessed vast and deep technical knowledge related to the machines it designed, manufactured, and serviced, the company lacked an effective way of applying this fragmented expertise at scale and connecting it with customers' business operations to arrive at new commercially viable solutions. Siemens filled this gap by creating the MindSphere platform referenced in previous chapters. As an open cloud platform for IoT applications, MindSphere stores operational data from devices like trains and wind turbines, making it accessible via digital apps. Accessing this data and drawing on its vast technical knowledge, Siemens can spot formerly hidden insights about its customers' operations across geographies, turning those into exciting new products and services.

In addition to the MindSphere platform itself, Siemens has built the MindSphere Application Centers (MACs) described earlier in the book, locations where Siemens's technical experts work side by side with customer teams as well as digital talent (data scientists, analysts, user experience specialists, and so on). Because of Siemens's global presence and extensive expertise, the company has managed to rapidly expand MindSphere around the world, creating new algorithms, analytics, insights, and solutions. At the MACs, teams consider customers' top business challenges and opportunities, collaborating on new solutions. To date, these solutions have unlocked tremendous value for Siemens's customers while creating new revenue streams for Siemens (or protecting older ones).

For example, Siemens's Power Diagnostics Services leverages large amounts of data to enhance the operation of electricity-generating wind turbines around the world. Siemens builds the wind turbines, installs them at local sites, and collects thousands of data points from sensors embedded on each wind turbine. Applying its expert understanding of wind-turbine design and operations, Siemens can analyze the data to provide advice at a massive scale, helping its customers improve the reliability and performance of wind turbines and even extending their life spans. Today, the company monitors almost eight thousand wind turbines, processing 200 GB of data every day. Since 2008, it has prevented some 97 percent of potential turbine breakdowns and reduced required service visits to wind turbines by 85 percent.[43]

Siemens has done something similar for power plants and public transportation systems. At individual plants, the company collects approximately one hundred thousand data points each day (temperatures, pressures, turbine speeds, and so on), diagnosing problems on turbines before they happen so that customers can take preventative measures and improve performance. The company likewise collects large amounts of data from the high-speed trains it supplies to countries like Germany, Spain, and Russia, using algorithms to spot certain problems before they happen and recommend how best to maintain the equipment. In the future, Siemens will integrate data from all its trains worldwide, as well as external data about weather, track conditions, and so on, gleaning insights to further help customers improve fleet performance and lower cost.[44]

As of 2019, Siemens generated over €16 billion in revenue from its digital industries operating company, a number that is expected to rise substantially.[45] "As more value migrates to software, MAC's will

become increasingly powerful in driving profitability," chief strategy officer Dr. Horst Kayser told us.[46] Siemens is hardly alone in deploying data
to leverage expertise at scale. The Dutch paint maker AkzoNobel has
developed InteracVision, a consulting service in which the firm uses data
and its technical know-how to predict how much fuel a customer in the
shipping industry would save by applying an industrial coating on its
ship's hull. Likewise, the Finnish crane manufacturer Konecranes analyzes global data to predict how its cranes will perform at sites around
the world and to perform predictive maintenance, leveraging its deep
knowledge of how construction cranes operate.

Platform Pathway #3: Collaboratively Create and Amplify Solutions to a Global Customer Base

Global data architectures and cloud-based data platforms allow companies to instantly deploy new solutions in domains and geographies that
previously would have been out of reach. A third pathway companies
are pursuing to grasp the opportunity generated by global data is to use
these platforms to look for patterns in the data, identify potential innovations that might benefit particular customers, develop these solutions,
and then quickly spread these solutions to specific groups of customers
around the world to unlock exponential value. Such a use of cloud-based
platforms amounts to a completely new community-based way of solving problems, one in which experts from a vast array of fields build on
one another's capabilities to produce pathbreaking, elegant, and efficient
solutions that no one entity working alone could have engineered.

One company that has mobilized a cloud platform to create and disseminate new solutions rapidly and at scale is the French energy company Schneider Electric. Historically, the company has acquired, stored,
and used data in a fragmented way, segregating it according to its products and services or the regions in which it operates. It has also treated
data as exhaust, capturing it in select instances and analyzing it after the
fact to optimize operations. More recently, as value has migrated toward
digital solutions, the company has sought to develop a capacity for building and deploying a wide range of solutions quickly and at scale.

The company's first step was to create its EcoStruxure platform—an
open, scalable, and interoperable IoT architecture that "enables Schneider Electric, its partners and end-user customers to develop scalable and

converged IT/OT solutions that deliver innovation at every level to an organization or enterprise."[47] This architecture allowed Schneider Electric to engage with a broad spectrum of participants in its ecosystem and to collect data off devices. Customers could also use software on the platform to better deploy the equipment they had purchased—what the company called "smart operations"—and to access applications, services, and more from Schneider Electric via the cloud.[48] As of 2018, some 650,000 local partners were using the platform, working with Schneider Electric on developing new solutions. In 2018, the company was managing some two million assets around the world on the platform and using EcoStruxure to help customers reduce their CO_2 emissions. The company was well on its way to achieving its 2020 goal of reducing emissions by 120 million metric tons.[49]

In addition to EcoStruxure, Schneider Electric in 2019 launched another platform called Schneider Electric Exchange, billed as "the world's first cross-industry open ecosystem dedicated to solving real-world sustainability and efficiency challenges."[50] "We've always had an ecosystem and network of partners," Schneider Electric's chief digital officer, Herve Coureil, told us, "which has proved to be a very strong asset in the past. As we went digital, we wanted to continue the same and hence built Schneider Electric Exchange, which allows a wide variety of partners to leverage our platforms to collaborate and build solutions for our customers. We didn't want to be at the center of the ecosystem, but to orchestrate it."[51] Coureil further noted that "no company has a technology stack that can cover everything for every efficiency and sustainability use case on any customer. There is a clear need for an ecosystem to accelerate innovation for customer-driven R & D, that is, developing technology to solve concrete problems instead of for technology's sake."[52]

Schneider Electric Exchange is in effect an opening up of EcoStruxure that enables collaboration between a wider set of participants from different industries and geographies. It's a digital marketplace for efficiency and sustainability, convening multidisciplinary experts to design solutions using technical tools and resources Schneider Electric provides. "We look at Schneider Electric Exchange from the perspective of solving actual customer challenges with a combination of technology and subject-matter expertise," Coureil said. A customer might post a problem on the site, sparking a conversation among platform participants who contribute their own particular expertise and help the customer develop a solution. Other customers can then access these solutions, so long as the original customer has agreed. Schneider Electric's customers can accelerate their innovation, accessing a broad array of talent.[53]

Because of the global data architecture and cloud-based platform enabled by EcoStruxure, solutions developed by customers in one part of the world can spread almost instantaneously to customers elsewhere with the click of a button. Companies can monetize platforms like EcoStruxure and Schneider Electric Exchange by selling access to the data itself, to analytics, to specific insights or actions generated by the analytics, or to benefits users might glean from deploying insights. So far, Schneider Electric has benefited from EcoStruxure and Schneider Electric Exchange by selling specific actions derived from insights, packaging these as a service provided to customers. Early indications are that Schneider Electric Exchange will prove successful. Within just a few months of its launch, more than thirty thousand participants joined the platform, creating more than a thousand new solutions.[54] As Schneider Electric's chief innovation officer, Emmanuel Lagarrigue, told us, the company sees Exchange as a unique source of competitive advantage for customers seeking solutions to extremely complex energy-related problems.[55] "Being partner centric," Coureil said, "we understand that we have to grow the GDP of our overall ecosystem, and we want to do so at scale, digitally."[56]

Platform Pathway #4: Build a New Business by Attacking Large Value Pools

It isn't just incumbents that can gain advantage from globalizing their data and turning it into fuel. New entrants can do so as well, mobilizing data as a strategy to disrupt existing players and capture value. Consider the shipping industry. As we've seen, globalization in the twentieth century arose in part because of cheaper shipping, which made it possible for companies to manufacture products at scale in low-cost countries and send them to markets around the world. Yet for all its benefits, the roughly $5 trillion global logistics industry was far from efficient.[57] Customers couldn't track shipments down the supply chain in real time and so couldn't optimize their operations (say, by keeping the right number of warehouse staff on duty in line with fluctuating demand) or inventory.

Since companies had to contract with different companies for the handling, loading, and transportation of freight, coordination between these vendors at each stage wasn't easy, and companies couldn't always hold these vendors accountable for their performance. The heavy bureaucratic requirements of shipping physical products slowed commerce, with each individual shipment generating more than thirty pieces of paper documentation, many containing the same information.

Flexport, a small San Francisco–based freight-forwarding start-up founded in 2013, has sought to solve many of these problems via a state-of-the-art data and analytics platform. Uploading data about a company's customer purchases, one of their products, OceanMatch, enables shippers to lower costs by allowing companies to consolidate shipments and occupy portions of containers that would have previously gone empty. Customers can follow the progress of their cargo around the world on an ongoing basis, allowing them clarity about when shipments will arrive. Thanks to data analytics, supply chains become more visible; customers can understand how much of their containers they're really using, how much of a carbon footprint their shipping is generating, and what their total shipping costs are, making more informed decisions as a result.[58] One plumbing fixture company saw its shipping costs decline by 10 percent thanks to the operational efficiencies and flexibility it achieved via Flexport, while a European smart-travel brand achieved a 35 percent monthly growth rate with almost no stock-outs.[59] As of 2020, Flexport had almost ten thousand clients and suppliers across 116 countries. In 2018, it generated revenues of $441 million.[60]

Large established companies are also turning to global data to attack existing value pools or create new ones as industry challengers. In 2017, the Anglo-Dutch oil and gas behemoth Shell saw the potential to use "smart sensors and next generation analytics" to help customers get the most out of their fleets of vehicles.[61] Imagine you're a construction company that runs a fleet of dozens of excavators, trucks, and other machinery. Shell's idea was to give you a little black box that would attach magnetically to a piece of machinery. Sensors within the box would collect information, which once analyzed would allow you to reduce the time that machines spent idling, improve maintenance practices, and take other steps. The result for customers: greater efficiency and lower costs. Within months, Shell had launched a venture, MachineMax, that delivered this value proposition commercially in the United Kingdom.[62]

Build Your Digital Architecture

Once you've considered how you might best use global data strategically to fuel your business, the next step is to round out your digital operating model by designing a digital architecture or supply chain.

A digital supply chain contains a number of key elements, including two-way connectivity between customers and the company, a cloud data/storage capacity for both data and software applications, an analytics capability, virtual global teams of experts who work with the data and create digital solutions, third-party developers who also help develop solutions, and logistics providers that deliver any physical products associated with the offering.

In building a digital supply chain, it can be difficult for companies to integrate all data generated from sites around the globe and create a holistic portrait of the business. As more firms build data-advantaged operating models, the number of sources and types of data increase exponentially and also become more diverse.[63] On the other hand, rapid advances in technology allow for ever more integration. Digital companies like Amazon, Spotify, and Netflix have the easiest time integrating their data and rendering it truly global, as they've built global digital architectures from the outset. Incumbents, by contrast, have to build their own global architectures either on top of or in addition to the legacy IT infrastructure they already have, since the latter is rarely integrated globally. This is by no means a straightforward task.

Additionally, global data architectures are not all created equal. Privacy laws and the strategic goals companies pursue might require that they collect, store, analyze, share, transfer, visualize, query, and update data in different ways. Other considerations that inform how an incumbent creates a data architecture includes the nature of its legacy IT assets, the structure of the data that the company will generate and store, and existing cultural norms inside the company relevant to data. From our discussions with a number of companies that have begun to build architectures of their own, we've uncovered three high-level decisions that companies must make in designing the technical handling of data.

First, *companies must decide how to craft a platform for their data and, specifically, whether it should incorporate older legacy data systems.* For incumbents with more extensive legacy data systems, the cost and time required to incorporate these systems is prohibitive. Fortunately, an effective shortcut is to build so-called distributed data and digital platforms, a structure that keeps only master data and some basic transaction data in existing core systems while moving other data suitable for analytics to a newer platform, where it can be accessed globally.

Once companies put a platform in place to organize their data, *they must decide how to organize data flows into the platform.* Should they establish an open architecture that combines internal data with external data from social media or other third parties? Or should they establish a closed architecture that uses only internal data and hence need not include interfaces to the outside world? The answer depends on the strategies companies are hoping to pursue and the solutions they're hoping to offer. Whirlpool has chosen to build an open architecture for its global data platform, seeking to build ecosystems and collaborate with other platforms to deliver an array of value-added services.[64] By contrast, Siemens's MindSphere is a focused, semiclosed platform designed to collect proprietary data and combine it with its technical expertise to generate unique solutions for customers. Both strategies can generate data advantage, and enterprises must choose carefully which makes the most sense given their competitive contexts.

A third design choice companies must make concerns people—*how much tech talent companies should employ themselves as opposed to accessing via third-party vendors.* Outsourcing is becoming an increasingly attractive option; data architecture has become a $75 billion industry and is growing rapidly.[65] Many companies prefer to rely on third-party vendors, while others opt to bring much of their architecture in-house not merely for security reasons but also to better integrate their data sources and to allow users the ability to sign on to multiple systems with a single password. In considering what to keep in-house, leaders should seek to protect elements of the data architecture that afford them a current or future competitive advantage.

Advice for Leaders

In the years ahead, companies everywhere must treat data for what it is: a preeminent source of global competitive advantage and means of building more resilience. The more customer data you collect and operationalize, the more easily you can deliver on the innovative digital value propositions described earlier. The more data from employees and teams you possess, the more efficiently and nimbly you can operate internally and the more you can optimize performance. As one data specialist told us, Amazon's ability to know its consumers intimately and personalize its offers via its numerous digital touch points is giving it a tremendous advantage over Walmart and other retailers that track only consumer shopping patterns in their brick-and-mortar stores. Netflix and Uber, too, designed their businesses from the start to collect data so they could develop more targeted offerings to consumers over time.

Despite the examples we've developed in this chapter and elsewhere in this book, many companies still have a long way to go to integrate their data into such a single well-functioning digital supply chain. One study found that most company data—over three-quarters of it—remains fragmented, "either siloed, scattered or located in multiple copies all over an organization's IT system."[66] As some data experts have observed, fragmented data within organizations and data of uneven quality are slowing efforts to bring valuable artificial intelligence solutions online, a situation that one has described as akin to owning a Ferrari but lacking the right fuel.[67] Commenting on the phenomenon of "mass data fragmentation," one expert warned that "there's a vast canyon of corporate and personal data that is unknown to IT leaders, organizations or even consumers, whether it's on a personal device, on the largest storage arrays in the data center or in popular cloud storage services like Amazon S3."[68]

To develop a well-functioning global data architecture, ponder the four platform pathways discussed in this chapter, deciding which to prioritize and adopt. Consider as well the following questions:

1. **Where do the greatest opportunities lie for your company to create value through data?** Further, which applications or use cases are the most feasible given their cost and your present capabilities, and which are the most promising?
2. **How might your company best pursue these opportunities?** What data will you require? How much must you invest in order to build the required infrastructure? What data can your company access, and what will you have to acquire from others? Where will you store the data, and in what form?

3. **What capabilities and expertise do you currently have when it comes to global data, and what do you lack?** How digitally mature is your organization across its businesses and functions? Do employees have sufficient experience in understanding, managing, and manipulating global data sets?

4. **How might you build strong data governance capabilities so that your customers can trust in the security of their data?** What data localization and security laws exist in the geographies where you operate? What existing rules govern data collection, storage, and usage in your organization, and how might you need to modify them as you build a global data architecture?

In this chapter and the two preceding, we've reviewed the radically new operational assets that global enterprises must assemble to prosper in the twenty-first century. But leaders can't engineer and exploit them well unless they also transform themselves internally. They must organize their teams differently, bring on different kinds of talent, and engage those employees in new ways. They must also run their businesses through a bigger lens, striving to enhance their total social impact rather than simply maximizing shareholder returns. Let's explore the tremendous internal evolution that leading-edge companies are quickly embracing, starting with their creation of nimbler, more responsive teams organized around that most important of stakeholders: the customer.

Key Insights

- Leading-edge firms are going beyond by building powerful global data architectures capable of turning the fuel of digital information into more efficient processes, better pricing, and more valuable products, services, and experiences. Connecting users seamlessly to platforms and partners around the world, these data architectures comprise a new kind of supply chain for the twenty-first-century enterprise, designed strategically to drive growth and unlock massive amounts of value.

- Your firm can mobilize data as a springboard for leaping ahead of the competition, even if your existing strategies and IT systems are out of date and your legacy data is local and fragmented. The first step is to build the right data-advantaged operating model for your business.

- In the course of our research and client work, we uncovered four distinct platform pathways companies are pursuing when turning data into fuel. Understanding these pathways can help you orient your company and shape its efforts to build a powerful digital supply chain of its own. These pathways are as follows: (1) reimagining your business processes and internal operations, (2) leveraging expertise at scale, (3) collaboratively creating and amplifying solutions to a global customer base, and (4) building a new business by attacking large value pools.

- Once you've considered how you might best use global data strategically to fuel your business, the next step is to round out your digital operating model by designing a digital architecture or supply chain. This entails making three high-level decisions: (1) how to craft a platform for your data, (2) how to organize data flows, and (3) how to source your tech talent.

PART III
ORGANIZING BEYOND

CHAPTER 7

GET FOCUSED, FAST, AND FLAT

Global companies remain hamstrung not only by legacy IT but by organizational forms that leave them mired in bureaucracy and slow to respond to changing customer needs. To grow in the twenty-first century, firms must go beyond the familiar matrix structure and reconfigure themselves in more flexible and fluid ways.

As leaders embrace innovative digital strategies, their organizations will need to evolve as well. We've seen that connected customers are more demanding than ever, expecting the latest, most innovative offerings as well as more complex integrated solutions and experiences. Most organizations, however, were designed not for quick customer responsiveness but rather for efficiency. As a result, large global companies today can't move quickly enough to meet changing customer needs.

To remain competitive, these companies will have to develop new levels of coordination and collaboration across and beyond their formal organizations. They will have to render their organizations more dynamic, fluid, and even amoeba-like in their formation of teams and allotment of resources, all in the service of staying close to customers and delivering on their defining purpose or reason for being (a topic we'll cover in the next chapter).

For a sense of what nontraditional organizational models might look like, we can look to the Chinese internet technology start-up

ByteDance. Best known for its popular content platforms TikTok and Toutiao, ByteDance has raised $7.45 billion as of 2019 on the back of an aggressive globalization strategy (by November 2019, ByteDance's products were available in seventy-five languages and in more than 150 countries).[1] Underpinning such momentous growth has been an organizational structure that from the very beginning was designed to deliver speed, customer responsiveness, and what Mojia Li of the ByteDance Management Institute has termed a "start-up mentality."[2]

Instead of a rigid pyramidal hierarchy with multiple lines of responsibility lacing up through each level, ByteDance maintains a flat structure, with more than one hundred executives occupying the top two levels of management below the CEO. The environment is democratic and nonbureaucratic, with employees at all levels working in open offices, avoiding the use of formalities such as *sir* and *Doctor* in conversation, and operating without knowledge of one another's official titles. Coupled with highly collaborative, agile ways of working (described later in this chapter), a deemphasis on hierarchy encourages employees to take ownership of projects themselves and propel them forward without bothering to seek approval from bosses. As ByteDance founder and CEO Zhang Yiming has explained, his company believes in its people and their ability to make wise decisions—"therefore we are dedicated to [avoiding] bureaucracy during daily work."[3]

To further enhance customer responsiveness, employees at ByteDance work in an array of fluid self-formed cross-functional teams dedicated to specific initiatives or processes, such as managing one of the company's platforms, taking a new app global, and so on.[4] Because of ByteDance's flat structure, employees have unique insight across the company, enabling them to rotate according to their desires and the company's needs. Collaboration spans geographies, with local teams and managers in foreign markets working remotely with China-based developers. An objectives and key results tool aligns the organization by making public each individual's goals, with the information updated every couple of months to enhance information efficiency.

When it comes to developing new products, ByteDance aggressively exploits the gray area of informal conversations that typically take place inside organizations. Employees toss out ideas for new products using an internal communications platform, then form informal virtual teams to develop them, again using collaborative web-based communication tools. Eventually, these teams grow into more elaborate cross-functional groups dedicated to bringing the product to market. Only in the later stages of maturity do these teams become formalized and assigned to a preexisting department. Emphasizing the gray area allows employees to break free from their daily work and innovate so that the entire company can stay alert to new opportunities and respond quickly.[5]

The fluidity and flexibility of ByteDance's fifty-thousand-people-strong organization is a far cry from that of most global incumbents. But as we'll see in this chapter, a few leading-edge firms are beginning to reconfigure themselves to allow for far greater speed and customer responsiveness. They're experimenting in three complementary and tightly interconnected areas: (1) customer-focused teams, (2) agile ways of working, and (3) horizontal enablement platforms (encompassing data, technology, and processes) that enhance collaboration across boundaries, spread knowledge across the organization, render the enterprise more adaptable, and allow companies to make the most of their scale advantage.

Companies have tried customer-focused frontline teams in the past, but only on a one-off basis for specific projects, such as a new piece of business they were pursuing. Companies have adopted agile, but only for IT-related processes. Firms must now make agile customer-focused teams permanent fixtures inside their organizations, and they must support these teams by deploying enablement platforms. Further, they must give frontline teams authority to make decisions, as well as financial responsibility, so that team members feel incented to solve customer problems quickly and comprehensively. To supercharge their responsive customer-centric organizations, companies should equip leaders with new skills and behaviors and build strong digital cultures that instill and support new ways of working.

If incumbents don't update their organizations in the years ahead, adopting all three of the interwoven experiments—customer-focused teams, agile ways of working, and enablement platforms—as well as the supportive leadership skills and culture, they'll jeopardize their ability to execute the other strategies covered in this book.

However, companies that become more fluid and flexible will transform themselves into innovation dynamos capable of tapping into new digital value pools. To borrow a metaphor from Nick Jue, CEO of ING bank's German operations, these revamped global organizations will still be the big "elephants" they are today, but they will become "as fast and flexible as a greyhound," able to compete with the nimblest and most innovative digital companies.[6] We'll end the chapter by suggesting how you can begin to turn your organization into a speedier, more responsive "elephant" capable of supporting your innovative growth strategies.

Focusing on Customers

To explore the first area in which leading-edge firms are experimenting with customer-focused teams, let's stick with ING for a moment. As we've seen in previous chapters, asset-light digital banking solutions are rapidly disrupting large commercial banks. Between 2010 and 2017, retail deposits at digital banks in the United States grew by 11.3 percent annually, far outpacing growth at national banks (6.3 percent) and regional banks (3.3 percent).[7] As one large 2018 study found, over half of consumers reported trusting one or more technology companies to handle their money more than they did banking institutions.[8] "Customers' expectations are set by Uber and SkyScanner," one banking executive has observed. "How people can do things so quickly in other industries plays a role in how we do things in banking."[9] Fintech is poised to gobble up far more business in the years ahead. While digital challengers currently account for about 3 to 5 percent of industry revenues, BCG estimates they could capture up to half of revenues by 2025.[10]

Confronted with the threat posed by digital innovators, whose presence served to elevate customer expectations, leaders at ING Netherlands might have pointed to their company's strong financial performance and shrugged off the need to change. To their credit, they opted for bold action, in line with the ambitions of the broader ING Group.

In 2014, the group had adopted a new vision: to achieve "global digital leadership" in banking.[11] "We want to be a tech company with a banking license," ING's CEO Ralph Hamers later put it.[12] Leaders recognized that this transformation would not come quickly and that it would entail deep organizational changes. As Nick Jue, then CEO of ING bank's Netherlands operations, noted, the transformation would fundamentally change the nature of work inside the organization, encompassing col-laboration, the empowerment of the workforce, and cultural change that extended to "every detail in the organization"[13] As we'll see in this book's final chapter, the need for change in the twenty-first century is open ended, and companies in the years ahead must become adept at what we call *always-on* transformation, as ING Netherlands has striven to be.

A key part of the bank's efforts was to depart from its matrix organiz-ational structure and form small customer-centric teams that could stay in touch with the local market. Dating from the 1970s and 1980s, the matrix is a pyramidal hierarchy defined by multiple lines of accountabil-ity and reporting, usually across business lines, geography, and function. Since their adoption, matrix structures have confronted leaders with a range of unintended consequences related to organizational confusion and excessive bureaucracy.[14] But global firms largely stuck with the mat-rix because they regarded it as a means of maintaining efficiency and control as their operations became ever more far flung and complex thanks to globalization. If your operations spanned numerous countries, replicating your organizational structure in specific countries or regions facilitated decision-making by allowing for a degree of standardization. At the same time, retaining hierarchical levels within geographical, func-tional, and product organizations allowed you to maintain oversight over operations. Information across your sprawling global footprint was scat-tered and fragmentary; you needed layers of management within geog-raphies or product organizations to process information into reports and send those reports up the chain of command so that you and others at the top could hold managers accountable and make informed decisions.

For all its benefits, the matrix was never designed to focus the organi-zation's attention on customers and their needs. In most matrix organ-izations, knowledge of the customer has been fragmented between operators in marketing, sales, service, and elsewhere. Product or geog-raphy and functions have become the main focus, as that's where the P&L has been. The presence of silos and bureaucracy have further impeded efforts to understand customers.[15] At ING Netherlands, silos prevented leaders and teams from truly knowing and understanding the customer. Employees at the company were organized into functional silos located in different spaces, buildings, and cities. Incentives were aligned with functional areas of expertise rather than multidisciplinary teams, and employees pursued their own individual performance targets.

To address these issues, the company reorganized thousands of professionals and sales and call-center employees over a three-year period, dividing them into hundreds of "squads," small teams responsible for a specific customer-related project from beginning to end. These squads in turn belonged to "tribes," each of whom pursued a single, more expansive mission. Squad members also belonged to "chapters" based on their functional area of expertise. Individuals still reported to multiple bosses, both chapter and squad heads, but instead of pursuing individual targets on an annual basis, employees were assigned short-term team targets. They were also evaluated based on their personal contribution to group results (as measured by 360-degree assessments) and their ability to boost their own skill level (as assessed by chapter heads).[16]

ING's transformation initially focused on its flagship Netherlands retail banking business, which accounted for about 40 percent of its global retail banking business.[17] Afterward, the bank introduced agile ways of working and customer-centric teams into other geographies and business units. The largely colocated multidisciplinary squads have demolished silos and allowed employees and leaders across functions to focus singularly on customer value. Even in back-end functions like IT, work became more customer centric. Employees could react more quickly when specific challenges arose, with increased trust and less hierarchy.

While ING's efforts to introduce customer-centric teams have focused primarily on the branch level in specific markets, Unilever has taken the next step and begun to reorganize itself globally to allow for quicker decision-making and more responsiveness to consumers' shifting needs. In recent decades, some large multinationals have focused primarily on thinking and acting globally, building and leveraging powerful global brands and products in local markets. Others like Unilever have endeavored to *think global* but also *act local.* That is, they've sought to uncover big ideas for new products and services, pilot them in a few markets to show that they work, and then introduce them into markets around the world, localizing them to some extent to reflect local needs and taste. Finding its brands challenged by savvy, nimble local start-ups attuned to fast-changing consumer needs, Unilever has turned this familiar model on its head, reorganizing itself to *think* locally (so as to respond to consumers' changing needs) and *act* globally (to exploit advantage at scale).[18] As part of its Connected for Growth program, the company has created 240 country-category business teams (CCBTs)—local, cross-functional entrepreneurial units that possess full decision-making authority and are responsible for their own profit and loss.[19]

Describing this new organizational concept, Sanjiv Mehta, chairman and managing director of Hindustan Unilever and president of Unilever South Asia, told us that these CCBTs function as "mini-boards."[20] Because they run all aspects of day-to-day operations, they can react more quickly to local market shifts and rapidly roll out locally relevant innovations.[21] Hindustan Unilever, for example, has sixteen such CCBTs led by young cross-functional managers.[22] Leaders focus on enabling these teams, providing them with resources required to operate like start-ups in local markets and win. By delegating day-to-day responsibility, leaders can focus on longer-term goals, inorganic opportunities, and management of disruptions.[23] With their evolving understanding of local consumer needs, teams can tap the power of Unilever's global scale to find the best solutions from across the organization. Recognizing India's cultural and regional heterogeneity, Sanjiv Mehta launched the Winning in Many Indias (WiMI) strategy, dividing the country into fourteen regional clusters.[24] Each cluster can customize its product propositions, supply chains, and media deployment, enabling faster decision-making, closer consumer connect, and rapid response to regional challenger brands. WiMI clusters act as regional business teams, working with CCBTs to make Hindustan Unilever more agile and nimble. Thanks to this structure, the company has hastened its decision-making and rolled out innovations faster.

To further enhance responsiveness, leaders at Unilever have taken two additional steps. First, they've flattened the organization, moving from thirteen layers of management between the CEO and the front line to just six, with plans to go even flatter. The company has done away with that hallmark of twentieth-century multinational corporations: regional management. Key country heads now report not to an intermediate level of regional managers but directly to the global chief operating officer, Nitin Paranjpe. He in turn can more quickly and efficiently shift resources as needed by local teams with fewer bureaucratic requirements. "Instead of optimizing how we allocate resources within a large region like Southeast Asia," Paranjpe explained, "we can now optimize it globally, or as we say, we can 'act global.'"[25]

Second, Unilever has decentralized certain of its key business functions, a move designed to bring these functions in closer contact with local teams and consumers. Unilever has continued to benefit from global scale in its operations, adopting global platforms in many areas (a topic we'll cover a bit later). But it has also moved strategically to relocate some functions like e-commerce and marketing that used to reside at global headquarters to the most important regions in the organization for that function. Relocation allowed these functions to operate at scale while freeing functional employees from the more distanced *headquarters* mentality. Functions like innovation and supply chain were merged into global category teams, granting them more proximity to local businesses and markets. In a departure from the matrix model, local countries were given formal control over part of R & D budgets, allowing them to more quickly bring to market products and services that local consumers desire. As Paranjpe noted, even global functions like data and governance "have to be built with a mindset of how it will benefit the local markets."[26]

Taken together, these adjustments have dramatically increased Unilever's responsiveness. As of 2018, Unilever's time to market was 40 to 50 percent faster than it had been in 2016, with more experimentation and collaboration taking place.[27] Whereas in 2016 Unilever delivered operating margins of 14.8 percent, by 2019 its margins had reached 16.8 percent.[28]

Agile Ways of Working

> The movement from product- to customer-focused teams is closely bound up with an embrace of new so-called agile ways of working.

Decades ago, the late John Clarkeson, former CEO of BCG, opined that twenty-first-century companies would have to resemble small jazz combos as opposed to orchestras. Their members have to become skilled in improvising quickly with one another to achieve shared objectives rather than following a rigid script.[29] Ever prescient, Clarkeson was right. To stay ahead of changing technologies, consumer needs, political conditions, and social expectations, global firms today must build teams that have a jazz combo's capacity to pivot quickly, experiment, and iterate on the go. Jazz musicians are resiliency personified in the face of unexpected challenges. Companies can be like that too.

Agile approaches to work allow for precisely this ability. Introduced in recent decades among software developers to supercharge innovation, the agile philosophy mobilizes small interdisciplinary teams, challenging them to rapidly iterate and evolve new product and service ideas via short-term cycles, or sprints.[30] Whereas teams in traditional matrix organizations tested products exhaustively before launch, agile teams adopt a *fail fast* mentality to arrive quickly at minimally viable products. Agile also incorporates tactics such as the trialing of initial versions of a product or service with customers and the colocation of team members.[31] Think of the US military and its small, tightly knit special-operations teams that maneuver stealthily behind enemy lines. These teams are highly agile, possessing the diverse skill sets and work processes required to improvise solutions quickly in the field as problems arise. Companies need high-performance teams like that if they are to build breakthrough solutions for the new global customer.

Many large firms today are struggling to become more agile. But the relatively few companies that are agile see dramatic results.[32] At ING Netherlands, leaders embraced agile ways of working, encouraging teams to work in quick, iterative sprints. These would flush out defects before a new offering was scaled up. Since 2014, the time it takes ING Netherlands to bring new ideas to market has become shorter and shorter. Instead of just a few product or service releases per year, the bank has managed to push out new releases every few weeks.[33] Buurtzorg, a Dutch nursing company with more than ten thousand employees, has organized itself into small, highly autonomous frontline teams of about a dozen multidisciplinary nurses serving a particular geographic area.[34] Instead of a corps of middle managers, the company relies on coaches who help spread best practices among disparate teams and provide training and tools to help with decision-making.[35] The point is to liberate teams from bureaucracy, allowing them to administer themselves within certain rough boundaries.[36] The system has allowed for considerable success in recent years: the company was named the Netherlands' best place to work for four years between 2011 and 2015.[37] "We feel more liberated, appreciated, and fully in control of how we can provide the best possible healthcare to our clients," one employee remarked. "Instead of having to work with lots of frustrating bureaucracy, we can now do what we love to do: delivering care to clients."[38]

Some leading-edge companies are using agile methodologies to stay
close to internal customers as well as external ones. The financial services
firm Fidelity piloted agile in 2017 as part of its ongoing drive to offer
the "best customer experience in the financial services industry."[39] Like
ING, the company created a more fluid organizational structure that
mobilized small, nimble, autonomous teams to improve the customer
experience. The push toward agile improved the firm's marketing and
innovation functions, allowing the company to iterate its advertising
efforts to incorporate customer input and to develop new products and
services more quickly in response to external trends.

But leaders also deployed agile internally to improve end-user experience and efficiency. Fidelity's internal audit team began to experiment
with agile, organizing auditors into small, dedicated teams that worked
in two-week sprints with the business groups being audited. Although
the deployment of agile required earlier and more frequent input from
business groups, they supported the change after realizing how much
agile sped up the auditing process and increased transparency, leaving
them with no surprises at the end of the audit. The audit group's leadership was likewise impressed with how the agile pilot elevated trust
between the business and internal audit functions and re-energized auditors by creating career development benefits. In early 2019, the entire
internal audit group embraced agile methodology and is currently working to identify KPIs that best support its new way of working.[40]

As global incumbents seek to become more agile, they face the challenge of doing so while still retaining the advantages of their global scale.
Agile work processes are difficult enough to sustain when all team members are physically present in the same location. The challenge becomes
far greater when they are spread around the world and must largely
interact by virtual means.

To manage this problem, leading-edge companies are experimenting
with so-called distributed agile, an approach that allows them to achieve
the benefits of both agile and global scale. A number of firms have successfully mobilized distributed agile, from global automotive companies
to investment banks to IT giants. One European aircraft manufacturer
implemented distributed agile at scale in its development function, with
two-thirds of its team (the software developers) located in India and
the other one-third with product-focused roles in Europe. Initially,
everyone came together in person to create a distributed agile playbook,

collaborating afterward using digital tools such as digital scrum boards, virtual conferences, and a cloud-based development platform. Communities of practice were created to enable team members to share information informally regardless of their physical location. Thanks to this transformation, time to market improved by 50 percent, and defects were removed 20 percent faster, again without sacrificing the cost advantage of large offshore software-development teams.

Build Horizontal Platforms

Customer-facing teams and agile ways of working enable companies to address customer needs more rapidly by doing away with traditional boundaries and silos. Hard boundaries still exist in organizations with customer-facing teams and agile ways of working, only now it is the customer journey rather than products or geography that defines specific teams and separates them from one another.

> To ensure that collaboration takes place across organizational boundaries in support of customer-facing teams, and to exploit the scale advantages of large organizations, leading-edge companies are implementing new horizontal enablement platforms encompassing data, technology, and processes.[41]

Consider Natura, Brazil's largest cosmetics company. To grow its beauty retail capabilities, to expand its global footprint, and to acquire local talent, knowledge, and experience, Natura embarked on a bold acquisitions strategy. They snapped up the Australian retailer Aesop and the British retailer the Body Shop, companies that deeply aligned with Natura's own values on sustainability. More recently, Natura has closed its acquisition of Avon, creating the world's fourth-largest beauty group, Natura &Co. In integrating these new acquisitions, leaders at Natura &Co saw an opportunity, as Natura &Co chairman and chief executive of the group, Roberto Marques, put it, to "create [a governance and operational structure] from scratch."[42]

Leaders were determined that the company not become a conventional multinational corporation (MNC) in which acquired companies merged more or less indistinguishably with the acquiring firm. In fashioning an alternative, they had three priorities. First, leaders wanted to craft an organizational schema that would build on the company's long tradition of building strong personal, collaborative relationships with stakeholders. Second, leaders sought an organization that allowed for more entrepreneurialism and that steered away from the feel of a big, centrally driven corporation with burdensome structures and processes. And third, leaders wanted to challenge the MNC's traditional focus on directives issued from a centralized headquarters. Instead, they sought to create *centers of gravity* around the company's individual businesses, locating resources there. In sum, they wanted their global organization to respect each brand's unique competitive advantages, afford each brand a significant amount of autonomy, and minimize bureaucracy while also enabling strong fluid collaboration across the brands.

Leaders decided on a group structure, creating a group brand— Natura &Co—that allowed each constituent company to operate with autonomy. To ensure collaboration across the boundaries of the member companies while leveraging economies of scale, leaders created three different supportive horizontal collaboration platforms linking the constituent companies, each with varying degrees of integration:

- "Networks of Excellence" were created when a specific functional priority for the group arose and focused on strengthening group-wide capabilities. Originally these networks existed in three areas: (1) sustainability, (2) digital, and (3) retail. An executive was selected to orchestrate executives across the companies in articulating a common group agenda. The time commitment required to participate in these networks was about two to four days a month.

- "Functional Networks" were created in areas like procurement, human resources, and investor relations where synergies existed and where the team set out to set group-wide policies. Functional heads in the companies also served as group leaders in a given function (for example, the chief human resources officer at Aesop also was the group human resources leader) and were referred to as "dual hats." Functional networks were designed to deliver economies of scale and standardization across the group without creating large and rigid central functions. Networks undertook specific projects, short sprints requiring eight to ten days per month.

- "Group Hubs," the most integrated form of collaboration, consolidated certain functions such as finance and legal across the group to integrate and execute group processes and monitor for performance. To further ensure collaboration across boundaries, Natura &Co created a group operating committee (GOC) composed of senior leaders from each company. Meeting quarterly for two days, this group worked in a collaborative agile way to help align the group's companies on topics that affected all of them, such as innovation.

Although some of these elements are still being implemented, early indications are that this more flexible, fluid, platform-based, cross-organizational structure is enabling the cross-pollination of ideas and spawning productive collaborations.

Enablement platforms might encompass specific functions or business processes, as the case of Natura suggests, but they can also include the underlying technology and data required to deliver on emerging consumer needs. Although traditionally the need for oversight and control prevented companies from organizing into horizontal, frontline, customer-focused teams, new data and technology platforms allow for just that. Not only can local teams draw on vast amounts of global data to design new solutions; these platforms empower leaders to access performance data from the front lines in real time, with algorithms translating a maddeningly diverse and discontinuous set of information into a consistent, coherent data stream to aid decision-making. Armed with such data and algorithms, leaders can bypass layers of management and still keep track of far-flung operations. Companies are poised to become simpler and flatter as they reorganize around customers and their needs, with leaders engaging directly with frontline operations.

Alibaba's customer-facing teams are empowered by so-called middle platforms of technological and process-related or functional capabilities (the latter related to marketing, content production, merchant recruitment, and so on) that Alibaba's businesses can customize to fit their needs. Businesses build up their own individual platforms from standardized components or develop and add their own components. An administrative unit called a *middle office* works to standardize the newly developed components for use by other businesses. Each functional platform consists of several dozen employees working in small teams. The company's middle office synthesizes customer insights from the various businesses, which its ecosystem partners can leverage to create value. This allows the company to break down informational silos, spot patterns in the data, and enable better decision-making by leaders.[43]

Across industries, collaboration technologies adopted by leading-edge companies enable a range of capabilities, including integration of customer feedback data, the tracking of team performance, and the sharing of service-related knowledge. Buurtzorg's autonomous teams of nurses rely not just on informal networks of nurses to coordinate and share information but also on an intranet they call the "Buurtzorg web."[44] As we've seen in previous chapters, industrial companies such as the industrial conglomerate Siemens and the aircraft-engine manufacturer Rolls-Royce use sophisticated technology platforms to monitor, disseminate, and analyze the performance of customer machinery in real time. With this technology, frontline teams can communicate and coordinate with centralized teams of experts to make repairs.

Data, technology, and process-related platforms figure prominently in the efforts of leading-edge companies to build wider networks of participants beyond their organizations. Agile customer-focused teams also are more potent because they draw on relationships with like-minded external partners—the ecosystems and value networks described in Chapter 3. At Rolls-Royce's R^2 Data Labs, described in Chapter 2, small teams of interdisciplinary experts collaborate with other teams across Rolls-Royce to develop new data-based services customers might find valuable. In addition to adopting agile methods (for instance, the work is organized into short sprints lasting fewer than ninety days), teams at R^2 call on a large ecosystem of partners, including, as per the company's website, "OEM partners, tech providers, cutting edge data innovation start-ups and academics."[45] As of this writing, the ecosystem has more than five hundred participants globally and is powered by a technology platform created in collaboration with Microsoft and Tata Consultancy Services.[46] Ecosystems make a world of difference as companies seek to respond to customers, and an underlying technology platform brings diverse ecosystem players together across distances and boundaries.

Readers might wonder how enablement platforms differ from the centers of excellence (CoE) global organizations have traditionally deployed. Unlike CoEs, which were independent of business units that owned parts of the value chain, platforms share responsibility for the success of frontline teams and exist only by virtue of their ability to add value by innovating and scaling what they deliver. Teams don't have to use these platforms. If platforms don't deliver value, companies decline to fund them. Employees often rotate between frontline teams and the platform, ensuring that they understand them both. Since platforms are innovative, they are just as entrepreneurial and fast moving as frontline teams, a magnet for ambitious talent inside the organization. Whereas CoEs were designed to centralize and own processes and capabilities (often so as to act as checks on individual businesses), companies use platforms to standardize data models and operations to allow for more speed and autonomy. Fluid and dynamic platforms, often distributed globally, are the flexible spines that help responsive customer-focused organizations to not merely function but shine.

Ultimately, we can think of platforms as new twenty-first-century solutions to a long-standing problem global firms have faced: how to derive benefits from both a global *and* a local orientation. Global firms long tended either to centralize functions at corporate headquarters so as to build expertise and scale or to disperse their functional capabilities at the regional or country levels. In the first case, firms sacrificed proximity to local customers and the ability to respond to their needs. In the latter, they sacrificed scale benefits and the ability to build deep expertise. Enablement platforms allow companies to connect distributed and fragmented front-end customer teams with global-scale functional expertise. In effect, these platforms help to distribute decision-making between local customer teams and global platforms as needed to arrive at the most desirable mix of local responsiveness and global scale. Decision rights are not rigidly specified; discretion and a bit of fuzziness built into the system allow leaders to meet evolving business needs, representing a huge advantage over how traditional multinational corporations operated. The organization can productively sustain such fuzziness if it has a supportive culture of collaboration in place, as well as leaders who understand and support that culture, enabling people to work between the lines of reporting, not just through them.

In the future, many global firms will become platform organizations oriented fundamentally around enablement platforms. These organizations will have many small, largely or fully autonomous agile teams armed with capacities and able to innovate quickly in response to market demands. Large enablement platforms will back these teams up, providing shared service centers that modularize and standardize functions, that pool resources, and that provide shared tools and support. Covering operational processes at both the front and back ends, these platforms will allocate resources as needed to front-end teams, which will hold decision-making rights and customize modular functional elements to fit their needs. As colleagues of ours have observed, these platforms will be "bionic," combining humans and technology.[47] Critically, these platforms will support external partners in surrounding ecosystems, enhancing the value they can create.

The Essential Role of Culture and Leadership

As companies move beyond the matrix and adopt customer-focused teams, agile ways of working, and enablement platforms to become more fluid, they're attending to two essential supportive areas: (1) cultural change and (2) leadership development.

The small agile customer-focused teams now cropping up inside organizations are so powerful because members of these teams and the wider organization are also adopting a mindset of innovation, openness, boldness, and intense customer focus, as well as related behaviors, and because leaders are utilizing the skills and behaviors required to generate rapid and effective solutions for customers.

In the rush to meet shifting customer needs, leaders of global companies might feel tempted to update their organizational structures without attending to people and culture. That's a big mistake. Companies seeking to develop an external customer-focused orientation require a very different culture to animate, engage, and orient their people. Simply put, it's not a digital transformation without a digital culture.[48] BCG research has found that companies do much better with digital transformations when they focus on culture. Of companies BCG tracked that pursued digital transformations, the vast majority (almost 80 percent) of those that had focused on culture "sustained strong or breakthrough performance," whereas none of the companies that neglected culture did.[49]

Much has been written about the kinds of cultural attributes incumbents must incorporate in order to win in a digital world. While companies will obviously maintain diverse cultures depending on their organizational purposes, industries, strategies, and so on, they will want to infuse their existing cultures with the following five key elements:

- A strong focus on empathizing with and understanding customers, rather than on the primacy of the firm's internal processes
- Delegation, rather than micromanaging and command and control
- Swift action, rather than perpetual planning that results in stasis
- Boldness and risk-taking when making decisions, rather than an excess of caution
- Collaboration, rather than a closed, siloed mindset

Each of these elements will be familiar to anyone who has worked inside a fast-moving digital start-up, but they traditionally have not defined workplace environments inside large global incumbents. That needs to change. These cultural elements help customer-focused teams to spot changing customer needs and move quickly and decisively to address them. If teams don't adopt entrepreneurial, change-oriented, customer-focused mindsets and behaviors, any well-intended changes in the organizational structure will prove ineffectual.

ING Netherlands prioritized cultural change from the outset when shifting to new ways of working. For instance, to render its culture better suited to agile customer-centric ways of working, the bank implemented a three-week onboarding program for all its employees in operations, mandating that they spend at least one of those weeks at a customer-loyalty-team call center taking customer calls. The company implemented open offices, creating environments similar to campuses at tech companies, and introduced more fluid peer-to-peer hiring protocols. Communications became more frequent and open, with the organization encouraging dialogue and informal interactions. Senior leaders set the tone for cultural change, spending significant time with the team spearheading the organizational transformation and working from a large table in a single open space themselves. This is as it should be. As colleagues of ours have observed, "Agile starts—or stops—at the top."[50]

With that precept firmly in mind, leading-edge companies are ensuring that leaders have the skills and behaviors they need to lead fluid customer-centric organizations. As colleagues of ours have noted, leaders in successful global organizations increasingly won't be "controllers of hardwired organizational structures, processes, and rules" but rather "more like jazz conductors, setting up the parameters of a flexible and dynamic system that unleashes employees' initiative and allows them to cooperate to achieve the organization's goals."[51] Rather than exercising command and control, leaders at many of the exemplar organizations described in this book are focusing more on empowering and coaching employees. Rather than sending decisions up the hierarchy for resolution, leaders are giving teams more operational autonomy while ensuring that they are aligned around company objectives. Rather than defining success in terms of the size of a team or organization, leaders are judging it in terms of the value a team or organization delivers. And rather than moving slowly and avoiding risk, leaders are prioritizing speed and ongoing improvement.

Advice for Leaders

Updating an organization, its culture, and its leadership is hard work, and most global incumbents have scarcely begun to tackle this task. As we've seen, however, doing so is vital if companies are to succeed with the other strategies in this book. Companies must make frontline teams permanent fixtures inside the organization. They must spread agile work practices throughout the organization. And they must build enablement platforms that facilitate collaboration across both internal and external boundaries. They must also put in place the soft enablers of responsiveness—culture and leadership. Experimenting with some of these changes is better than nothing, but firms like ING that embrace most or all of them at once position themselves to lead their markets going forward. As Bob Black, a BCG senior adviser and former executive at Kimberly-Clark, has suggested, companies must take a fundamentally different approach to their modes of organizing, designing organizations "from front to back, starting from the front lines" rather than the traditional top to bottom with the most power at the top.[52]

Look critically at your current organization, considering the pain points that flare up when it comes to responding quickly to customers. From there, imagine broadly how you might revamp your organization, defining key design principles that the new organizational structure must solve for. Many companies opt for organizations that allow them to achieve goals like driving growth, improving service levels, and reducing cost. Then think about specific organizational changes you might make to adapt some of the experiments we've described. Ponder the following questions:

- In implementing local customer-focused teams, how might you strike the balance between flexibility and frontline autonomy on the one side and control and risk management on the other? What must remain uniform across local teams, what might local teams borrow from others and adapt in their own ways, and what should local teams run entirely on their own?
- Which teams should you place in the same location, and which can viably remain virtual?
- What enablement platforms might you put in place to manage the transfer and sharing of knowledge and expertise across the organization? How might you best ensure that the organization is applying the right expertise where it needs it?
- How might you best allocate and reallocate resources (including capital, talent, technologies, and so on) in a fluid organization?
- If you've been strengthening your culture, have you been incorporating the specific values and behaviors you'll need to render your organization more responsive? If not, what specific gaps exist, and how might you fill them?
- Given the magnitude of the organizational changes described in this chapter, do you have a sufficient change management capacity in place to pull them off? In particular, have you prepared leaders and managers, informing them about how they can best support customer-focused teams, agile ways of working, and enablement platforms?

If the transition to a more fluid and responsive organization seems daunting, remember that you don't need to do it all at once. As we'll see, transformation in the twenty-first century—organizational or otherwise—is not a one-off proposition but a constant ongoing evolution. One tech client of ours remarked that when his company conducts a reorganizational effort, they assume that the new organization has a shelf life of only eighteen months before it will become obsolete. Think of your transformation efforts as a process that will evolve organically, initially supplementing and over time perhaps supplanting the older organizational structures.

Relatedly, consider how you might best navigate a reality in which newer, more agile parts of the business engage with other parts of the business that locked into the traditional matrix model. As colleagues of ours have argued, "Leaders need to combine the agile ways of working used by startups with traditional, more rigid, corporate ways of working."[53] Recognizing that some parts of the bank would continue to operate in traditional ways, leaders at ING Netherlands created mechanisms that allowed agile teams to collaborate with nonagile parts. A set of meetings and informal forums were instituted to help nonagile parts of the bank adopt innovations created by agile teams, ensuring a continuity of operations. Key members of traditional teams that were collaborating with agile teams were assigned to ensure the squad's success, empowered to make independent decisions related to their function.[54]

One mistake leaders make when they contemplate organizational change is to become too coldly analytic about it. Organizations are not only about rational structures and processes. They're about *people* and how they might best collaborate and coordinate to achieve desired outcomes. Focusing on culture becomes critically important, but to fully execute on the twenty-first-century growth and operational strategies in this book, companies will need to attend more directly to their workforces, hiring and retaining a new generation of workers equipped to win in the digital economy. As many incumbents are now realizing, attracting, inspiring, and upskilling a digital workforce is quite challenging for incumbents, who face fierce competition for talent from digital firms. Incumbents can win in this area, but to do so, they'll need to transcend their traditional talent-management playbooks and embrace a new set of tactics—yet another way global companies can and must go *beyond*.

Key Insights

- To remain competitive, these companies will have to develop new levels of coordination and collaboration across and beyond their formal organizations. They will have to render their organizations more dynamic, fluid, and even amoeba-like, all in the service of a defining purpose or reason for being.
- If incumbents don't update their organizations in the years ahead, adopting three interwoven experiments—(1) customer-focused teams, (2) agile ways of working, and (3) enablement platforms—they'll jeopardize their ability to execute the other strategies covered in this book.
- As companies move beyond the matrix and adopt customer-focused teams, agile ways of working, and enablement platforms to become more fluid, they're attending to two essential supportive areas: (1) cultural change and (2) leadership development.

CHAPTER 8

THRIVE WITH TALENT

*Global companies have long underestimated the importance of talent,
regarding it as at best a secondary business asset. Today, with
the very nature of talent changing and the competition for the
right people so fierce, companies must attend more closely to what a
new generation of employees wants and needs. They must go beyond
traditional talent management and fundamentally shift how they find,
inspire, and develop a twenty-first-century workforce.*

The hot digital start-ups that have remade the global economy
don't just possess new technologies and visionary ideas. They have
highly skilled and engaged people capable of delivering on the changes
described in previous chapters. Global incumbents need these people
too. They need employees who understand the new global consumer,
are creative enough to devise exciting new value propositions to entice
them, wield the technical skills to build powerful digital solutions, possess a digital mindset (even if they're not directly involved in writing
code), collaborate well across silos, and feel comfortable contributing to
agile work processes. Most fundamentally, incumbents need employees
who are eager to reinvent themselves over time and develop entirely new
competencies as markets and the demand for specific skills and behaviors evolve. As if all this isn't enough, companies in the post-COVID era
also need people who are able to thrive while working collaboratively in
remote work environments.

Unfortunately, incumbents are finding it difficult to assemble
and engage a workforce that meets these criteria with their existing
talent-management strategies. This holds true even at companies and

within industries that have built large successful talent-management capacities. Unilever is a 150-year-old global consumer product company headquartered in London and Rotterdam, Wipro a forty-year-old Indian IT services firm. Known for its best-in-class HR practices, Unilever has created world-class training programs[1] and rotated employees across geographies and functions to develop a strong corps of managers. Its Indian business unit, Hindustan Unilever Limited, has become known as a "CEO factory" for other companies, with some five hundred corporate leaders having worked there at one point in their careers.[2] As for Wipro, the company pioneered a large-scale talent engine for itself during the 1990s and 2000s, recruiting and onboarding tens of thousands of recent graduates per year. Among other elements, Wipro mobilized an in-house university with a customized curriculum, providing eighteen million hours of training in fiscal year 2019, and maintained an internal job market.[3] Wipro's peers in the Indian IT industry adopted similar tactics and, like Unilever and Wipro itself, have grown thanks in part to their proven abilities to attract, deploy, and retain top talent. But as we'll see in this chapter, Unilever and Wipro have lately been revamping and updating their approaches to talent in a major way, as have other traditionally talent-savvy companies.

Two key forces are prompting this change. First, a significant global skills shortage has emerged thanks to the immense demand for employees skilled in developing and delivering digital solutions and capable of working in agile environments. As media outlets reported often in 2019, many companies were unable to fill a significant number of critical positions, sustaining millions of dollars in productivity losses as a result.[4] By 2030, companies around the world will have some eighty-five million skilled jobs unfilled—a gap that will exact a severe economic toll.[5] Making matters worse, educational systems aren't outfitting students with the skills and knowledge many employers need, forcing companies to provide additional training to new hires once they are on board and impacting productivity. This global skills mismatch affects some 40 percent of employees in OECD countries.[6] BCG managing director and senior partner Rainer Strack, a leading global expert on talent trends, has summed up the situation by observing that "in the near future, the world will face a global workforce crisis consisting of an overall labor shortage plus a skills mismatch. Every company needs a people strategy and to act on it immediately."[7]

Traditional talent strategies are coming under strain for a second reason: the global workforce's needs and desires are changing dramatically, forcing companies to rethink how they keep employees engaged, happy, and inspired on the job. Traditional talent management sought to maximize productivity by deploying primarily extrinsic motivators, like salary and promotions. But younger generations of employees no longer seek highly structured careers with ever-increasing responsibility and financial rewards as they climb the corporate ladder. They desire continuous experiential learning on the job as well as the chance to do meaningful work, make a difference in society, and find fulfillment outside of work. Research has shown that members of Generation Z will readily accept 10 percent less pay in exchange for shorter work hours and that scarcely more than a third of workers in this age group prioritize their career growth.[8] In a 2018 BCG survey of 366,000 people from almost two hundred countries, respondents ranked "good work-life balance" and "learning and training opportunities" as much more important to them than "financial compensation." These findings were especially pronounced among a subset of people surveyed who qualified as "digital experts."[9] One study of American professionals found that almost all participants surveyed—nine out of ten—would willingly sacrifice some of their earnings for more meaningful jobs.[10]

To gain advantage from talent in the face of these two shifts, firms are not only embracing new tactics—they're comprehensively transforming talent management. Unilever, for instance, has taken six broad actions, as chief human resources officer Leena Nair told us. It has done the following:

- Sought to make itself more attractive to top prospects by embedding its purpose—"better me, better business, better world"—into its recruiting efforts (the company also conveys that "companies with purpose last, brands with purpose grow, and people with purpose thrive")
- Broadened how it accesses talent, adopting what it calls the 4 Bs: not only developing people ("building" talent) and paying to acquire them ("buying") but also hiring people for short periods ("borrowing") and helping them migrate to new jobs ("bridge")
- Aimed to build systems, a culture, and the leadership capacity required to nurture talent
- Reorganized employees into agile teams

- Fostered continuous learning among its workforce
- Sought to upskill all its employees in digital skills[11]

To thrive in the years ahead, global enterprises must follow Unilever's example, changing their underlying mindset and reconceiving their strategies and tactics from top to bottom. Talent management has traditionally regarded employees instrumentally as a means to an end—the creation of business value. Companies sought to source talent, deploy it to the company's advantage, and control it.

In the years ahead, companies must take steps to thrive with talent, putting people and their needs first rather than regarding them as resources to exploit.

"When people are the priority," Microsoft chief people officer Kathleen Hogan has written, "everything else falls into place."[12] As per Hogan, leaders and companies alike should aim to not just ensure a steady supply of the talent they need but also create "an environment where people can do their best work—a place where they can proudly be their authentic selves, and where they know their needs can be met."[13] To understand how your company might accomplish this, let's review how leading-edge firms are unleashing new tactics in the three key strategic areas: (1) attracting, (2) inspiring, and (3) upskilling talent.

Attracting Talent

Companies have long tried to source talent by recruiting people with top educational credentials and industry-relevant experience and then having them relocate physically to work at their facilities. Today, that approach no longer suffices. First, locating talent today is trickier than it has been in the past. "When the pool [of people with specific skills] is so small," one chief technology officer said, "you have to hunt everywhere."[14] More positively, many people with nontraditional backgrounds have precisely the knowledge companies need to get ahead of disruption. That's because disruption frequently originates in far-flung industries, but it also owes to the more varied way people cultivate new skills in the twenty-first century. Instead of merely enrolling in a formal degree or certification program, ambitious professionals are potentially learning on the job, via online courses, and by completing collaborative projects on open digital platforms. Recognizing this reality, more leaders are taking a broader view of talent acquisition. One survey found that employers were increasingly willing to depart from traditional educational criteria when hiring. Over 40 percent of hiring managers anticipated that a coding "boot camp" would soon be just as good a credential as a college degree when evaluating candidates.[15]

> Creating a steady pipeline of top talent today means going beyond traditional tactics (career fairs, campus outreach programs, and lateral hires) and applying far more creativity and open-mindedness in whom you select, where you find them, and how you appeal to them.

We can survey the tactics leading-edge companies are deploying to attract a new generation of employees by borrowing Unilever's 4B framework. Let's briefly review how Unilever and other leading-edge firms are building, buying, borrowing, and bridging when it comes to talent.

Building

Companies have long focused on building a talent pipeline by hiring and developing new recruits. Although this remains a vital avenue for attracting talent, companies are now finding and hiring employees in exciting new ways. One Indian technology company we spoke with faced the challenge of quickly staffing up to fulfill a new contract it had signed. To obtain the specialized skills they needed, leaders bypassed the traditional job search and created a global contest in which they described the business problem they were dealing with and challenged programmers to propose potential solutions. The winner would have a chance to work with the company, in exchange for generous compensation. Although leaders expected little from this tactic, it delivered magnificently for them. And as they discovered, contest participants weren't motivated so much by money as by the chance to work on an interesting problem.

At another global technology firm, executives in the marketing function were discussing how to access new talent that could help them fundamentally rethink their strategies to distinguish themselves from competitors. As one leader observed, the best strategists in digital marketing didn't come from the most prestigious business schools where the company typically hired. Rather, they came from the gaming world. Given the skill it took to compete and excel in highly complex, dynamic game environments, top players were keenly versed in strategic thinking to an extent most people didn't realize. This talent was culturally much different from the company's typical hires (some top gamers are college dropouts, for instance, who don't begin working until the middle of the day), and leaders initially weren't sure how to tap into it. The company eventually experimented by creating a gaming lab that replicated a gaming culture but had participants work on real-life problems. As one leader told us, these so-called misfits improvised brilliant, highly creative solutions to marketing problems.

Companies are deploying a number of other innovative tactics to locate new hires and thus build their talent pools. When users type specific software-related terms into Google, they are shown a coding challenge that, when successfully completed, can prompt the company to offer a job interview. Companies are also accessing unconventional talent via online communities and platforms like the Muse (millennials), AngelList (start-up talent), and GitHub (programmers), and they're partnering with universities to build their employer brands with students. Many companies are also siting their global technology centers strategically to access digital talent pools. Although digital talent doesn't congregate in the same geographic locations as traditional talent, it turns out it isn't just concentrated in places like Silicon Valley, Israel, and Estonia either. BCG has tracked eighty digital hot spots around the world, extending into locations like Moscow, Shanghai, and Melbourne that many don't typically associate with digital talent. In considering which of these hot spots to enter, leading-edge companies are considering a wealth of factors, including their existing footprint, how easy it is to start new ventures in these locales, and the local economy.[16]

If companies are seeking out prospective hires in new ways, they're also revamping their screening processes, as these have often proven ineffective in gauging highly sought-after qualities such as adaptability and customer centricity. Some leading-edge firms are including assessments from online self-learning platforms or evaluating prospective employees by having them complete trial projects. Microsoft's LEAP program, for instance, invites participants from nontraditional backgrounds to pursue a semester-long internship at the company, combining classroom learning with hands-on projects.[17] Client reviews and online ratings on sites like Uber, StackExchange, and GitHub are also supplementing or replacing traditional screening. To appeal to a generation that is more interested in solving real problems than filling out long standardized aptitude tests, companies are increasingly gamifying their screenings and identifying talent via the online competitions and hackathons mentioned previously. Other nontraditional screening measures companies are deploying include expert interviewers, automatic application scanners, and people analytics.[18]

Buying

Companies have long bought new talent through mergers and acquisitions, and that trend has continued in recent years. In its efforts to build new digital mobility services, GM has struggled to attract and keep top talent. As one engineer was quoted as saying, "GM's problem now is that ... no one who wants to work on engines goes there." Instead, "good candidates go there and see their offices and team structure and walk straight out to Tesla/Mercedes/Google."[19] GM addressed that issue when it acquired the ride-share provider Sidecar in 2016, accessing what arguably was the company's greatest asset: its employees. This tactic is becoming so widespread it now has a name—"acquihiring"—with one journalist going so far as to call it "the new normal in talent acquisition."[20]

Another company that has pursued an aggressive acquihiring strategy is the Indian IT services company Wipro. Since 2005, when the company embarked on a growth strategy it dubbed the "string of pearls," Wipro has acquired about two dozen companies.[21] Although these acquisitions served a variety of strategic purposes, in recent years the chance to obtain employees skilled in specific areas has proven an important inducement to dealmaking. In 2019, the company acquired the digital engineering firm International TechneGroup, a move designed to "add value to its core services in industry."[22] In 2016, Wipro snapped up the IT technology company Appirio, a move that gave it new capabilities in cloud technology. In addition to adding thousands of employees to Wipro's workforce, the Appirio transaction also brought new talent-management knowledge into Wipro, in particular the notion of a "virtuous cycle" of positive reinforcement between employees and customers.[23] The year before, Wipro acquired Danish strategic-design firm Designit and its more than three hundred employees, giving it design and user-experience capabilities that complemented Wipro's own capabilities in areas like digital strategy and architecture.[24]

In addition to acquisitions, leading-edge firms are buying talent by making early-stage investments in start-ups. In 2014, Unilever announced the launch of Foundry, a platform to structure and host the company's collaboration with start-ups.[25] As of 2020, Unilever had invested $20 million in start-ups through the platform.[26] In addition to giving Unilever access to innovative business concepts, Foundry enables it to tap external digital talent without having to formally acquire a company. Other large companies—Shell, Nike, Procter & Gamble, and IBM among them—are reputed to have set up corporate incubators.[27] As of 2016, 44 percent of the world's thirty biggest companies used incubators or accelerators.[28]

Borrowing

To access talent, companies have traditionally sought to hire or acquire full-time formal employees. Today, more companies are relying on contractors and hence *borrowing* talent for short stints or on a project basis. Borrowing carries the advantage of making companies more resilient. They can quickly address pressing challenges without having to shoulder the overhead of hiring and training employees. An important driver behind the use of contractors is the rise of global crowdsourcing platforms and a broader gig economy. Although as of 2018 relatively small percentages of workers in developed countries relied on the gig economy, our survey of eleven thousand employees around the world found that in countries like China, Indonesia, India, and Brazil, sizable proportions of workers do so (in China, almost half of respondents reported turning to gigs for primary or secondary income, while in India about 40 percent did).[29] A 2018 survey of executives found that some two-fifths anticipated that their organizations would rely more heavily on gig workers in the years to come.[30]

In the media world, leading film studios and other content producers have traditionally drawn from a familiar talent pool of writers, directors, and other professionals, while young unproven talent has had great difficulty breaking in. To increase their access to talent, content producers have begun crowdsourcing solutions for specific projects, turning to communities of freelancers on digital platforms. One such platform, Tongal, boasts 160,000 freelancers from 168 countries and clients that include 20th Century Fox, National Geographic, Disney, and Mattel.[31] The work process is straightforward: creative talent and corporate clients connect on the site with clients submitting briefs for upcoming projects and creators their own original ideas. Clients pay the creators to execute the agreed-upon work.[32] Companies don't replace full-time employees with talent gleaned on Tongal but rather borrow them for a short time period and for specific needs.

Bridging

To help secure needed talent, leading-edge companies are taking new steps to bridge talent by helping employees continuously move on to new opportunities internally. In 2019, Unilever launched FLEX Experiences, an internal talent marketplace that used AI to help current employees find jobs tailored to their unique skills and goals. As one Unilever HR executive remarked, the company was "driving new ways of working to gain rapid access to the best skills and business ideas available both internally and externally." FLEX Experiences didn't just help the company meet its own needs but also increased employees' access to growth and learning opportunities. "We believe that our people are much more than their job title," this executive said. "If our people thrive, we thrive as a business."[33]

As this last example suggests, attracting talent isn't just about locating people to hire or with whom to contract. It's about creating attractive opportunities so that people *want* to work with your enterprise. Departing from traditional talent sourcing, leading-edge companies are offering much more compelling employee value propositions to appeal to a new generation of talent. For instance, it's no secret that many young people recoil at the thought of working in a stodgy office. Global companies are creating more open, noncorporate environments to entice and inspire young, digitally native employees. The global software company Kronos recently opened a glittering new Boston-area headquarters, complete with an espresso bar and full-length basketball court.[34] LinkedIn features music rooms at its locations that allow employees to play together,[35] while Nestlé's offices in the United Kingdom allow employees to bring their dogs to work.[36]

At the extreme, companies are creating environments separate and apart from their existing operations to lure digital talent. The carmaker Renault felt that its identity as an industrial company could hamper efforts to attract employees and quickly launch a digital center. So it partnered with a renowned outside provider to create a center administered separately from the main organization under a "build, operate, transfer" model. In just six months, this center attracted young, ambitious talent, allowing Renault to build up an enviable digital capacity. Over time, these new employees would transition to Renault's global team. Companies such as John Deere and Siemens have likewise chosen to establish digital centers of excellence that are physically and organizationally separate from their legacy operations. John Deere established an Intelligent Solutions Group (ISG) at its headquarters, augmented by a digital lab in San Francisco and a precision agriculture start-up it had acquired in the Bay Area. The work environment at the ISG is much less formal than at other departments of the company, and policies such as performance management and compensation structures differ as well in ways designed to appeal to digital talent.[37] As one employee put it, ISG has "an environment of a 'software company.'"[38]

As important as it is, the physical workplace environment is just one element among many that makes for a compelling job or employer in the eyes of employees with in-demand skills. Companies are also attending to important elements of the workplace that motivate them, engage them, and allow them to grow their careers. Let's take a look.

Inspiring and Empowering Talent

Companies have long motivated their workforces by focusing on extrinsic incentives, such as salary increases and bonuses. Such incentives still matter for new talent, but leading-edge companies are also working hard to ensure that work is meaningful.

When employees find their work meaningful, they tend to stick around longer. One study found that these employees are almost 70 percent less likely to leave their jobs over the subsequent six months and stay at their jobs for over seven months longer on average than employees toiling away at less meaningful jobs.[39] Mindful of such realities, global companies are transforming their cultures to emphasize purpose at work, infusing purpose into their strategic decision-making and screening new hires to ensure that they understand the corporate purpose well and that their own personal beliefs and goals align with it. These companies are also framing talent policies to ensure that once employees are on board, the purpose is continually reinforced and employees understand their own work as deeply meaningful and connected with the company's overarching reason for being.

A critically important component of Unilever's efforts to inspire and empower employees (and also attract them to begin with) has been its much-admired focus on purpose. As the company's chief human resources officer, Leena Nair, confirmed, "Purpose is at the heart of everything we do," including how the company has managed its workforce.[40] When recruiting, the firm follows the mantra "better me, better business, better world," neglecting to hire people who aren't passionate about making a better world. The careers page on the company's global website emphasizes purpose and its role at the company: "Whether you're a human spark ignitor, a talent catalyst, or a digital disrupter, we encourage our employees to live their purpose everyday."[41] Once on board, employees participate in "life purpose workshops" to help them uncover their own personal purpose.[42] The company has also built purpose into the identity of each of its brands, a tactic that not only helps it appeal to customers but attracts and engages employees. The company's Dove brand, for instance, is dedicated to making "a positive experience of beauty universally accessible to every woman." This means challenging stereotypes "to ensure every woman feels seen and represented in the world of beauty," a goal that energizes employees.[43]

As Nair has remarked, "We know that companies with purpose last, brands with purpose grow, and people with purpose thrive."[44] The company's emphasis on purpose has certainly had a profound and even pivotal impact on its talent pipeline, helping the company lower its recruitment costs by 90 percent and the average time required to recruit a new hire by sixteen days.[45] "The number one reason people apply to Unilever is because they perceive that we are helping to make the world better," Nair said. As of 2019, Unilever was ranked the most attractive employer in more than three dozen of its hiring markets.[46] As a measure of its popularity with younger, technology-savvy professionals in 2019, Unilever ranked among the top ten most followed organizations on LinkedIn, counting more than six million followers.[47]

Another company that has mobilized purpose to engage its workforce is the Brazilian global cosmetics company Natura. As a certified B Corporation (a designation for companies dedicated to delivering social and environmental goods in addition to profits) in its industry, Natura has embraced a business model focused on ensuring sustainability and enhancing biodiversity, sourcing its ingredients in sustainable ways from local producers and achieving a carbon-neutral certification for its manufacturing.[48] As Keyvan Macedo, Natura's sustainability manager, told us, a significant portion of employee bonuses reflects their performance on environmental and social measures. Natura's organization of daily work around purpose has proven a significant draw for talent. At the leadership level, Macedo notes that "executives have joined Natura because they want to work for a company [like this] and share a common understanding of the sustainable business model."[49] The company's purpose also helps the company inspire and engage its sales representatives, even prompting some to make sacrifices themselves to better help the company achieve its objectives. As Macedo noted, "We see that there are so many consultants whose main reason for selling is not just to achieve higher level but because they like the brand and what it stands for. Some are even giving up the higher profit margin to promote the cause."[50]

In addition to purpose, companies are inspiring employees by promoting cultural values like collaboration, diversity, agility, and learning. These values at once support twenty-first-century business models and appeal to the sensibilities of younger employees. Take diversity. As companies move toward horizontal agile teams, cultures that welcome diversity will become increasingly important, as employees in local teams will be called to collaborate closely with colleagues located elsewhere around the world. But younger employees also seek out workplaces that emphasize diversity and that are respectful and welcoming, and employees in general are more engaged in such workplaces.[51] Leading-edge companies are moving aggressively to make their own workplaces more welcoming and to promote their warm, inclusive cultures to employees and prospective hires. Intel, for instance, set aggressive goals for hiring women and minorities,[52] while SAP prepares and recruits students attending Historically Black Colleges and Universities (HBCUs), trains and places neurodiverse candidates in its company, and has pledged to increase women in management roles by 1 percent annually.[53]

Another critically important way leading-edge companies are inspiring and empowering employees is by enhancing the career-development opportunities they offer and providing more autonomy and tools to excel on the job. Young, digitally savvy employees value learning and career development. In a study of almost twenty-seven thousand digital experts, respondents listed "learning and training opportunities" and "career development possibilities" as among the most important elements of their jobs, with only work-life balance ranking higher.[54] Members of this group also spend a great deal of their time on learning.[55] As BCG senior adviser and former Kimberly-Clark executive Bob Black noted, millennial and Generation Z employees tend to want a series of enriching on-the-job learning experiences rather than formal "careers." They value continuous learning and the chance to make a difference in their jobs. "What companies are not thinking about," he noted, "is that over time, as this generation settles down and starts families, they will also seek certainty. So companies should help them seek to balance that need for certainty with the desire for enriching experiences."[56] The strongest companies in this area are thinking about the entire employee journey just as they are the customer journey, analyzing methodically how they can attract, acquire, onboard, develop, and promote employees.

Mindful that many younger employees favor self-directed learning, companies are taking an increasingly expansive approach to learning and developing, incorporating on-demand learning, virtual training, feedback, coaching, mentoring, and experiential learning. Leading-edge firms are providing young talent with more opportunities to work on interesting projects, promoting entrepreneurialism, experimentation, and a fail-fast culture. Walmart has created an internal incubator that organizes large-scale innovation events.[57] Google's gThanks tool allows employees to recognize others for their good ideas and proffer small financial rewards.[58]

As we discussed in Chapter 6, leading-edge firms are also rendering work more stimulating, engaging, and enriching day to day by embedding agile ways of working and by mobilizing digital technology to improve the workplace experience. Prior to the COVID crisis, some companies were using digital collaboration tools, which includes messaging, content sharing, and the hosting of group discussions. Once the pandemic struck, these tools proliferated as large swaths of the work-force shifted to working from home. In the years ahead, companies will need to further empower people by measuring and rewarding outcomes rather than activities and "face time." Hybrid arrangements that include both remote and onsite work and that use technology to enable seam-less collaboration and teaming will afford an advantage. To make the most of these arrangements, companies will need to define new behav-iors and expectations and reinforce them with new forms of recognition and reward. They'll have to imagine new ways to build relationships and develop employees that emphasize digital tools rather than daily face-to-face contact.

But collaboration tools are just the beginning. The analytics software company Humanyze is issuing sociometric badges to employees, using the resulting data and insights to improve collaboration, time usage, and other elements bearing on productivity. Another firm, VMware, is using predictive analytics to spot workers in danger of leaving the company, alerting managers so that they can take preemptive action. GE is sup-plementing the standard annual performance review, allowing employ-ees to monitor their performance in real time via a smartphone app. Firms like Kimberly-Clark are using analytics to improve the diversity of their workforce. Such tools are important for engaging workers, but leading-edge companies understand that they will go astray if they don't genuinely embrace them as a vital way of making work better, more fulfilling, more stimulating, and more enriching. At these companies, leaders truly thrive with talent, through both technological and nontech-nological means. They elevate talent, transforming it from a peripheral topic to a core part of business strategy.

Upskilling the Talent Pool

> Attracting and inspiring talented young employees won't be enough for most companies to meet their talent needs. Companies must take steps to teach their existing workforce new skills and behav-iors, what some have termed *upskilling*.

The World Economic Forum has observed that "by 2022, no less than 54% of all employees will require significant re- and upskilling."[59] Skills and behaviors required on the job will change dramatically, with a new emphasis on analytic thinking, creativity, technology design, emotional intelligence, and problem solving, among others.[60] Unfortunately, companies aren't yet rising to the challenge of upskilling their workforces: a majority of employees most in need of such training aren't receiving it.[61]

If your firm hasn't embarked on a major upskilling initiative, you should bear in mind that you might have the skills and behaviors on hand to achieve your current business outcomes, but your business five to ten years from now will likely look much different than it does today. The sheer number of digital and agile-friendly employees you'll need can make upskilling a more cost-effective option than replacing most of your workforce. Existing employees also afford an advantage on account of their familiarity with the organization's mission, vision, values, and purpose. As BCG research has found, large majorities of workers profess an openness to learning new skills relevant to their jobs.[62] One of our colleagues put the situation this way: "Our research paints a picture of a global workforce that is aware of the coming changes, and is ready to meet the challenge."[63]

Such considerations, as well as the recognition that large numbers of existing employees will see their existing jobs rendered less relevant thanks to technology,[64] are prompting leading-edge companies and even entire industries to embark on aggressive upskilling programs. In the Indian IT industry, analysts have projected that roughly 40 percent of the workforce will require new skills training as technology shifts toward areas like virtual reality, blockchain, and cloud technologies, as regulation and globalization render work more complex, and as jobs become increasingly automated.[65] Although in 2019 the industry counted about eight hundred thousand digitally skilled professionals, the National Association of Software and Services Companies (NASSCOM), the industry's trade association, anticipated that by 2023 companies would need 2.7 million people.[66] Given that only a portion of India's engineering graduates every year possess the right skill mix, the industry foresees a skills shortage. To address it, companies will have no choice but to upskill large swaths of their workforces.[67]

NASSCOM has launched a massive upskilling program called FutureSkills with the goal up upskilling four million people in a number of key technological areas by 2025.[68] Among many other elements, FutureSkills created a curriculum of courses linked to skills in dozens of specific job roles, making it accessible to leading IT firms in the form of an open marketplace platform. The course's goal: "to enable discovery, continuous learning and deep skilling in 10 emerging technologies."[69] In 2018, Indian prime minister Narendra Modi formally launched NASS-COM at an event attended by IT industry leaders and delegates from around the world.[70]

Among its peers, Wipro has been especially aggressive in pursuing upskilling, playing a high-profile role in NASSCOM's FutureSkills initiative.[71] Despite possessing state-of-the-art training programs, Wipro was unable to find sufficient digital talent to cater to the growing demand for rapidly evolving digital disruptions. Younger employees didn't respond well to traditional classroom instruction; they wanted training experiences that were more flexible and that offered quick results. The organization launched an ambitious program to reskill its workforce across business units. However, business teams were looking for employees with relevant project experience on these new skills. While thousands of employees were learning new skills, an imbalance arose in which too many employees were trained in some skills and too few in others. Wipro's business teams wanted a reliable pipeline of relevantly reskilled employees with good hands-on project experience.

Wipro needed a new, more dynamic approach to find and match digital talent in a timely manner that would enable it to execute short-term projects while also building its talent base over the long term. The company reimagined its reskilling program with the goal of creating a workforce that possessed in-depth skills in multiple areas along with strong hands-on experience. The new program deployed a four-step methodology, providing training courses through multiple channels, enabling learning through hands-on assignments, certifying employees using assessments and coding challenges, and crystallizing learning by providing live project experience.

In designing this new program, Wipro first mapped its anticipated skill needs for each role, creating an inventory of future skills. The company then identified which skills and behaviors the upskilling program should prioritize, focusing on training for those that were high value and also used in high volumes. Using AI algorithms, Wipro matched employees with skill needs. Recognizing that it also had to make upskilling attractive to employees, Wipro enabled them to build critical competencies through a gamified competency framework and immersive digital programs. Leveraging a crowdsourcing platform, the new program provided hands-on experience on live projects, motivating employees, fostering a growth mindset, and embedding employees in a broader learning ecosystem. The effort to arrive at a thoughtful and effective program design paid off. By March 2020, this program had played a significant role in helping the company fill 75 percent of its talent demands with internal candidates.[72]

Wipro is hardly alone in unveiling ambitious upskilling programs. Since creating a chief digital officer role in 2014, L'Oréal has launched a digital upskilling initiative designed to build grassroots digital expertise across functions. As of 2018, about two thousand experts supported digital programs across the company, and more than twenty-one thousand employees had received digital upskilling.[73] AT&T has invested $1 billion in an initiative with the goal of retraining one hundred thousand employees in high-demand skills by 2020.[74] The program includes an online platform that employees can use to browse various jobs, their salary levels, and the skills required, as well as a tool that assesses their current skills and diagnoses which skills they need to work on to achieve their desired goals. In partnership with educational institutions, AT&T offers short online courses and certification programs.[75] After one year, the program allowed AT&T to fill more than 40 percent of open job listings with existing employees.[76] One former project manager became a senior scrum master via the program.[77] Another transitioned from network operator to data scientist.[78] Firms like Google, Accenture, and Cognizant have also developed leading-edge upskilling programs. In 2020, American manufacturing companies expected to spend upwards of $26 billion upskilling current and new employees.[79]

These examples evoke some of the strategic best practices leading firms are following as they develop upskilling programs. But leading-edge companies are also considering the emotional dimensions of training in new-talent skills and behaviors. As companies embrace digital cultures and agile ways of working, the pace of learning increases. Employees often find themselves learning new skills and behaviors before they've had a chance to master existing ones. Realizing that this process can fluster and even frustrate employees, leading-edge companies develop cultures of learning, give employees safe spaces to learn on the job (for example, by giving them sufficient time off to learn), deliver knowledge in ways that employees find most comforting, and help employees to manage the emotions they experience. They also recognize that not every existing employee can morph into "new talent."

Advice for Leaders

We've focused in previous chapters on the technical side of twenty-first-century global business: digitally enabled value propositions, digital ecosystems, Industry 4.0–equipped factories, data architectures, and technological platforms. But as the headline of an article presented as part of the World Economic Forum annual meeting observed, "Talent, not technology, is the key to success in a digital future."[80] Likewise, colleagues of ours have argued that the "bionic" tech-heavy companies of the future will derive their strength from "further unleashing the power of human creativity," as "machines are only enablers."[81] They are right. Global companies can't hope to execute many of this book's other strategies unless they have people with the relevant skills and behaviors. And as we've seen in this chapter, they won't be able to tap that talent unless they go beyond traditional talent management and attract, inspire, and upskill people in new ways.

In addition to ensuring companies a steady supply of people wielding in-demand skills and behaviors, the tactics described in this chapter afford a whole range of additional benefits for companies. As Gallup has found, organizations that invest in developing their people are more profitable than other organizations and retain more of their employees.[82] Instilling a purpose can impact productivity and lower labor costs, since employees who find meaning in their work tend to work longer hours and stay at their jobs longer.[83] Indeed, given the ever-quickening pace of business, communicating and embedding purpose and values can also allow companies to orient new employees more quickly. Attending to the tactics described in this chapter can in many cases also lead to higher employee engagement, with the many benefits that yields. When companies thrive with talent, they usually find that their people become more committed to the organization's success, not merely their own.

If you find the prospect of moving beyond traditional talent management daunting, you're not alone. A survey by the Conference Board found that talent attraction and retention was the top "hot-button issue" globally inside companies that concerned CEOs in 2020.[84] You can get started on the task of reimagining your people strategies by considering the following key questions:

- Given anticipated changes in your business over the next three to five years, what kinds of skills do you anticipate needing—and in what quantities? Will your existing talent-management tactics be enough?
- What kinds of nontraditional talent might be right for your company? Do you have a plan in place for attracting these individuals? What new tactics might you try? And what's the right mix of temporary, permanent, and virtual talent for your business?
- Have you thought seriously enough about your company's purpose? If you do have a purpose, have you gone beyond surface purpose to a reason for being that is real for your workforce? How might you deepen your commitment to it?
- How might you upgrade your culture, paying attention to values and behaviors like collaboration, agility, continuous learning, and diversity?
- Assess your talent needs against the supply of top talent in your industry. Can you make an economic case for investing in a significant upskilling initiative for existing employees?
- Given the magnitude of the changes required, have you prepared leaders and managers, informing them on the new roles they will play in attracting, inspiring, and upskilling talent?

As you ponder these questions, bear in mind that the leading-edge companies we researched didn't simply embrace a series of innovative tactics. Their leaders changed their underlying mindsets about talent, committing themselves to putting people first and working comprehensively to make it happen. As a measure of their seriousness, these companies didn't fool themselves into thinking that they would entirely replace their existing talent-management practices, and they didn't attempt to do so in a single bold stroke. They layered on new tactics over a period of years, making it one of a number of transformations they were pursuing company-wide on an ongoing basis. Peter Drucker once predicted that "the only skill that will be important in the 21st century is the skill of learning new skills. Everything else will become obsolete over time."[85] Stepping back from the chapters we have covered thus far,

successful twenty-first-century enterprises will need to deploy one more
meta strategy in order to apply the first eight strategies presented in
this book. As we'll see in the next chapter, continuous transformation
is a strategy that leading-edge companies are also racing to develop and
deploy.

Key Insights

- In the years ahead, companies must strive to thrive with talent, putting people and their needs first rather than regarding them as resources to exploit.
- Creating a steady pipeline of top talent today means going beyond traditional tactics (career fairs, campus outreach programs, and lateral hires) and applying far more creativity and open-mindedness in whom you select, where you find them, and how you appeal to them. Leading-edge firms are building, buying, borrowing, and bridging when it comes to talent.
- Companies have long motivated their workforces by focusing on extrinsic incentives, such as salary increases and bonuses. Such incentives still matter for new talent, but leading-edge companies are also working hard to ensure that work is meaningful.
- Attracting and inspiring talented young employees won't be enough for most companies to meet their talent needs. Companies must take steps to teach their existing workforce new skills and behaviors, what some have termed *upskilling* and others *reskilling*.

CHAPTER 9

EMBRACE ALWAYS-ON TRANSFORMATION

Leaders have traditionally approached organizational
transformation as an episodic one-and-done proposition.
They mobilized people around the change, and when it was accomplished,
everyone resumed business as usual. That won't suffice any longer.
To compete and win in volatile, rapidly evolving business environments,
global companies must become adept at pursuing
multiple transformations on an ongoing basis. They must embrace
always-on transformation as an operating norm.

In our era of rapid, revolutionary, and open-ended change, you can't just go *beyond* once or even twice. The three disruptive forces described in this book are unfolding simultaneously, confronting companies with market changes, evolving customer expectations, and competitor actions—volatility that is only compounded by COVID-19, tsunamis, and other shocks. To achieve advantage and sustain it over time, you'll have to pursue many or all of the eight strategies we've covered so far, executing them diligently, efficiently, and well. Each strategy requires decisive top-down intervention and mobilization of resources, and you must thoughtfully integrate the strategies with one another, allowing for interdependencies. Further, you'll have to maintain a steady tempo of transformation, prioritizing among the strategies, pivoting quickly between change initiatives, and conceiving of the broader change process as holistic, ongoing, and ever evolving. Transformation, in other words, must become an *always-on* proposition, an essential part of operating your business. As Tata chairman N. Chandrasekaran remarked to us, "Innovation and change has to be deeply embedded in the DNA of the company."[1]

Always-on transformation might sound exhausting, even impossible and inadvisable. Traditional transformation initiatives are discrete one-off events in the life of an organization where, over a period of twelve to eighteen months, leaders construct a plan to achieve a clear goal and the organization executes in a disciplined way until the goal is realized. Leaders then disband the transformation teams and infrastructure, and the firm goes back to business as usual. As relatively straightforward as this approach is, companies struggle mightily with it. By some accounts, up to 70 percent of business change efforts fail to deliver.[2] So how can companies possibly pursue overlapping change initiatives on an ongoing basis and hope to succeed?

A few leading-edge companies are reimagining their approach to transformation, with exceptional results. In 2014, when Satya Nadella became Microsoft's CEO, the company was in solid shape, with healthy revenues, operating margins just shy of 35 percent, and $76 billion in cash and short-term investments.[3] Yet the company's share price had stagnated, its market capitalization hovered around $314 billion, and its future prospects were unclear.[4] Although Microsoft's legacy businesses were performing well, the company had missed almost every major technology trend over the past decade, including mobile phones, search engines, and social networking. It now seemed poised to miss yet another massive trend—the cloud—as its competitors were far outpacing it in that area. Underlying this sluggishness was a classic innovator's dilemma dynamic. Although leaders at Microsoft spotted new trends on the horizon as well as anyone, an insular, arrogant, and internally competitive culture—as well as leaders' obsession with the company's traditional cash cow, the Windows operating system—prevented Microsoft from aggressively entering new markets. Employees and leaders across the company felt fearful, vigorously defended their turf, and resisted new ideas and initiatives.[5] "The company was sick," Nadella wrote in his 2017 book *Hit Refresh*. "Employees were tired. They were frustrated. They were fed up with losing and falling behind despite their grand plans and great ideas."[6]

Microsoft needed to change, and under Nadella, a career Microsoft engineer, it has. Over the next several years, the company underwent a remarkable turnaround that included a new mission, vision, and strategy. Instead of obsessing over PCs, the company focused on developing cloud- and mobile-related offerings with the mission, articulated by Nadella in 2015, of empowering "every person and every organization on the planet to achieve more" and the vision of "mobile-first, cloud-first."[7] In effect, it updated its strategy to support the kinds of digital value propositions described in Chapter 2. Investments were shifted away from Windows toward Azure (Microsoft's cloud offering) and its AI and business apps. Eventually, Windows was merged into the Office organization. Microsoft was no longer in the business of protecting Windows. In 2017, the strategy and vision had evolved somewhat, with a new emphasis placed on AI (articulated as "intelligent cloud, intelligent edge") instead of mobile. As the company stated in its annual report, "Our strategy is to build best-in-class platforms and productivity services for an intelligent cloud and an intelligent edge infused with artificial intelligence ('AI')."[8]

Microsoft's pivot toward the cloud and AI didn't occur as a single dramatic rupture with the past. Rather, it comprised a number of dramatic transformations undertaken in parallel and on an ongoing basis over a number of years. Microsoft created a dynamic portfolio of transformation initiatives that evolved over time as some were completed, some continued, and others were launched. These initiatives were as varied as they were ambitious. To empower employees, the company shifted from an adversarial, competitive culture toward one focused on collaboration, individual growth and development, and the pursuit of social purpose (Chapter 8). Instead of a company of "know-it-all" personnel, as Nadella put it, Microsoft endeavored to fill itself with "learn-it-all" personalities.[9] At the same time, the company reorganized itself to become more responsive to and collaborative with its customers (Chapter 7). It embraced data, adding a range of metrics to reinforce its new customer focus (Chapter 6). Externally, Microsoft abandoned its harsh rivalries with competitors and joined forces with them in a collaborative ecosystem (Chapter 4), becoming home to the world's largest number of open-source code contributors and forging partnerships with companies including archrivals like Apple, Google (Android), and Salesforce.[10] As Nadella said, "It is incumbent upon us, especially those of us who are platform vendors to partner broadly to solve real pain points our customers have."[11]

Collectively, these and other initiatives touched every part of the organization, amounting to what one journalist has called a "Nadellaissance."[12] The company has massively grown its cloud platform and services businesses while cutting billions in cost and making important acquisitions, such as GitHub and LinkedIn. Behind the scenes, Microsoft has become more dynamic and entrepreneurial, breaking down stifling product and leadership silos, implementing agile work processes in its engineering function, and turbocharging its go-to-market capability. The company's financial results have been extraordinary. Since 2014, Microsoft's total shareholder returns have outpaced the S&P 500 by 60 percent, and market capitalization has increased from around $300 billion to over $1.6 trillion (as of July 2020),[13] making Nadella the first CEO in Microsoft's history to create over $1 trillion in market cap.

As Microsoft's story suggests, today's successful change efforts aren't a sprint as yesterday's were. They're a never-ending triathlon. Finish one stage, and you're immediately on to another very different one, making for an intense experience of near-constant change. As of 2020, Microsoft was six years into its transformation, and its journey continues. Winning at such an endurance contest means building up a fundamentally new kind of transformation capacity inside your organization. Inspired by Microsoft's story as well as research into transformation programs at more than one hundred companies, we've developed an approach you can use to increase your odds of success with always-on change.

Companies that are going *beyond* are embracing an always-on transformation model that we describe as the "Head, Heart, and Hands" of transformation.[14] The model calls on companies to tackle three distinct tasks: (1) envision the firm's desired future and how you'll get there ("head"); (2) inspire and empower the workforce behind ongoing transformation efforts ("heart"); and (3) build the capability to execute and innovate with agility ("hands"). To excel at always-on transformation, leading-edge companies are rigorously attending to all three of these elements (which relatively few firms have traditionally done). But our research reveals that they're also going much further, making powerful adjustments to the three tasks that collectively reimagine transformation for an age of volatility.

In particular, leading-edge companies are dramatically enhancing the attention they pay to the heart so as to help employees avoid transformation fatigue, they're broadening their approach to the head to elucidate a longer-term path to change, and they're building up new muscles that allow the hands to execute more quickly. By attending to all three elements and making these adaptations, you can transform your firm's transformation efforts, empowering and emboldening your enterprise to go—and stay—beyond great.

Place the Heart of Transformation at the Center

The success of the transformations has hinged on leaders' ability to get people inspired and empowered to make the change real. Unfortunately, most companies neglected to do this. As our research has found, firms have focused only about half as much attention on the heart as they have the hands and only about a third as much as they have on the head.[15] Most companies have tended to treat people as a means to an end when it comes to change—or, worse, as collateral damage. One study of two hundred executives found most either were leading or would lead a change initiative, but half reported not having thought through how their people felt about the shift.[16] This is a shame and likely one of the biggest reasons companies have struggled to succeed with transformations. In our study, "of the companies with long-term high performance, twice as many had high heart scores."[17]

Companies can't take their people for granted if they hope to succeed with always-on transformation—they have to make them their central focus.

People will only sustain transformation over time, sticking with multiple initiatives and welcoming ongoing changes in the portfolio of initiatives, if they feel passionate about change. They must put their whole selves into transformation rather than viewing it as just another corporate initiative. In effect, they must become the beating heart powering transformation forward. To ensure that the workforce feels an enduring passion for change, leaders must take a series of measures to empower and inspire their workforces. Pulling four distinct *activation levers* is especially important.

Activation Lever #1: Purpose

Employees will become more enthused in transformation if they understand at a deep level why they're doing it. To build an always-on transformation capability, leading-edge firms take care to explicitly connect change efforts with the company's purpose. Purpose has always been important for transformation, but it becomes absolutely vital when change is always on. Purpose provides "much-needed alignment, clarity, guidance, and energy," serving to link "various transformation efforts in a way that is logical and accessible to everyone."[18] Satya Nadella recounted in his 2017 book how purpose played a critical role in Microsoft's ongoing transformation. Upon becoming CEO, Nadella called on the company to rediscover its "soul," as he put it, its purpose or core reason for being.[19] He spent months querying employees about the company's purpose. "To my first question, why does Microsoft exist, the message was loud and clear. We exist to build products that empower others. That is the meaning we're all looking to infuse into our work."[20]

In his July 2014 all-company email, Nadella called on the company to "rediscover our soul—our unique core" and defined a mission attached to that purpose: "We will reinvent productivity to empower every person and every organization on the planet to do more and achieve more."[21] The response from employees was overwhelming. From across the enterprise, they wrote to him, conveying that "the language of empowering everyone on the planet to achieve more inspired them personally, and they saw how it applied to their daily work, whether they were a coder, designer, marketer, or customer-support technician."[22]

To give everything they have to ongoing transformation efforts, to stick with those efforts during challenging moments, and to pursue open-ended change, people need to understand the ultimate point of the change. Not just *understand*—they must feel it in their bones each and every day as they do their work (an imperative we also discussed in Chapter 1). Transformation efforts must have meaning, and it's up to leaders to shape that meaning by discovering and communicating the deeper purpose.

Activation Lever #2: Culture

So many companies today are content to pursue purpose in a halfhearted or incomplete way—this is *surface purpose*. These companies fail to make the company's reason for being tangible and compelling for employees and customers.[23] As leading-edge companies also understand, you can't simply articulate the purpose in words and expect it to stick. People have to *live* the purpose in their daily work, which in turn means that the culture must change to evoke and support it. Further, the culture must liberate and empower people to take action in support of transformation efforts. As enthused as they might be about where the company is headed, employees' passion for change will evaporate if the culture prevents them from taking action in support of the company's strategy and goals. In our research, companies that emphasized culture during digital transformations were five times more likely to achieve strong or exceptional performance than those that didn't. Simply put, it's not a digital transformation without a digital culture.[24]

In guiding Microsoft's turnaround, Nadella understood the importance of culture and its close relationship with purpose. Influenced by Carol Dweck's book *Mindset: The New Psychology of Success*, he shifted Microsoft's culture away from one of competitiveness and conflict to one of personal growth, or, as he put it, "dynamic learning" rooted in a growth mindset. "Anything is possible for a company," he said, "when its culture is about listening, learning, and harnessing individual passions and talents to the company's mission."[25] For Nadella and Microsoft, a culture of dynamic learning would take on a number of expressions, including an obsessive curiosity about customers and their needs, diversity and inclusion internally, and collaboration across the organization, what Nadella termed "One Microsoft." "I talked about these ideas every chance I got," he recalled. "And I looked for opportunities to change our practices and behaviors to make the growth mindset vivid and real."[26]

One place Microsoft's culture and purpose have come alive is in the large hackathons it has held in recent years during the company's annual One Week event. The company's performance-management and organizational structure have also changed to reflect the growth mindset ideal,[27] and Microsoft has sought to empower people to grow via human resources policies that promote a positive and welcoming work environment, attract top and diverse talent, and provide collaboration-enhancing tools and technology. Nadella himself has worked tirelessly to instill a growth mindset, communicating with the company about interesting books he has discovered, letting leaders know when they're straying from the culture, and holding two-way conversations with employees.[28] He has also pushed leaders to live the culture and empower their teams to embrace a positive growth mindset as well.[29] Over time, the culture Nadella envisioned has taken hold and fueled the company's ability to pursue ongoing transformation. As Microsoft's chief marketing officer has said, "We went from a culture of know-it-alls to a culture of learn-it-alls. Everything we do now is rooted in a growth mindset."[30]

Activation Lever #3: Empathy

Traditional transformation has typically been challenging for employees. Always-on transformation is even more so, as now organizations are asking their people to step up, reach further, and run faster on an ongoing basis. Even if employees don't lose their jobs, they'll undergo the stress and strain of seeing colleagues depart, having to change how they operate, and potentially relocating to a new job within the company. Leading-edge firms show empathy for employees, anticipating the challenges transformations bring and helping their workforces to adapt. Satya Nadella, for instance, has often spoken of empathy. In his book *Hit Refresh*, he remarked, "My passion is to put empathy at the center of everything I pursue—from the products we launch, to the new markets we enter, to the employees, customers, and partners we work with."[31] In this spirit, not only do leading-edge firms offer the usual help to employees transitioning to new jobs and careers outside the company; they supply employees with coaching, various kinds of vocational training, and assistance with financial planning. Making life just a bit easier for employees, such measures show them that the company cares about their welfare and considers them more than just an expendable resource.

A good example comes from the Finnish technology firm Nokia. Having missed the smartphone revolution with significant financial consequences in terms of revenues, losses, and market capitalization, Nokia undertook a set of massive transformations that remade the company. Over several years, Nokia restructured and then sold its core mobile phone business to Microsoft and adopted network infrastructure as its new core business, acquiring the remaining half of its joint venture with Siemens in 2013 and then finalizing its acquisition of Alcatel-Lucent in 2016. The company also sold its mapping software business and strengthened its innovation-and-reinvention business. These changes helped to stabilize the company, launching it into a new phase of reconsolidation and integration that spanned the years 2015–2019. For many employees, however, the changes posed an immense challenge. While the company was trimming businesses, some employees had to continue at their jobs knowing that their time at the company was limited, while others who stayed had to witness their colleagues depart. As the company integrated new businesses, employees had to face uncertainties about the shape and form their eventual roles would take.

Still, as distressing as this transition was for employees, Nokia had their backs in ways that many companies undergoing transformations don't. Leaders strove for transparency, giving teams as much notice as possible of future layoffs so that employees could prepare. To help people transition to new careers, the company provided support through an extensive program called Bridge.[32] It's goal: maximize the number of employees who knew their next move after their employment with the company ended. Through Bridge, employees could locate new jobs inside Nokia and obtain access to coaching, help with their résumés, networking, money for skills training, and more. Those seeking to strike out on their own as entrepreneurs could apply for start-up money as well as connections to incubators. A special feature of Bridge was its flexibility: as employees' plans for the future evolved, they could access different parts of the program as they saw fit.[33] They could also obtain funding to help them achieve their own unique goals, such as volunteering.[34] For Nokia, Bridge was not merely altruistic but also good business. By treating employees well, the company could maintain morale among remaining employees, ensuring that they continued to put out their best effort. To ensure that Bridge met employees' needs, Nokia assigned key local managers who were also poised to leave the company to oversee it.[35]

All told, the company let go eighteen thousand employees during this phase of its turnaround, but thanks to Bridge, almost two-thirds of them had already determined their next career move before leaving the company.[36] Bridge funding helped employees found one thousand new businesses.[37] Checking in with employees some eighteen months after leaving the company, Nokia found that the vast majority—67 percent of participants in general (and 85 percent within Finland)—felt positively about the program's treatment of them.[38] The company fared well too. Thanks to Bridge, the company avoided any dips in engagement, productivity, and quality. In some cases, quality even improved. Meanwhile, Nokia's expenditures on Bridge represented just a tiny percentage (4 percent) of its total restructuring costs over the years 2011–2013.[39] As compared with 2012, Nokia's sales growth improved by almost ten percentage points, and its margins rose by almost twelve percentage points by 2015. Annualized total shareholder return had risen by over fifty percentage points during that same period.[40]

In 2015–2016, when Microsoft laid off former Nokia employees who'd come on board during its acquisition of the latter's mobile phone business, it chose a similarly empathetic approach. Under a program called Polku, Microsoft supplemented its severance program by offering start-up money and other resources to former Nokia employees in Finland interested in founding new companies.[41] Thanks to this effort and others coordinated by the Finnish government, virtually all (almost 90 percent) of the employees hit by layoffs managed to secure new employment.[42] As Polku's director related, "It was really reassuring to see so many of our former colleagues find new work through Polku. The programme earned high praise from participants and external actors."[43]

Activation Lever #4: Leadership

As we've seen, Nadella's personal involvement was vital to Microsoft's ability to sustain ongoing and open-ended transformation. Nadella served as the curator of the purpose or reason for being that gave rise and was embedded in its culture. To ensure that other leaders throughout the company supported its ability to transform, Microsoft implemented a transformational leadership model with three planks: "create clarity," "generate energy," and "deliver success." At other leading-edge companies as well, we've seen leaders help to create an always-on transformation capacity by making it their personal mission to inspire and empower employees and by ensuring that other leaders in the company do so as well. Companies we've studied have deployed a number of specific tactics to mobilize leaders behind the transformation, including enhancing their training function and performance-evaluation processes.

Make the Head of Transformation More Expansive

With a traditional transformation, the path ahead is fairly straightforward. Leaders identify a single operational change the organization needs to make and then put resources before the change for the next three to four years. Always-on transformation is far more complex and requires more effort on the part of leaders to establish and communicate an agenda for change. It's no longer enough to articulate a narrow operational goal—"cut costs by 10 percent" or "improve quality by 10 percent"—and then unleash the organization to go do it.

With change initiatives shifting, overlapping with, and impacting one another, companies and leaders must fundamentally reset their and the organization's ambitions. They must articulate a far broader, more comprehensive understanding of where they're going over the long term as well as how they'll prioritize and focus to reach this desired state.

To tackle this first task, leaders paint a clear, inspiring picture of all the enterprise can and will become with strong, concerted effort. This picture must be rooted in the company's long-term purpose and encompass the eight strategies described in this book. Leaders must promote this vision of transformation internally, making an inspiring case for change to the workforce and ensuring that key leaders buy into it. As time passes, leaders must also check in every year on the vision, updating and modifying it as external conditions change and as some transformation efforts conclude and others begin.

At Microsoft, Satya Nadella laid out the broad outlines of the company's desired state in a lengthy 2014 email. Whereas Microsoft had traditionally focused on providing customers with "devices and services," Nadella proclaimed it would become "the productivity and platform company for the mobile-first and cloud-first world. We will reinvent productivity to empower every person and every organization on the planet to do more and achieve more." In adopting this formulation, Nadella advanced the multistakeholder view we discussed in Chapter 1 rather than focusing exclusively or even primarily on shareholders. The email went on to explain what reinventing productivity would mean— not just enabling individuals and businesses to create but arming them with intelligent tools that are "more predictive, personal, and helpful." The company would deliver experiences that would "light up digital work and life experiences in the most personal, intelligent, open and empowering ways." To make this vision a reality, the company would revamp its culture, making it more dynamic, customer focused, and efficient, and allow each individual who worked at Microsoft to learn and grow. "We must each have the courage to transform as individuals. We must ask ourselves, what idea can I bring to life?"[44]

As inspiring as a comprehensive vision of the future can be, employees will find it overwhelming if leaders attempt to transform everything at once. In setting forth a program of always-on change, leaders must articulate clear priorities among our eight strategies based on the enterprise's unique needs, deciding what the company will address now and what can wait until later. These priorities must emerge, as we've suggested elsewhere in this book, out of an analysis of the company's present capabilities. What specific transformations are most urgent if the company is to create enduring value in the face of changing customer expectations, market trends, or competitor actions? Typical burning platforms include simplification of the company or its products, innovation of its business model, building leadership and talent, and developing digital products and services. In Microsoft's case, the company initially focused on growing its cloud business and developing the culture that would support that growth. It also worked to make the company more agile and to make the workforce leaner. As those changes took hold, the company moved to invest in growth, acquiring new companies (LinkedIn and GitHub) and expanding its AI research division. Most recently, it began a big push to make the company more sustainable.

Once companies map priorities, they should create a portfolio of initiatives, as Microsoft did, recognizing that this portfolio will evolve over time. Companies should integrate management of this portfolio with the company's operating model, as has apparel and footwear maker Nike. During the mid-2010s, leaders at Nike worried that the brand was losing its edge with consumers. The company's share in the lucrative US market was shrinking, and the retail vendors that had traditionally accounted for most of Nike's sales were being disrupted by Amazon, which was dominating online apparel retailing.

Determined to change multiple facets of its brand and supply chain, Nike created plans in 2016 for a wide-ranging transformation explicitly built around an embrace of digital technologies. To help the organization execute on this strategy, Nike created a governance framework and established a body inside the company, the digital transformation office, to create and run a portfolio of digital transformation initiatives. Nike charged its head of digital transformation and chief digital officer to oversee the portfolio, and it also appointed a steering committee composed of senior executives. To ensure that digital transformations became part of the company's operating model, Nike linked these initiatives to the annual development process of its enterprise strategy. Each year, leaders determined the digital capabilities Nike needed to deliver on its annual strategies, created budgets, oversaw expenditures, and allowed transformation efforts to incubate and scale up in its businesses alongside other strategic initiatives. In addition to enabling leaders to monitor the progress of digital initiatives, this process ensured that people, data, infrastructure, and budgets would all be aligned between the digital transformation efforts and Nike's businesses.

In recent years, Nike has maintained eight to ten corporate transformation initiatives in its portfolio at any given time, all at various stages of maturity. Leaders have reevaluated the initiatives on an ongoing basis and reprioritized them according to the demands of Nike's businesses and shifts in external conditions. Collectively, these initiatives have driven dramatic changes across the enterprise, allowing Nike to improve its consumer experience dramatically by digitizing the retail experience (Chapter 2) and revolutionizing its supply chain and manufacturing.

With Nike's popular app, consumers can now access the company's membership program and a range of benefits, including personalized workouts and exclusive offers. The company's running and training apps track consumers' fitness performance, offer personalized coaching, provide access to free workouts, and much more. But the apps are much more than a digital experience. Nike's House of Innovation concept stores (opened in New York and Shanghai in 2018, with another in Paris planned as of this writing)[45] are integrated with the company's Nike app, allowing consumers to scan bar codes and determine whether the store has their desired color and size, to summon store staff to help them try on a shoe with the touch of a button, and to pay quickly at checkout. As Nike has found, its concept stores have inspired more consumers to download and use their app, allowing the company access to a greater pool of user data while also building engagement and differentiating the Nike brand from its competitors.[46]

With the user data it collects (Chapter 6), Nike can improve the digital shopping experience for consumers. "With machine learning and AI, we're able to have every digital experience at Nike be unique and personal," said one Nike executive.[47] Consumer data also helps drive Express Lane, a supply-chain process that enables Nike to respond more quickly and flexibly to consumers' needs. Real-time data allows Nike to restock hot items more quickly and update products based on consumer feedback. Using rapid prototyping and 3-D printing (Chapter 5), Express Lane allows Nike to slash the time it takes to develop new products and get them on store shelves from months to ten days.[48] Express Lane in turn contributes to Nike's Consumer Direct Offense Strategy, designed to increase responsiveness in a dozen cities spread across ten countries, locations that collectively account for more than 80 percent of the company's anticipated growth through 2020.[49] Teams on the ground in these cities (Chapter 7) pay close attention to market demand, relying on Express Lane—and in turn, the data generated through Nike's apps—to create new products that consumers love.

Nike's portfolio of transformation initiatives has produced impressive results. Between 2016 and 2019, revenues mushroomed from $32.4 billion to $39.1 billion. In 2019, Nike's innovation platforms accounted for almost all of its total incremental growth. Investors are happy: Nike's total shareholder return since 2016 has significantly outpaced the S&P 500.[50]

Nike achieved such results by setting and adjusting its transformational priorities preemptively, before a major challenge, setback, or black-swan event required it. Research by our BCG colleagues have found that companies that get a jump on transformations produce better results, outpacing those that performed them reactively by 3 percent in total shareholder returns.[51] Preemptive transformations also cost less to execute and occur more quickly compared with those pursued reactively. Nevertheless, the vast majority of companies don't pursue preemptive transformations.[52] Global firms can thus gain advantage by doing what Nike did as part of the head of transformation: crafting and communicating an overarching long-term vision, merging transformation with the firm's operating model, and creating clear priorities. Leaders should stay alert to early warning signs and build in mechanisms for regularly assessing transformation initiatives and reprioritizing them as needed. Companies should also take care to control the narrative for investors and employees as changes in the transformation portfolio become necessary.

Build a More Agile Pair of Hands

When leaders lay out a clear agenda for change, always-on transformation efforts stand a far greater likelihood of succeeding. But companies would be remiss to neglect the actual execution of change efforts, what we term the "hands of transformation." Execution was relatively straightforward in traditional transformations. The capabilities required for execution were relatively clear at the outset, so the company trained its change muscles for a particular initiative and then took a break before it had to execute once again. In the volatile environments in which today's companies operate, leaders and teams can't anticipate every last executional requirement at the outset. They have to be able to innovate and adapt as they go and to pivot between multiple kinds or areas of change.

In order to perpetually reinvent itself, the enterprise must be able to proactively execute the strategies—they must build creativity and innovation into the system. At companies we studied, leaders equipped the organization for always-on change by attending to three areas in particular: (1) agile ways of working, (2) new capabilities, and (3) strong governance models.

As we saw in Chapter 7, the transition to agile ways of working is itself one of the key transformations companies must make to go beyond great during the twenty-first century. Agile figured centrally under BCG's original head-heart-hands model as a means of making traditional transformation as seamless and effective as possible, given rising volatility. But adoption of agile becomes even more critically important to firms attempting to conduct always-on transformation. As the company becomes nimbler, teams will be equipped to quickly spot resource gaps and other difficulties in the broader transformation process and to devise appropriate solutions. Key elements of agile methods, including cross-functional and colocated teams, sprints, minimally viable products, empowered decision-making, and fast-cycle learning, can help teams innovate quickly to advance change efforts. The digital tools used by agile customer-facing teams can likewise enhance transformation by fostering more collaboration and the rapid spread of ideas. In general, agile injects an intensity and speed into execution that enables companies to supercharge the execution of multiple and shifting change initiatives.

Microsoft's transformation was likewise powered by agile. "Every team across Microsoft must find ways to simplify and move faster, more efficiently," Nadella proclaimed in his July 2014 letter to the company. "We will increase the fluidity of information and ideas by taking actions to flatten the organization and develop leaner business processes."[53] Parts of the company had been embracing agile for years, notably the developer division that Nadella had previously run.[54] As one visitor to the developer division reported in 2015, "Everyone we talked to—including unscripted conversations with the developers—is living, thinking, talking and acting with Agile values. It is not only *doing* Agile. It is *being* Agile. There is a pervasive Agile *mindset* in which respecting, valuing and engaging those doing the work in response to customers' needs is at the core."[55] Now the virtues of agile would be spread throughout the organization, greatly facilitating the company's change efforts. Nadella asked senior leaders to "evaluate opportunities to advance their innovation processes and simplify their operations and how they work."[56]

In addition to embracing agile, leading-edge companies should go beyond the original head-heart-hands model and build transformation into the operating model and leadership of the organization. In particular, they should create governance models that enable leaders and board members to review progress and to continue to push change forward. These models include dedicated transformation offices to drive, monitor, support, and communicate about change, as well as sustained involvement on the part of key leaders. As we saw earlier, Nike integrated transformation tightly into its annual strategic-planning process and established a digital transformation office to spearhead and monitor change efforts. The company also created a digital steering committee that included executives reporting directly to the CEO. Likewise, Microsoft placed an emphasis on transformational leadership, conceiving it as one of five key elements that would help energize its workforce behind change.

Leading-edge companies further enhance their execution of ongoing always-on change initiatives by ensuring that the organization possesses the necessary capabilities it needs to operate in new ways, including tools, expertise, processes, skills, and behaviors (see Chapter 7). When planning transformations, leaders at these firms think ahead, beginning to build capabilities for a forthcoming transformation even before they have finished an existing one. For its transformation, Adobe opted not to rely primarily on hiring new talent but instead to rely on rigorously upskilling its employees. Adobe has grown dramatically in the past five years both through organic hiring and acquisition, and the company continues to focus on internal development and mobility of employees to ensure a strong pipeline of talent. Adding to its internally designed leadership-development programs, Adobe has partnered with the University of California at Berkeley's Haas School of Business to create a new training program for leaders dedicated to helping them develop the new skills they will need to drive change.

Advice for Leaders

Change in the twenty-first century can't be something you do only sometimes, reactively, and in a disconnected way. Dedicate your organization to making change a constant preoccupation—an obsession, even—and an integral part of your operating model, and you'll dramatically hasten your enterprise's ability to compete, grow, and win in the years ahead. Rather than feeling besieged by the three forces affecting markets, you'll master them and ride the wave of opportunity they present. Although shocks like COVID-19 will on occasion unsettle you, you'll ultimately survive them better and bounce back more quickly than your peers. Instead of viewing your company as a behemoth rendered stagnant by its own previous success, the outside world will see you as a resilient and relevant leader of innovation. Microsoft's transformation was so successful that other companies today regard the organization not only as a leader in cloud, AI, and other technologies but as a leader in transformation. They knock on Microsoft's door seeking to learn about their turnaround and how they might evolve their own enterprises to succeed in the digital age.

Like many leaders, you might find it easiest to focus on one element of our model in particular, the head, sketching out a vision of the future and determining the organization's change priorities. But you neglect the other two at your peril. As we found in our research, companies pursuing traditional transformations that moved decisively to fully embrace and include all three elements were much likelier to see their change initiatives succeed over an extended period. Virtually all of these companies—96 percent—achieved sustained performance improvement, a rate nearly three times that of companies that did not engage all three elements.[57] Similar results should hold for companies pursuing ongoing always-on change.

To begin the transition toward always-on transformation, consider the transformations you've attempted in recent years, those that have succeeded and those that haven't. Reflect on the following questions:[58]

- Do your people dread the thought of embarking on a transformation journey, or do they perceive it as inspiring and empowering? If they dread it, you almost certainly aren't embracing an always-on transformation mindset.
- When it comes to the all-important heart, do you place most of your attention here, attending to all four of the heart's chambers—purpose, culture, empathy, and leadership? If you think you do, are you sure your actions are resonating with the workforce?
- When it comes to the head, do you stake out a vision of your company's future state, develop a dynamic portfolio of transformation initiatives, communicate a powerful case for change, and align your leadership team?
- As for the hands, have you embraced agile as fully as you might? Are you building the right internal capabilities proactively? Do you have the right governance system and control mechanisms in place?
- Are you personally leading with the head, heart, and hands? Which do you find most natural, and which is the most difficult? What two or three actions might you take going forward to ensure a better balance?

Traditional one-off change initiatives feel confusing, scary, and painful to employees and leaders. People can't wait for the change initiative to wrap up so that they can finally return to business as usual. It's a different story when change becomes permanent and woven into the fabric of everyday life at a company and when the head, heart, and hands of transformation are fully developed.

Imagine what might happen at your firm if leaders were to transfix employees with an alluring vision of what everyone might accomplish together, breaking down the change process into manageable parts and connecting it with the enterprise's operating model. Imagine what might happen if leaders were to inspire employees by connecting change with the company's reason for being, and if they were to further energize them by rendering the culture more empowering, by taking care of them when they become displaced, and by enlisting leaders throughout the organization to empower the workforce as well. Finally, imagine what might happen if leaders were to cut away the bureaucracy and make work far more productive and collaborative via agile teams, enhanced capabilities, change management, and governance. Taken collectively, such measures revolutionize the workforce's experience of change, rendering it exciting, fulfilling, and intensely meaningful. Who *wouldn't* want to help turn a stodgy incumbent into an innovative market leader that is finally capable of delivering for *all* stakeholders? And who wouldn't want to contribute his or her full intellectual and creative powers to make it happen?

You owe it to your people and yourself to make transformation not merely a habit but an invigorating way of living and working in your organization. By attending to the head, heart, and hands, you enable your people to not merely survive but thrive as they move the enterprise relentlessly toward the future. In the end, going beyond great entails not reaching a specific destination but rather embracing transcendence, reinvention, and evolution as a permanent mindset and state of being. Great organizations of the twentieth century changed when and if they had to. They changed in order to live. Organizations that venture beyond great live to change. Pursuing a purpose that extends beyond shareholder value, leaders and employees discover that work is more enriching when they push both to develop themselves and perpetually increase the value they create for the enterprise and its stakeholders. Organizations that go beyond great seize the full potential of our century's more volatile, less predictable business environment. Instead of perceiving it as a threat and shrinking back in fear, they boldly embrace it as an opportunity to make the enterprise more of what it was always meant to be: productive, compassionate, and useful to humanity.

So what are *you* waiting for? Pick your priorities and get started reinventing your company for the twenty-first century. The greatest journey you and your people have ever taken is about to begin—the journey beyond great.

Key Insights

- Transformation must become an always-on proposition, an essential part of operating your business. As Tata chairman N. Chandrasekaran put it, "Innovation and change has to be deeply embedded in the DNA of the company."
- Winning at such an endurance contest means building up a fundamentally new kind of transformation capacity inside your organization. Inspired by Microsoft's story, as well as research into

transformation programs at more than one hundred companies, we've developed an approach you can use—an adaptation of BCG's head-heart-hands model of transformation—to increase your odds of success with always-on change.

- Companies can't just attend to their people (the heart of traditional, best-practice transformation) in hopes of succeeding with always-on transformation. They have to make the heart their central focus by attending to purpose, culture, empathy, and leadership.

- With change initiatives shifting, overlapping with, and impacting one another, companies and leaders must fundamentally reset their and the organization's ambitions (the head part of traditional transformation). They must articulate a far broader, more comprehensive understanding of where they're going over the long term as well as how they'll prioritize and focus to reach this desired state.

- Traditional, best-practice transformation held that companies proactively cultivate agile ways of working (the hands of traditional transformation). To execute ongoing always-on transformation, companies must double down on agile and build an even nimbler set of hands by cultivating new capabilities and adopting strong governance models.

BEYOND GREAT LEADERSHIP

S o here you have them: the nine strategies you need to build a new business-operating model for global companies, one that enables them not merely to survive but to thrive in an era of social tension, economic nationalism, and technological revolution. These strategies level the playing field for large incumbents, giving companies as diverse as John Deere, Whirlpool, Microsoft, TCS, and ING (to name a few) the tools they need to thrive and grow. Firms employing our nine strategies gain a new ability to remain resilient in the face of unpredictable, rapidly changing market conditions, positioning themselves for enduring success. But we have yet to address an important question: What does our new era mean for leadership? Let's say you're the new CEO of a global firm, or you've just been nominated by the board's selection committee to become one, or you aspire one day soon to receive a nomination. What specific leadership traits or mindsets will you need to succeed? How should you best approach leadership so as to leave a strong legacy of growth, financial success, and meaningful social impact?

We wish we could offer a simple framework that encapsulates everything you'll need to do, but that would trivialize the task at hand, and it would also fly in the face of what we have learned from the many leaders who have contributed to *beyond great*. Instead, we close the book by offering some reflections gleaned from our many interviews with leaders who were, in one way or another, moving swiftly to go beyond great. These conversations suggest that beyond great leadership would appear to consist, in its essence, of six fundamental imperatives.

First, leaders must *lead with conviction to positively impact society*. As we saw in Chapter 1, stakeholders are demanding more of companies.

If they want their firms to thrive, leaders must abandon traditional strategies bent only on maximizing returns to their shareholders and measure themselves against a higher bar: the ability to impact *all* stakeholders positively. With pandemics and pandemonium to contend with, employees and customers are increasingly desperate for meaning, and they long to associate themselves with organizations that are inspired and guided by a sense of purpose. They also look skeptically on organizations that have espoused purpose in the past but have stopped at surface purpose—posters and slogans but nothing more. Employees and customers are looking to—and longing for—leaders who understand their human need for meaning and are taking the actions required to benefit society in profound ways.

Reflect seriously on how you and your firm might engage to address social and environmental problems. To deliver total societal impact, you'll have to take it personally. It's not enough to simply believe in TSI—you must become your firm's chief purpose officer. As Siemens's CEO elect Dr. Roland Busch told us, "The leader has to define what the company stands for, which goes above and beyond the latest and greatest technology, and [he or she has] to give something meaningful to the company." In particular, the CEO must galvanize operational leaders and managers. Otherwise, a disconnect will emerge, and business units will pursue business as usual.[1] Satya Nadella put it starkly as well, remarking, "The most useful thing I have done is to anchor us on the sense of purpose and mission and identity. There is a reason we exist."[2]

Second, leaders must *pivot from a command-and-control mindset to a more collaborative, agile-friendly approach.* For centuries, leadership has largely entailed some form of command and control. Leaders have set the direction, commanded people to follow it, and instilled a set of controls to ensure that they comply. This orientation remains deeply embedded in the psyche, experience, and practice of most leaders today. Because going beyond great requires speed in a volatile world, leaders must break with the past and take a much more open and collaborative approach. Rather than trying to exert control at every turn, leaders must focus on gaining alignment and then granting autonomy. They must empower and coach, pursuing pace over perfection. Beyond great leadership also requires leaders to role model agile ways of working for others in the organization.

Natura &Co chairman and chief executive of the group Roberto Marques pointed out to us that no leader can hope to have all the answers in a world that is changing as rapidly as ours. Instead, leaders have to recruit others with the capacity to develop solutions, amplifying and expanding their efforts rather than directing them. "You have to empower your teams," he said, "understanding that there are going to be people on the ground business and functional areas that will have the right answers, and that will know more than I do."[3] As he further remarked, leadership today entails having the self-awareness to acknowledge you don't even know what you don't know and the humility to listen to others. Leaders have to communicate well, "reaching out to the organization in a way that will allow you to get information back that will help you make the right decisions and course correct when necessary."[4]

Third, leaders must *guide their firms to become far more open-minded toward their peers—small and big, in the industry and beyond—than they were previously*. Firms long have sought to deliver value to customers by deploying strategies limited almost exclusively to the firm itself. Relationships between companies that did exist were formal, and partnerships with customers and competitors were rare. Leaders regarded their companies as operating within a closed system, with competitors located squarely outside. It wasn't uncommon to see banners in production facilities exhorting workers to beat the *enemy*—the primary competitor.

As we saw throughout this book but especially in Chapter 4, companies today are increasingly delivering value by participating in open constellations or ecosystems of companies across industries, sizes, and geographies that can include competitors. As Tata Group chairman (and former CEO of Tata Consultancy Services) N. Chandrasekaran remarked, the power in markets "is shifting from companies to ecosystems."[5] Each company must decide what role it might play in its ecosystems so as to create a favorable balance between the value it contributes and gleans. Leaders today must not only embrace this radical new mindset, sourcing ideas and talent from beyond the firm and constantly seeking out partnerships to deliver greater value. They must also help their people to do so as well. Natura's Roberto Marques noted that constant open two-way communication across a broader ecosystem (which in Natura's case includes tens of thousands of employees as well as millions of customer-facing sales consultants) is "the oxygen for the organization to continue to evolve."[6]

Fourth, leaders must *elevate and embed a continuous learning mindset.* Going beyond great challenges many implicit and explicit assumptions about what it takes to succeed and thrive. Leaders must unlearn old ways of seeing, thinking, and acting in favor of something new, and they must do it on an ongoing basis. As colleagues of ours have pointed out, the capacity for constant ongoing learning will undergird a company's (and an individual's) ability to compete.[7] As a leader, you must be prepared to spend far more time and energy learning than you have in the past. With technology, customers, and external conditions evolving so rapidly, you can no longer take for granted your existing assumptions about your business. As Tata Group's N. Chandrasekaran reflected, "Every company has to ask this, from the perspective of my product or service—what is my new value chain? Or what ecosystem do I fit in? Unless you have clarity in this, you can't build a good strategy."[8] Leaders must also model for the rest of the workforce the intellectual flexibility and dynamism that employees, too, will need to display during their careers as they partake of upskilling and reskilling.

As Siemens's Dr. Busch related, staying tuned and learning is the only way to stay abreast of technology. Accordingly, he makes a point of traveling once or twice a year from Germany to the West Coast of the United States to meet with both large IT firms and start-ups, simply to gain an understanding of their activities. He encourages middle managers at Siemens to do the same. "I really care about this," he said, "and hope that the layers [of management] below me are mimicking me, saying, 'Oh, if this guy does it, I have to do the same.'" On one occasion, Busch took his core leaders to a two-day workshop in San Francisco to meet with technology firms. "We talked about technology development and how they see Siemens and our ecosystem, what its shortfalls are, how we might be able to improve it. It was really a 360-degree meeting, so to say, it was amazing." Busch added that learning in his view encompasses not simply technology but personal growth as well. Leaders have to "stay curious and [embrace] lifelong learning. If you give up on this, you have lost already."

Fifth, leaders must *embrace transformational leadership.* As we've seen, always-on transformation has to become business as usual in our era of disruption and change. The risk, of course, is that people in organizations attempting such an ongoing never-ending evolution will become overwhelmed and fatigued. To avoid such malaise and buttress an organization's capacity to thrive on constant change, every leader must become a transformational leader, embracing a holistic human-centered approach that entails engaging simultaneously with the head, heart, and hands. Leaders must provide clarity of direction, pursuing an iterative process in which they take stock of the disruptions the company faces, envision a future across the nine strategies, and align the organization to embark on the journey (head). They must motivate and inspire teams to behave more confidently and perform at their best, demonstrating care and empathy, actively listening, and coaching and empowering everyone (heart). Finally, leaders must mobilize their organizations in the more open, collaborative approach to executing and innovating with agility described previously, encouraging practices that foster creativity and agility (such as colocation, daily stand-ups, working in sprints, and fast-cycle learning) and emphasizing the need to invest in and develop much-needed capabilities both human and digital (hands). Microsoft's Satya Nadella has embodied a head-heart-hands leadership model at Microsoft, describing respectively how important it is for leaders to "create clarity," "generate energy," and "deliver success."

Sixth, leaders in the twenty-first century must *develop a new ability to navigate through ambiguity, tension, and paradox.* If you think back through the three disruptive forces, the nine strategies, and the specific ways that the companies we studied have approached and implemented these strategies, you find that they confront leaders with a number of significant paradoxes. Leaders must steer their organizations to learn, rethink, and experiment 'on the one hand *and* ground their organizations in elements of the business that are stable and unchanging. They must compete ferociously with their peers *and* collaborate with them as never before. They must push their companies to be both global *and* local. They must cultivate fluidity *and* stability in the organization. *Great* during the twentieth century meant pushing hard on one element of a binary and excelling. To go *beyond great*, leaders must feel comfortable with handling both elements of a binary, and they must help their people feel comfortable as well.

When leaders go beyond great, they embolden their companies to take charge of their own destinies and master our volatile global business environment rather than remain imprisoned in it. Rather than simply growing their existing businesses, their companies broaden their horizons and launch boldly into entirely new competitive spaces. Each of the leaders consulted here—Chandrasekaran, Marques, Busch, and Nadella—exemplifies beyond great leadership. Each has led his firm to execute a number of the nine strategies, delivering peer-leading shareholder returns while creating an organization that is resilient, socially responsible, and a magnet for young talent. Each has fundamentally transformed his firm: Chandrasekaran made TCS more agile, innovative, and entrepreneurial; Marques led Natura to build a unique relationship-driven operating model founded on the idea of collaborative networks; Busch is helping his organization adapt its strong, internally focused, technology-driven culture to become more open and sensitive to global issues and local markets; and Nadella rallied Microsoft around a bold new purpose.

What legacy will *you* leave? As you pursue the nine strategies for building new forms of competitive advantage, galvanize your people to pursue a broader social impact as well as shareholder returns. Become more collaborative and less directive. Treat others in your space as collaborators as well as competitors. Exemplify a growth mindset. Become a transformational leader. Embrace ambiguity, tension, and paradox. The journey beyond great is wonderfully fulfilling and enriching for everyone involved. And it all starts with you.

ACKNOWLEDGMENTS

One of the great joys in completing a book like *Beyond Great* is the opportunity to acknowledge the many outstanding people who helped us along the way. We are particularly indebted to Seth Schulman for his brilliant work in helping us conceptualize, write, and edit the manuscript for this book. Seth is a consummate professional, and we could not have completed this work without him.

Rajah Augustinraj and Kishore Seetharam's able leadership of our exceptional research team was vital to the book's development. Rajah and Kishore partnered with us unwaveringly over the last eighteen months, codeveloping the strategies and supporting them with relevant, well-researched stories and thought-provoking interviews. Their ability to orchestrate the multitude of contributors was critical to ensuring the manuscript's timely development at every key milestone. Likewise, our heartfelt thanks go out to the tireless and talented team working with Rajah and Kishore. Alejandro Assam and Stephanie Rich provided the research behind our early arguments and helped us identify the most exciting stories to tell. Paul Pavel and Ina Foalea developed deep outlines for the "Growing Beyond" section. Akash Sehra, Heather Cameron-Watt, and Laura Vasconcellos researched the "Operating Beyond" and "Organizing Beyond" sections. Sophia Lugo and Afreen Ghauri helped us research the TSI, leadership, and resilience topics and apply the finishing touches. Our thanks also to Hiba Warrach for helping find many of the finer facts that the team leveraged and to Rachel Gostenhofer for her fact-checking prowess.

We would like to thank our agent, Todd Shuster, and our editor, Colleen Lawrie, for their strong, invaluable support of this project. Todd served as a true thought partner, shaping the book concept at the outset and guiding us through the intricate process of bringing a book to market. Colleen patiently guided us through the many months of writing and editing, showing us new ways to make the argument concise, direct, and provocative. Thank you both!

We were fortunate to count a number of our senior colleagues as thought partners throughout this journey. First and foremost, thank you to our CEO, Rich Lesser, for carefully reading and contributing to the manuscript. It is much better for your insights. We are also deeply indebted to BCG's global chairman, Hans-Paul Bürkner; BCG's India chairman, Janmejaya Sinha; and BCG's global people chair, Dinesh Khanna, who shaped our thinking on changes in globalization. We thank Martin Reeves and François Candelon, the chairman and the director of the BCG Henderson Institute, where the three of us as fellows researched the ideas that eventually developed into *Beyond Great*. Practice area leaders and topic experts at BCG helped us bring out the nuances of each strategy and pointed us to exceptional companies to research. Special thanks to sixteen topic experts for their especially intensive involvement: Sylvain Duranton, Karalee Close, and Rajiv Gupta (global data and digital); David Young (sustainability); Massimo Russo and Konrad von Szczepanski (ecosystems); Peter Rosenfeld, Daniel Küpper, and Michael McAdoo (flex delivery and global supply chains); Allison Bailey, Vikram Bhalla, Martin Danoesastro, Diana Dosik, Julie Kilmann, Deborah Lovich, and Sumit Sarawgi (people and organization).

We extend our deep thanks to the eminent business leaders who spent many hours with us sharing their personal stories and insights with us. We feel greatly in their debt and hope that the book truly captures the perspectives they shared. We also wish to thank a number of worldwide partners and client officers at BCG—including Daniel Azevedo, Douglas Beal, Jan Philipp Bender, Aparna Bharadwaj, Ted Chan, Ajay Chowdhury, Marc Gilbert, Volker Hämmerle, Nimisha Jain, Ryoji Kimura, Satoshi Komiya, Justin Rose, Abheek Singhi, Peter Tollman, Tomer Tzur, and John Wenstrup—for helping us gain access to these leaders.

Three BCG senior advisers—Bob Black, Bernd Waltermann, and David Michael—critically reviewed our work and served as our sounding board. Their insightful feedback and encouraging appraisals give us great confidence that *Beyond Great* will be a highly relevant book for our times. This book would also not have been possible without the sponsorship of BCG's Global Advantage Practice. We thank Kasey Maggard, the practice's global director, for assembling the necessary resources and relentlessly navigating all internal and external processes to enable this book's successful completion. Thank you as well to Massimo Portincaso, who, along with Belinda Gallaugher, Eric Gregoire, and Sarah McIntosh, shepherded our efforts to bring *Beyond Great* to the widest possible audience.

Finally, and most importantly, we wish to thank each of our families for their constant support, encouragement, and faith, which has sustained us during the arduous process of writing a book. Without you by our sides, we wouldn't have been able to tell the fascinating story of *Beyond Great* and introduce it to a global readership. Thank you for everything!

NOTES

Introduction: Great Is No Longer Good Enough

1. Marc Bitzer (former COO and current CEO of Whirlpool), interview with Boston Consulting Group research team, June 15, 2017.

2. We can think of total shareholder return (TSR) as consisting of three primary components: (1) profit growth, (2) increases in share price, and (3) the return of cash to shareholders. For a fuller discussion, please see Gerry Hansell et al., "The Dynamics of TSR Turnarounds," BCG, July 15, 2014, downloaded April 6, 2020, at https://www.bcg .com/publications/2014/value-creation-strategy-dyamics-tsr-turnarounds.aspx.

3. Scott D. Anthony et al., "2018 Corporate Longevity Forecast: Creative Destruction Is Accelerating," Innosight, accessed December 10, 2019, https://www.innosight .com/insight/creative-destruction/.

4. Martin Reeves and Lisanne Püschel, "Die Another Day: What Leaders Can Do About the Shrinking Life Expectancy of Corporations," BCG, December 2, 2015, https://www.bcg.com/publications/2015/strategy-die-another-day-what-leaders-can -do-about-the-shrinking-life-expectancy-of-corporations.aspx.

5. John D. Stoll, "CEO Tenure Is Getting Shorter. Maybe That's a Good Thing," *Wall Street Journal*, October 4, 2018, https://www.wsj.com/articles/ceo-tenure-is-getting -shorter-maybe-thats-a-good-thing-1538664764; Lauren Silva Laughlin, "Many C.E.O. Tenures Are Getting Shorter," *New York Times*, October 23, 2018, https://www .nytimes.com/2018/10/23/business/dealbook/ceo-tenure-kimberly-clark.html.

6. Hans-Paul Bürkner, Martin Reeves, Hen Lotan, and Kevin Whitaker, "A Bad Time to Be Average," BCG, July 22, 2019, https://www.bcg.com/publications/2019/bad -time-to-be-average.aspx.

7. TCS's IPO prospectus, June 2004, 67, http://www.cmlinks.com/pub/dp/dp5400 .pdf.

8. Jochelle Mendonca, "TCS Restructures Its Business Units to Focus on Long-Term Strategy," *Economic Times*, last updated October 22, 2018, https://economictimes .indiatimes.com/tech/ites/tcs-restructures-its-business-units-to-focus-on-long-term -strategy/articleshow/66309922.cms.

9. "Blazing a Trail," Tata, accessed April 2, 2020, https://www.tata.com/newsroom /titan-diversity-blazing-a-trail.

10. Market capitalization of $115 billion as of December 30, 2019. All numbers derived from BCG ValueScience database, accessed December 30, 2019.

11. N. Shivapriya, "How N. Chandrasekaran's Second Term at TCS Will Be Different from His First," *Economic Times*, September 4, 2014, https://economictimes.indiatimes .com/tech/ites/how-n-chandrasekarans-second-term-at-tcs-will-be-different-from-his -first/articleshow/41650912.cms.

12. Paul Laudicina, "Globalization Is Dead: What Now?" *World Economic Forum*, January 20, 2016, https://www.weforum.org/agenda/2016/01/globalization-is-dead -what-now/.

13. "2019 Edelman Trust Barometer Reveals 'My Employer' Is the Most Trusted Institution," Edelman, January 20, 2019, https://www.edelman.com/news-awards/2019 -edelman-trust-barometer-reveals-my-employer-most-trusted-institution.

14. See, for example, Richard Baldwin, *The Great Convergence: Information Technology and the New Globalization* (Cambridge: Belknap, 2016).

15. "While almost every economy faces headwinds, the poorest countries face the most daunting challenges because of fragility, geographic isolation, and entrenched poverty," said World Bank Group vice president for equitable growth, finance, and institutions, Ceyla Pazarbasioglu (World Bank, "Global Growth to Weaken to 2.6% in 2019, Substantial Risks Seen," press release, June 4, 2019, https://www.worldbank.org/en/news /press-release/2019/06/04/global-growth-to-weaken-to-26-in-2019-substantial-risks -seen).

16. Erdal Yalcin, Gabriel Felbermayr, and Marina Steininger, "Global Impact of a Protectionist U.S. Trade Policy," ifo Institute, October 2017, 29–30, https://www.ifo.de /DocDL/ifo_Forschungsberichte_89_2017_Yalcin_etal_US_TradePolicy.pdf.

17. Vanessa Gunnella and Lucia Quaglietti, "The Economic Implications of Rising Protectionism: A Euro Area and Global Perspective," *ECB Economic Bulletin* 3 (2019), https://www.ecb.europa.eu/pub/economic-bulletin/articles/2019/html/ecb.ebart201903 _01~e589a502e5.en.html#toc3.

18. Emma Cosgrove, "'Economic Nationalism' Is a Growing Challenge for Manufacturers, Survey Says," Supply Chain Dive, November 13, 2018, https://www .supplychaindive.com/news/economic-nationalism-risk-for-manufacturers/542137/.

19. Figures compiled by TeleGeography database, November 2019, accessed December 12, 2019.

20. BCG Henderson Institute: Center for Macroeconomics, proprietary analysis, 2019.

21. Luke Kawa, "Traders Are Wagering the VIX Hits Triple Digits on Tuesday," Bloomberg, March 9, 2020, https://www.bloomberg.com/news/articles/2020-03-09 /traders-are-wagering-the-vix-hits-triple-digits-on-tuesday.

22. "Vix-Index," CBOE, accessed June 5, 2020, http://www.cboe.com/products/vix -index-volatility/vix-options-and-futures/vix-index/vix-historical-data#.

23. "Business Roundtable Redefines the Purpose of a Corporation to Promote 'An Economy That Serves All Americans,'" Business Roundtable, August 19, 2019, https://www.businessroundtable.org/business-roundtable-redefines-the-purpose-of -a-corporation-to-promote-an-economy-that-serves-all-americans.

Chapter 1: Do Good, Grow Beyond

1. Douglas Beal et al., "Total Societal Impact: A New Lens for Strategy," BCG, October 25, 2017, https://www.bcg.com/publications/2017/total-societal-impact-new -lens-strategy.aspx; Douglas Beal et al., "Insights on Total Societal Impact from Five Industries," BCG, October 25, 2017, https://www.bcg.com/publications/2017/corporate -development-finance-strategy-insights-total-societal-impact-five-industries.aspx.

2. Andrea Álvares (chief marketing, sustainability, and innovation officer at Natura), interview with BCG research team, March 18, 2020.

3. "About Us," Natura, accessed March 29, 2020, https://www.naturabrasil.com/pages /about-us; "Cosmetics & Relationships," Natura, accessed March 29, 2020, https://www .naturabrasil.fr/en-us/our-values/our-essence.

4. As Seabra has recounted, "At age 16, I was given this quote from Plato: 'The one is in the whole; the whole is in the one.' That was a revelation to me. This notion of being part of a whole has never left me." Michael Silverstein and Rune Jacobsen, "Take Giant Leaps (Because You're Not Going to Win with Timid Steps)," BCG, October 7, 2015, https://www.bcg.com/publications/2015/marketing-sales-consumer-products -take-giant-leaps-not-going-win-timid-steps.aspx.

5. "Natura &Co," Natura Co., 2018, https://naturaeco.com/report_2018_en.pdf.

6. "Natura: Multi-Level Sales for Multi-Level Impact," Business Call to Action, accessed March 29, 2020, https://www.businesscalltoaction.org/sites/default/files /resources/bcta_casestudy_natura_web.pdf.

7. "Natura &Co," 37.

8. "Natura: Multi-Level Sales for Multi-Level Impact"; "Natura &Co," 57.

9. Geoffrey Jones, "The Growth Opportunity That Lies Next Door," *Harvard Business Review*, July–August 2012, https://hbr.org/2012/07/the-growth-opportunity-that -lies-next-door.

10. Keyvan Macedo (sustainability manager, Natura Cosmeticos SA), interview with BCG team, March 20, 2019.

11. Luciana Hashiba, "Innovation in Well-Being," Management Exchange, May 18, 2012, https://www.managementexchange.com/story/innovation-in-well-being.

12. "Our Engagements," Natura, accessed April 1, 2020, https://www.naturabrasil.fr /en-us/our-values/sustainable-development.

13. "Natura Presents Campaign with New Positioning of the Brand: The World Is More Beautiful with You," Cosmeticos BR, February 12, 2019, https://www.cosmeticosbr .com.br/conteudo/en/natura-presents-today-a-campaign-with-new-positioning-of-the -brand-the-world-is-more-beautiful-with-you/.

14. BCG company research; Andres Schipani, "Beauty Company Natura Balances Profitability and Sustainability," *Financial Times*, December 4, 2019, https://www.ft.com /content/4795bbe2-e469-11e9-b8e0-026e07cbe5b4.

15. "Impact Case Study: Natura's Commitment to Ethical BioTrade," Union for Ethical BioTrade, accessed April 1, 2020, https://static1.squarespace.com/static /58bfcaf22994ca36885f063e/t/5d1a1b3ecff76800013e65d2/1561992003982/Natura -impact+study-july+2019.pdf; Guilherme Leal, "Exploiting Rainforest Riches While

Conserving Them," *Telegraph*, June 10, 2019, https://www.telegraph.co.uk/business/how
-to-be-green/exploiting-and-conserving-rainforest-riches/.

16. Keyvan Macedo, interview with BCG team, March 20, 2019.

17. "Natura's Carbon Neutral Programme | Global," United Nations, accessed March
31, 2020, https://unfccc.int/climate-action/momentum-for-change/climate-neutral
-now/natura.

18. Andrea Álvares, interview with BCG research team, March 18, 2020.

19. Hashiba, "Innovation in Well-Being," https://www.managementexchange.com
/story/innovation-in-well-being.

20. Andrea Álvares, interview with BCG research team, March 18, 2020.

21. "About Us," Natura, accessed March 29, 2020, https://www.naturabrasil.com
/pages/about-us.

22. "Care About the Planet," Natura, accessed April 19, 2020, https://www.naturabrasil
.com/pages/care-about-the-planet-a-sustainable-timeline.

23. Keyvan Macedo, interview with BCG team, March 20, 2019.

24. Data derived from investing.com., accessed January 15, 2020.

25. Katharine Earley, "More Than Half of All Businesses Ignore UN's Sustainable Development Goals," *Guardian*, September 30, 2016, https://www
.theguardian.com/sustainable-business/2016/sep/30/businesses-ignore-un-sustainable
-development-goals-survey.

26. Scott Tong, "How Shareholders Jumped to First in Line for Profits," MarketPlace,
June 14, 2016, https://www.marketplace.org/2016/06/14/profit-shareholder-value/.

27. Tony O'Malley, "Business for Good: How Fujitsu Believes CSR Is Essential for Business Success," Business & Finance, accessed March 29, 2020, https://
businessandfinance.com/business-for-good-fujitsu/.

28. Roberto Marques (Natura &Co chairman and chief executive of the group),
interview with BCG team, March 10, 2020.

29. Governance & Sustainability Institute, "Flash Report: 86% of S&P 500 Index®
Companies Publish Sustainability / Responsibility Reports in 2018," press release, May
16, 2019, https://www.ga-institute.com/press-releases/article/flash-report-86-of-sp
-500-indexR-companies-publish-sustainability-responsibility-reports-in-20.html.

30. BCG analysis based on MSCI annual report (2018), Crunchbase, S&P investor
fact book (2019), and Vigeo Eiris estimation (2017).

31. Alana L. Griffin, Michael J. Biles, and Tyler J. Highful, "Institutional Investors
Petition the SEC to Require ESG Disclosures," American Bar Association, January
16, 2019, https://www.americanbar.org/groups/business_law/publications/blt/2019/01
/investors/.

32. "China Mandates ESG Disclosures for Listed Companies and Bond Issuers,"
Latham & Watkins, February 6, 2018, https://www.globalelr.com/2018/02/china
-mandates-esg-disclosures-for-listed-companies-and-bond-issuers/.

33. "CGS Survey Reveals 'Sustainability' Is Driving Demand and Customer
Loyalty," *CGS*, accessed March 30, 2020, https://www.cgsinc.com/en/infographics
/CGS-Survey-Reveals-Sustainability-Is-Driving-Demand-and-Customer-Loyalty;
"Study: 81% of Consumers Say They Will Make Personal Sacrifices to Address

Social, Environmental Issues," Sustainable Brands, accessed March 31, 2020, https://
sustainablebrands.com/read/stakeholder-trends-and-insights/study-81-of-consumers-
say-they-will-make-personal-sacrifices-to-address-social-environmental-issues.

34. "Sustainability Futures," *The Future Laboratory*, 6, 13, https://www
.thefuturelaboratory.com/hubfs/Sustainability%20Futures%20Report.pdf.

35. "Americans Willing to Buy or Boycott Companies Based on Corporate Values, According to New Research by Cone Communications," Cone, May 17, 2017,
https://www.conecomm.com/news-blog/2017/5/15/americans-willing-to-buy-or-boy
cott-companies-based-on-corporate-values-according-to-new-research-by-cone-com
munications.

36. "Performance with Purpose: Sustainability Report 2017," PepsiCo, 2, https://
www.pepsico.com/docs/album/sustainability-report/2017-csr/pepsico_2017_csr.pdf.

37. "Performance with Purpose," PepsiCo, 1.

38. "Performance with Purpose," PepsiCo, 3; "Indra K. Nooyi on Performance with
Purpose," BCG, January 14, 2010, https://www.bcg.com/en-in/publications/2010/indra
-nooyi-performance-purpose.aspx.

39. "Performance with Purpose," PepsiCo, 3.

40. "Performance with Purpose," PepsiCo, 3–4; "Helping to Build a More Sustainable
Food System: PepsiCo Sustainability Report 2018," PepsiCo, 8, https://www.pepsico
.com/docs/album/sustainability-report/2018-csr/pepsico_2018_csr.pdf.

41. "Helping to Build a More Sustainable Food System," PepsiCo, 3.

42. "Performance with Purpose," PepsiCo, 3.

43. "Helping to Build a More Sustainable Food System," PepsiCo, 3.

44. "World of Business Must Play Part in Achieving SDGs, Ban Says," United
Nations, January 20, 2016, https://www.un.org/sustainabledevelopment/blog/2016/01
/world-of-business-must-play-part-in-achieving-sdgs-ban-says/.

45. By law, Indian companies beyond a net worth, sales, or profit threshold must dedicate 2 percent of their profits to funding development activities benefitting society. See
Stephen Kurczy, "Forcing Firms to Do Good Could Have a Negative Impact," Colum-
bia Business School, November 13, 2018, https://www8.gsb.columbia.edu/articles/ideas
-work/forcing-firms-do-good-could-have-negative-impact.

46. Lee Ann Head, "Getting and Keeping A-List Employees: A Bonus Benefit of
Sustainability Efforts," Shelton Group, September 6, 2013, https://sheltongrp.com/posts
/getting-and-keeping-a-list-employees-a-bonus-benefit-of-sustainability-efforts/.

47. Susan Warfel, "ESG Investing Survey Reveals 3 Social Goals Investors Value
over Profits," *Investor's Business Daily*, November 20, 2019, https://www.investors.com
/research/esg-investing-survey-reveals-social-goals-investors-value-over-profits/.

48. "Sustainable Investing's Competitive Advantages," Morgan Stanley, August 6, 2019,
https://www.morganstanley.com/ideas/sustainable-investing-competitive-advantages.

49. Nicolas Rabener, "ESG Investing: Too Good to Be True?" Enterprising Investor,
January 14, 2019, https://blogs.cfainstitute.org/investor/2019/01/14/esg-factor-invest
ing-too-good-to-be-true/.

50. Gordon L. Clark, Andreas Feiner, and Michael Viehs, "From the Stockholder
to the Stakeholder," Smith School of Enterprise and the Environment, September

2014, https://www.smithschool.ox.ac.uk/publications/reports/SSEE_Arabesque_Paper _16Sept14.pdf.

51. "A Fundamental Reshaping of Finance," BlackRock, accessed March 31, 2020, https://www.blackrock.com/corporate/investor-relations/larry-fink-ceo-letter.

52. BCG analysis, led by Vinay Shandal (managing director and partner, global leader in sustainable investing).

53. For an extensive treatment of TSI, please see Beal et al., "Total Societal Impact." This chapter relies heavily on the concepts and language in this article.

54. Beal et al., "Total Societal Impact."

55. Ajay Banga, "Contributing to a Sustainable and Inclusive Future," Mastercard, August 20, 2019, https://www.mastercardcenter.org/insights/doing-well-by-doing -good-with-Ajay-Banga.

56. Tara Nathan, interview with BCG team, December 13, 2019.

57. Mohammed Badi et al., "Global Payments 2018: Reimagining the Customer Experience," BCG, 6, 9, https://image-src.bcg.com/Images/BCG-Global-Payments -2018-Oct-2018_tcm9-205095.pdf.

58. "The Private Sector Is Becoming a Major Catalyst for Sustainability," Master-card Center for Inclusive Growth, August 22, 2018, https://www.mastercardcenter.org /insights/private-sector-becoming-major-catalyst-sustainability.

59. Tara Nathan, interview with BCG team, December 13, 2019.

60. Ryan Erenhouse, "Financial Inclusion Commitment: Reach 500 Million Peo-ple by 2020," Mastercard, https://newsroom.mastercard.com/news-briefs/financial -inclusion-commitment-reach-500-million-people-by-2020/; "Doing Well by Doing Good: Corporate Report 2018," Mastercard, 3, https://www.mastercard.us/content/dam /mccom/global/aboutus/Sustainability/mastercard-sustainability-report-2018.pdf.

61. "How Mobile Payments Can Help Keep Children in School," Mastercard Cen-ter for Inclusive Growth, June 10, 2019, https://www.mastercardcenter.org/insights/how -mobile-payments-can-help-keep-children-in-school.

62. Jake Bright, "Mastercard Launches 2KUZE Agtech Platform in East Africa," TechCrunch, January 18, 2017, https://techcrunch.com/2017/01/18/mastercard-launches -2kuze-agtech-platform-in-east-africa/.

63. "SASSA MasterCard Debit Card Grows Financial Inclusion in South Africa," Mastercard, press release, November 13, 2013, https://newsroom.mastercard.com/press -releases/sassa-mastercard-debit-card-grows-financial-inclusion-in-south-africa/; Cath Everett, "Technology for Social Good—Mastercard," Diginomica, August 10, 2017, https://diginomica.com/technology-social-good-mastercard.

64. BCG company research.

65. Tara Nathan, interview with BCG team, December 13, 2019.

66. "Mastercard Incorporating," Great Places to Work, accessed March 31, 2020, https://www.greatplacetowork.com/certified-company/1001388.

67. BCG analysis based on data from the Capital IQ database.

68. "Businessperson of the Year," *Fortune*, 2019, https://fortune.com/businessperson -of-the-year/2019/ajay-banga/.

69. Tara Nathan, interview with BCG team, December 13, 2019.

70. "The OMRON Principles," Omron, 2019, accessed April 1, 2020, https://www.omron.com/global/en/assets/file/ir/irlib/ar19e/OMRON_Integrated_Report_2019_en_Vision.pdf.

71. Seiji Takeda (Omron executive officer and director of business strategy in main global strategy unit), interview with BCG team, November 8, 2019; "Working for the Benefit of Society: The Corporate Philosophy Driving Omron's Value Creation," Omron, accessed April 1, 2020, https://www.omron.com/global/en/assets/file/ir/irlib/ar14e/ar14_02.pdf; "The OMRON Principles," 5.

72. "Automated Railway Ticket Gate System Named IEEE Milestone," Omron, November 27, 2007, https://www.omron.com/global/en/media/press/2007/11/c1127.html.

73. "Automated Railway Ticket Gate System."

74. "Enhancing Lifestyles in Japan," Omron, accessed April 1, 2020, https://www.omron.com/global/en/about/corporate/history/ayumi/innovation/#history1964; "History of Omron's Blood Pressure Monitor," Omron, accessed April 2, 2020, https://www.omronhealthcare.com.hk/en/article/ins.php?index_am1_id=7&index_id=25.

75. "Communities," Anglo American, accessed April 1, 2020, https://www.angloamerican.com/sustainability/communities.

76. Froydis Cameron-Johansson, interview with BCG research team, November 14, 2019.

77. Daniel Gleeson, "Anglo American's FutureSmart Mining on Its Way to Tangible Technology Results," International Mining (blog), June 7, 2019, https://im-mining.com/2019/06/07/anglo-americans-futuresmart-mining-way-tangible-technology-results/.

78. Froydis Cameron-Johansson, interview with BCG research team, November 14, 2019.

79. Paul Polman, interview by Christiane Amanpour, PBS, aired March 3, 2020, http://www.pbs.org/wnet/amanpour-and-company/video/bill-mckibben-impact-fossil-fuel-divestment-efforts-r1eszd-2/.

80. Mary Sigmond, "93% Of CEOs Believe Business Should Create Positive Impact Beyond Profit," YPO, accessed April 1, 2020, https://www.ypo.org/2019/01/93-of-ceos-believe-business-should-create-positive-impact-beyond-profit/; "2019 YPO Global Leadership Survey," YPO, 2019, https://www.ypo.org/global-leadership-survey/.

81. "The US Walking the Walk of a Circular Economy," ING, February 5, 2019, https://www.ing.com/Newsroom/News/The-US-walking-the-walk-of-a-circular-economy.htm.

82. "United Nations Global Compact Progress Report," United Nations Global Compact, 2017, https://d306pr3pise04h.cloudfront.net/docs/publications%2FUN+Impact+Brochure_Concept-FINAL.pdf.

83. Franklin Foer, "It's Time to Regulate the Internet," *Atlantic*, March 21, 2018, https://www.theatlantic.com/technology/archive/2018/03/its-time-to-regulate-the-internet/556097/.

84. Please see "What Empowerment Means to Us," Microsoft, accessed April 1, 2020, https://news.microsoft.com/empowerment/.

85. Brad Smith, "Microsoft Will Be Carbon Negative by 2030," Microsoft, January 16, 2020, https://blogs.microsoft.com/blog/2020/01/16/microsoft-will-be-carbon-negative-by-2030/.

86. For more guidance, please see Beal et al., "Insights on Total Societal Impact."

87. Elisha Goldstein, "What Is the Investment That Never Fails?" Mindfulness & Psychotherapy with Elisha Goldstein, PhD (blog), updated April 26, 2011, https://blogs.psychcentral.com/mindfulness/2011/04/what-is-the-investment-that-never-fails/.

Chapter 2: Stream It, Don't Ship It

1. Nick Ismail, "Servitisation: How Technology Is Making Service the New Product," Information Age, March 28, 2018, https://www.information-age.com/servitisation-technology-service-new-product-123471260/.

2. Russell Stokes, interviews with author, October 5, 2017, February 19, 2018, and June 12, 2019.

3. Marc Bitzer, interview with author, June 15, 2017.

4. BCG analysis based on data from United Nations UNCTAD.

5. Amy Watson, "Netflix—Statistics & Facts," Statista, February 6, 2020, https://www.statista.com/topics/842/netflix/.

6. "Netflix Is Now Available Around the World," Netflix, January 6, 2016, https://media.netflix.com/en/press-releases/netflix-is-now-available-around-the-world; Watson, "Netflix."

7. "Shared Micromobility in the U.S.: 2018," National Association of City Transportation Officials, accessed December 13, 2019, https://nacto.org/shared-micromobility-2018/.

8. "The Sharing Economy," PricewaterhouseCoopers, 2015, https://www.pwc.fr/fr/assets/files/pdf/2015/05/pwc_etude_sharing_economy.pdf.

9. Thales S. Teixeira, Unlocking the Customer Value Chain (New York: Currency, 2019), 251.

10. Keith Naughton and David Welch, "Why Carmakers Want You to Stop Buying Cars, Someday," Bloomberg, July 11, 2019, https://www.bloomberg.com/news/articles/2019-07-12/why-carmakers-want-you-to-stop-buying-cars-someday-quicktake.

11. Jack Ewing, Liz Alderman, and Ben Dooley, "Renault and Nissan Need Each Other to Thrive in Future, 2 Leaders Say," New York Times, July 21, 2019, https://www.nytimes.com/2019/07/21/business/renault-nissan-alliance.html.

12. BCG Henderson Institute: Center for Macroeconomics, internal proprietary analysis, accessed July 2019; "The Great Mobility Tech Race: Winning the Battle for Future Profits," Boston Consulting Group, January 11, 2018. This analysis was performed prior to the COVID-19 crisis. As of this writing, the crisis remains ongoing. We suspect that the shift to digitally delivered automotive services will only accelerate once the industry stabilizes.

13. Mike Colias and Nick Kostov, "After Defeat in Europe, GM Is Picking Its Battles," *Wall Street Journal*, April 1, 2017, https://www.wsj.com/articles/gm-signs-off-on -its-retreat-from-europe-1501573108?mod=e2tw.

14. General Motors, "General Motors Accelerates Transformation," news release, November 26, 2018, https://investor.gm.com/news-releases/news-release-details /general-motors-accelerates-transformation; David Goldman, "GM Is Reinventing Itself. It's Cutting 15% of Its Salaried Workers and Shutting 5 Plants in North America," CNN, November 26, 2018, https://edition.cnn.com/2018/11/26/business/gm-oshawa -plant/index.html.

15. "GM and Lyft to Shape the Future of Mobility," General Motors, January 4, 2016, https://media.gm.com/media/us/en/gm/news.detail.html/content/Pages/news /us/en/2016/Jan/0104-lyft.html; "GM to Acquire Cruise Automation to Accelerate Autonomous Vehicle Development," General Motors, March 11, 2016, https://media .gm.com/media/us/en/gm/home.detail.html/content/Pages/news/us/en/2016/mar /0311-cruise.html.

16. "GM Advances Self-Driving Vehicle Deployment with Acquisition of LIDAR Developer," General Motors, October 9, 2017, https://media.gm.com/media/us/en/gm /news.detail.html/content/Pages/news/us/en/2017/oct/1009-lidar1.html.

17. Andrew J. Hawkins, "GM's Cruise Will Get $2.75 Billion from Honda to Build a New Self-Driving Car," Verge, October 3, 2018, https://www.theverge.com/2018/10 /3/17931786/gm-cruise-honda-investment-self-driving-car.

18. In autonomous vehicles, GM was anticipating margins in the 20 to 30 percent range: Mike Colias and Heather Somerville, "Cruise, GM's Driverless-Car Unit, Delays Robot-Taxi Service," *Wall Street Journal*, July 24, 2019, https://www.wsj.com/articles/gm -s-driverless-car-unit-cruise-delays-robot-taxi-service-11563971401.

19. Andrew J. Hawkins, "Waymo Strikes a Deal with Nissan-Renault to Bring Driverless Cars to Japan and France," Verge, June 20, 2019, https://www.theverge.com/2019 /6/20/18692764/waymo-nissan-renault-self-driving-car-japan-france.

20. Philips, "New Study Demonstrates Significant Clinical Workflow and Staff Experience Benefits of Philips' Azurion Image-Guided Therapy Platform," news release, November 14, 2017, https://www.philips.com/a-w/about/news/archive/standard /news/press/2017/20171114-new-study-demonstrates-significant-benefits-of-philips -azurion.html.

21. "Reducing Procedure Time in Image-Guided Therapy with Philips Azurion," Philips, accessed December 27, 2019, https://www.philips.com/a-w/about/news/archive /case-studies/20180824-reducing-procedure-time-in-image-guided-therapy-with -philips-azurion.html.

22. "Reduction of Procedure Time by 17% with Philips Azurion in an Independently Verified Study," Philips, November 2017, 7, https://www.usa.philips.com/c-dam/b2bhc /master/landing-pages/azurion/philips-nieuwegein-case-study.pdf.

23. "Reduction of Procedure Time," 7.

24. "Reducing Procedure Time in Image-Guided Therapy."

25. "With Azurion, Performance and Superior Care Become One," Philips, accessed December 27, 2019, https://www.usa.philips.com/healthcare/resources/landing/azurion.

26. "Reduction of Procedure Time," 8.

27. "Aiming for Zero," Philips, accessed January 13, 2020, https://www.usa.philips .com/c-dam/b2bhc/master/landing-pages/aiming-for-zero/Infographic_remote _services_final.pdf.

28. "Five Ways in Which Healthcare Innovation Has Changed over the Past 15 Years," Philips, April 2, 2019, https://www.philips.com/a-w/about/news/archive /blogs/innovation-matters/20190402-five-ways-in-which-healthcare-innovation-has -changed-over-the-past-15-years.html.

29. Elizabeth Cairns, "Philips Uses Its Intelligence for Outcomes-Based Incomes," Evaluate, April 25, 2018, https://www.evaluate.com/vantage/articles/interviews/philips -uses-its-intelligence-outcomes-based-incomes.

30. "Value-Based Care: Turning Healthcare Theory into a Dynamic and Patient-Focused Reality," Philips, position paper, April 2019, 8, https://www.philips.com/c-dam /corporate/newscenter/global/whitepaper/20200128_Value-based_care_position_paper _FINAL.pdf; "Transforming Healthcare to a Value-Based Payment system," *Washington Post*, https://www.washingtonpost.com/sf/brand-connect/philips/transforming -healthcare/.

31. Frans van Houten and Abhijit Bhattacharya, "Company Update and Performance Roadmap," (investor presentation, Philips internal documents), slide 21, https:// www.philips.com/corporate/resources/quarterlyresults/2016/Capital_Markets_Day/01 _VanHouten_Bhattacharya_Company_update_and_performance_roadmap.pdf; "Royal Philips Third Quarter 2019 Results," Philips, October 28, 2019, 8, https://www.results .philips.com/publications/q319/downloads/files/en/philips-third-quarter-results-2019 -presentation.pdf.

32. Van Houten and Bhattacharya, "Company Update," slide 16.

33. "Jeroen Tas on the Importance of Long-Term Relationships," Philips, April 1, 2019, https://www.philips.com/a-w/about/news/archive/standard/news/articles/2019 /20190401-jeroen-tas-on-the-importance-of-long-term-relationships.html.

34. "Jeroen Tas."

35. Andrew Ross, "Digital Transformation in Manufacturing Is Driven by Customers," Information Age, May 4, 2018, https://www.information-age.com/digital -transformation-manufacturing-customers-123471810/.

36. "Power by the Hour," Rolls-Royce, accessed December 28, 2019, https://www .rolls-royce.com/media/our-stories/discover/2017/totalcare.aspx.

37. "Power by the Hour."

38. "Power by the Hour."

39. "Rolls-Royce Opens New Airline Aircraft Availability Centre—Supporting Its 'On Time, Every Time' Vision," Rolls-Royce, press release, June 6, 2017, https://www .rolls-royce.com/media/press-releases/2017/06-06-2017-rr-opens-new-airline-aircraft -availability-centre.aspx.

40. Company website, press releases; http://www.mro-network.com/engines-engine -systems/rolls-royce-opens-new-service-center-airline-support, https://www.rolls-royce .com/sustainability/performance/sustainability-stories/totalcare.aspx. "Rolls-Royce and Microsoft Collaborate to Create New Digital Capabilities," Microsoft, accessed January

13, 2020; Anna-Maria Ihle, "Encouraging Rolls-Royce Power Systems to Create an Innovation Culture," SAP, August 24, 2018, https://news.sap.com/2018/08/rolls-royce-power-systems-innovation-culture/.

41. Ian Sheppard, "Rolls-Royce Launches 'IntelligentEngine' Concept," AIN Online, February 5, 2018, https://www.ainonline.com/aviation-news/air-transport/2018-02-05/rolls-royce-launches-intelligentengine-concept.

42. "R² Data Labs Ecosystem," Rolls-Royce, accessed January 9, 2019, https://www.rolls-royce.com/products-and-services/ecosystem.aspx.

43. Sheppard, "Rolls-Royce Launches."

44. "Digital Innovations for a Sustainable World," Schneider Electric, 2019, https://www.se.com/ww/en/assets/564/document/124836/annual-report-2019-en.pdf.

45. Marco Annunziata, "Digital-Industrial Revolution: Ready to Run After Very Slow Start, New Survey Shows," Forbes, February 28, 2019, https://www.forbes.com/sites/marcoannunziata/2019/02/28/digital-industrial-revolution-ready-to-run-after-very-slow-start-new-survey-shows/#770250d777dd.

46. Madeleine Johnson, "Starbucks' Digital Flywheel Program Will Use Artificial Intelligence," Zacks, July 31, 2017, https://www.zacks.com/stock/news/270022/starbucks-digital-flywheel-program-will-use-artificial-intelligence?cid=CS-NASDAQ-FT-270022.

47. Kevin R. Johnson, Starbucks Corporations Q2 2017 earnings call, April 27, 2017.

48. Kevin R. Johnson, Starbucks Corporations Q2 2017 earnings call, April 27, 2017.

49. Howard Schultz, Starbucks Corporation Q3 2016 earnings call, July 21, 2016.

50. Tim Hardwick, "Apple Pay Overtakes Starbucks as Most Popular Mobile Payment Platform in the US," Mac Rumors, October 23, 2019, https://www.macrumors.com/2019/10/23/apple-pay-overtakes-starbucks-in-us/.

51. Amanda Mull, "The Future of Marketing Is Bespoke Everything," Atlantic, June 11, 2019, https://www.theatlantic.com/health/archive/2019/06/special-orders-dont-upset-us/591367/.

52. Mull, "The Future of Marketing."

53. Katrina Lake, "Stitch Fix's CEO on Selling Personal Style to the Mass Market," Harvard Business Review, May–June 2018, https://hbr.org/2018/05/stitch-fixs-ceo-on-selling-personal-style-to-the-mass-market.

54. "Stitch Fix Annual Report, 2019," Stitch Fix, October 2, 2019, https://investors.stitchfix.com/static-files/96389147-1dbe-444a-b2cf-880a1bf7f99f.

55. For the profile, I'm indebted to "L'Oréal Unveils Perso, an AI-Powered At-Home System For Skincare and Cosmetics," L'Oréal, press release, January 5, 2020, https://www.lorealusa.com/media/press-releases/2020/ces2020.

56. "L'Oréal Unveils Perso," L'Oréal.

57. Mull, "The Future of Marketing."

58. Ellen Byron, "We Now Live in a World with Customized Shampoo," Wall Street Journal, April 17, 2019, https://www.wsj.com/articles/we-now-live-in-a-world-with-customized-shampoo-11555506316; "Introducing Gx," Gatorade, accessed January 13, 2020, https://www.gatorade.com/gx/.

59. Chantal Tode, "Burger King Builds Mobile Platform to Quickly Scale Up in Payments," Retail Dive, accessed December 29, 2019, https://www.retaildive.com /ex/mobilecommercedaily/burger-king-builds-mobile-platform-to-quickly-scale-up-in -payments.

60. Nick Babich, "The Next Level User Experience of Tesla's Car Dashboard," Adobe Blog, October 24, 2017, https://theblog.adobe.com/the-next-level-user-experience-of -teslas-car-dashboard/.

61. Babich, "The Next Level User Experience."

62. Jason Udy, "Tesla Model S Software Update Increases Personalization," *Motor Trend*, September 22, 2014, https://www.motortrend.com/news/tesla-model-s-software -update-increases-personalization/.

63. Udy, "Tesla Model S Software."

64. Udy, "Tesla Model S Software."

65. Fred Lambert, "Tesla Reveals How It Will Use Camera Inside Model 3 to Personalize In-Car Experience," Electrek, July 24, 2019, https://electrek.co/2019/07/24 /tesla-use-camera-inside-cars-personalize-in-car-experience/.

66. Fred Lambert, "Tesla Vehicles Can Now Diagnose Themselves and Even Preorder Parts for Service," Electrek, May 6, 2019, https://electrek.co/2019/05/06/tesla -diagnose-pre-order-parts-service/.

67. "Advancing Automotive Service," Tesla, accessed December 29, 2019, https:// www.tesla.com/service.

68. Jacob Kastrenakes, "Spotify Is Personalizing More Playlists to Individual Users," Verge, March 26, 2019, https://www.theverge.com/2019/3/26/18282549/spotify -personalized-playlists-curation-more-songs.

69. Sarah Perez, "Spotify Expands Personalization to Its Programmed Playlists," Techcrunch, March 26, 2019, https://techcrunch.com/2019/03/26/spotify-expands -personalization-to-its-programmed-playlists/; Monica Mercuri, "Spotify Reports First Quarterly Operating Profit, Reaches 96 Million Paid Subscribers," *Forbes*, February 6, 2019, https://www.forbes.com/sites/monicamercuri/2019/02/06/spotify-reports-first -quarterly-operating-profit-reaches-96-million-paid-subscribers/#61bde1ed5dc9.

70. Matt Burgess, "This Is How Netflix's Secret Recommendation System Works," *Wired*, August 18, 2018, https://www.wired.co.uk/article/netflix-data-personalisation -watching; Sameer Chhabra, "Netflix Says 80 Percent of Watched Content Is Based on Algorithmic Recommendations," Mobile Syrup, August 22, 2017, https://mobilesyrup .com/2017/08/22/80-percent-netflix-shows-discovered-recommendation/.

71. Chhabra, "Netflix Says 80 percent of Watched Content."

72. Nicole Nguyen, "Netflix Wants to Change the Way You Chill," Buzzfeed, December 13, 2018, https://www.buzzfeednews.com/article/nicolenguyen/netflix -recommendation-algorithm-explained-binge-watching.

73. Tom Gerken, "Fortnite: 'Millions Attend' Virtual Marshmello Concert," BBC, February 4, 2019, https://www.bbc.com/news/blogs-trending-47116429.

74. Tec 2 News Staff, "Pokemon Go Earns $950 Million in 2016, Breaks Records: Report," Tech 2, January 17, 2017, https://www.firstpost.com/tech/gaming/pokemon-go -earns-950-million-in-2016-breaks-records-report-3724949.html.

75. "NBA," *Fast Company,* accessed December 29, 2019, https://www.fastcompany.com/company/nba.

Chapter 3: Refine Your Global Game

1. Eva Dou, "Xiaomi Overtakes Samsung in China Smartphone Market," *Wall Street Journal,* August 4, 2014, https://blogs.wsj.com/digits/2014/08/04/xiaomi-overtakes-samsung-in-china-smartphone-market/?mod=article_inline.

2. BCG analysis, based on an extensive review of secondary sources and annual reports.

3. Kenny Chee, "China Phone Maker Xiaomi Setting Up International Headquarters in Singapore," *Straight Times,* February 19, 2014, https://www.straitstimes.com/business/china-phone-maker-xiaomi-setting-up-international-headquarters-in-singapore; Savannah Dowling, "The Rise and Global Expansion of Xiaomi," Crunchbase, February 12, 2018, https://news.crunchbase.com/news/rise-global-expansion-xiaomi/.

4. Daniel Tay, "Launch of Xiaomi's Redmi Note in Singapore Sees 5,000 Phones Sold Within 42 Seconds, Breaking Last Record," TechinAsia, July 7, 2014, https://www.techinasia.com/launch-xiaomi-redmi-note-singapore-42-seconds-record.

5. Dowling, "The Rise and Global Expansion of Xiaomi."

6. Anand Daniel, "[Podcast] Manu Kumar Jain on Scaling Xiaomi and Disrupting the Indian Electronics Space," *Your Story,* September 20, 2019, https://yourstory.com/2019/09/accel-podcast-manu-kumar-jain-jabong-xiaomi-anand-daniel.

7. Team Counterpoint, "India Smartphone Market Share: By Quarter," *Counterpoint,* November 27, 2019, https://www.counterpointresearch.com/india-smartphone-share/.

8. Uptin Saiidi, "The 'Apple of China' Expanded into 80 New Markets in Four Years. Here's How Xiaomi Grew So Rapidly," CNBC, updated September 10, 2019, https://www.cnbc.com/2019/09/09/xiaomi-how-the-apple-of-china-grew-rapidly-into-80-new-markets.html.

9. Komal Sri-Kumar, "Hot Emerging Markets May Be in for a Shock," Bloomberg, March 27, 2019, https://www.bloomberg.com/opinion/articles/2019-03-27/emerging-markets-are-hot-but-face-a-shock.

10. Martin Fackler, "Putting the We Back in Wii," *New York Times,* June 8, 2007; "Europe Gets Wii Last," Nintendo World Report, September 15, 2006, http://www.nintendoworldreport.com/pr/12069/europe-gets-wii-last.

11. Sameer Desai, "Nintendo Wii and DS to Launch in India on September 30," Rediff, September 16, 2008, https://www.rediff.com/getahead/2008/sep/16wii.htm; Siliconera staff, "Wii Launches in South Korea on April 26 with Even Cheaper Virtual Console Games," *Siliconera,* April 14, 2008, https://www.siliconera.com/wii-launches-in-south-korea-on-april-26-with-even-cheaper-virtual-console-games/; Matt Martin, "Wii to Release in Taiwan July 12," Games Industry, June 26, 2008, https://www.gamesindustry.biz/articles/wii-to-release-in-taiwan-july-12; "Wii," Wayback Machine, December 12, 2009, https://web.archive.org/web/20100306012826/http://www.nintendo.com.hk/wii_console.htm.

12. Tech2 News staff, "Pokemon Go Earns $950 Million in 2016, Breaks Records: Report," Tech2, January 17, 2017, https://www.firstpost.com/tech/gaming/pokemon -go-earns-950-million-in-2016-breaks-records-report-3724949.html; Alina Bradford, "Here Are All the Countries Where Pokemon Go Is Available," Cnet, January 24, 2017, https://www.cnet.com/how-to/pokemon-go-where-its-available-now-and-coming-soon/.

13. Louis Brennan, "How Netflix Expanded to 190 Countries in 7 Years," *Harvard Business Review*, updated October 12, 2018, https://hbr.org/2018/10/how-netflix -expanded-to-190-countries-in-7-years.

14. "Emerging Markets Powering Airbnb's Global Growth," Airbnb, accessed January 3, 2020, https://press.airbnb.com/wp-content/uploads/sites/4/2019/02/Final _-Emerging-Markets-Powering-Airbnbs-Global-Growth-.pdf; Shawn Tully, "Why Hotel Giant Marriott Is on an Expansion Binge as It Fends Off Airbnb," *Fortune*, June 14, 2017, https://fortune.com/2017/06/14/marriott-arne-sorenson-starwood -acquisition-airbnb/; "Number of Marriott International Hotel Rooms Worldwide from 2009 to 2018," Statista, March 20, 2019, https://www.statista.com/statistics/247304 /number-of-marriott-international-hotel-rooms-worldwide/.

15. James Brumley, "If Fitbit Finds a Willing Suitor, It Should Take the Offer," Motley Fool, September 28, 2019, https://www.fool.com/investing/2019/09/28/if-fitbit -finds-a-willing-suitor-it-should-take-th.aspx; Robert Hof, "How Fitbit Survived as a Hardware Startup," *Forbes*, February 4, 2014, https://www.forbes.com/sites/roberthof /2014/02/04/how-fitbit-survived-as-a-hardware-startup/#204121341934.

16. "FY 2017 Earnings Deck," Fitbit, February 2018, https://s2.q4cdn.com /857130097/files/doc_financials/2017/Q4/Q4'17-Earnings-Presentation.pdf.

17. For more on Fitbit and a few of its partnerships, please see Simon Mainwaring, "Purpose at Work: How Fitbit's Giveback Is Strengthening Its Business," *Forbes*, February 12, 2019, https://www.forbes.com/sites/simonmainwaring/2019/02/12/purpose-at -work-how-fitbits-giveback-is-strengthening-its-business/#11fac05058d2.

18. "Fitbit Authorized Retailers," Fitbit, accessed January 3, 2020, https://www .fitbit.com/content/assets/legal-pages/FITBIT%20AUTHORIZED%20RETAILERS %20Q2%202016.pdf.

19. Matt Swider, "Fitbit OS 3.0 Is Giving the Ionic and Versa Smartwatches New Powers," Tech Radar, December 17, 2018, https://www.techradar.com/in/news/fitbit-os -3-0-new-versa-ionic-features.

20. Chaim Gartenberg, "Google Buys Fitbit for $2.1 Billion," Verge, November 1, 2019, https://www.theverge.com/2019/11/1/20943318/google-fitbit-acquisition-fitness -tracker-announcement.

21. It had exported opportunistically since the 1970s.

22. "The World's Favourite Indian," *Bajaj Auto Limited* (12th Annual Report) 2018–2019, 9.

23. "The World's Favourite Indian," *Bajaj Auto Limited* (12th Annual Report) 2018–2019, 18.

24. "The World's Favourite Indian," *Bajaj Auto Limited* (12th Annual Report) 2018–2019, 10, 18–19.

25. BCG company research; Tom Brennan, "Alibaba.com Opens Platform to US Sellers," Alizila.com, July 23, 2019, https://www.alizila.com/alibaba-com-opens-platform-to-us-sellers/.

26. Gene Marks, "Is Now the Time to Start Selling on Alibaba?" *Inc.*, July 25, 2019, https://www.inc.com/gene-marks/is-now-time-to-start-selling-on-alibaba.html.

27. See Tmall global's website, https://merchant.tmall.hk/.

28. François Candelon, Fangqi Yang, and Daniel Wu, "Are China's Digital Companies Ready to Go Global?" BCG Henderson Institute, May 22, 2019, https://www.bcg.com/publications/2019/china-digital-companies-ready-go-global.aspx.

29. John Detrixhe, "Americans Are Splurging on Personal Loans Thanks to Fintech Startups," Quartz, July 24, 2018, https://qz.com/1334899/personal-loans-are-surging-in-the-us-fueled-by-fintech-startups/; Wendy Weng, "Despite Rapid Digitisation of Payments in China, Credit Card Usage Will Reach New Heights by 2020," Asian Banker, February 28, 2019, www.theasianbanker.com/updates-and-articles/despite-rapid-digitisation-of-payments-in-china,-credit-card-usage-will-reach-new-heights-by-2020; "Allied Wallet Adds WeChat Pay with 900 Million Active Users," Mobile Payments Today, October 12, 2018, https://www.mobilepaymentstoday.com/news/allied-wallet-adds-wechat-pay-with-900-million-active-users/; Kate Rooney, "Fintechs Help Boost US Personal Loan Surge to a Record $138 Billion," CNBC, February 21, 2019, https://www.cnbc.com/2019/02/21/personal-loans-surge-to-a-record-138-billion-in-us-as-fintechs-lead-new-lending-charge.html.

30. Jonathan Kandell, "Can Citi Return to Its Pre-crisis Glory?" Institutional Investor, January 8, 2018, https://www.institutionalinvestor.com/article/b15ywlgddl683f/can-citi-return-to-its-pre-crisis-glory.

31. Though please note that in 2009, the company claimed approximately 300,000 employees, while at the end of 2016 it comprised 241,000 part-time and full-time employees. "Strong, Steadfast, Sustainable," HSBC Holdings plc, Annual Reports and Accounts 2009, 10, 12, https://www.hsbc.com/-/files/hsbc/investors/investing-in-hsbc/all-reporting/group/2009/hsbc2009ara0.pdf; "Annual Report and Accounts 2016," HSBC Holdings plc, 8, 150, https://www.hsbc.com/-/files/hsbc/investors/investing-in-hsbc/all-reporting/group/2016/annual-results/hsbc-holdings-plc/170221-annual-report-and-accounts-2016.pdf.

32. Bruce Sterling, "Banks Thrilled to Be Free of Customers," *Wired*, July 27, 2016, https://www.wired.com/beyond-the-beyond/2016/07/banks-thrilled-free-customers/.

33. Martin Arnold and Camilla Hall, "Big Banks Giving Up on Their Global Ambitions," *Financial Times*, October 19, 2014, https://www.ft.com/content/95bed102-5641-11e4-bbd6-00144feab7de.

34. For Citibank's withdrawal from Japan, please see Stephen Harner, "Citibank to Quit Japan's Retail Market: Another QE Casualty," *Forbes*, August 19, 2014, https://www.forbes.com/sites/stephenharner/2014/08/19/another-qe-casualty-citibank-to-quit-japans-retail-market/#f8dd5bf67bb1; informal interview with former senior global business head at Citibank.

35. Kevin Lim, "Singapore's UOB to Launch Digital Bank in Thailand," *Nikkei Asian Review*, February 14, 2019, https://asia.nikkei.com/Business/Companies/Singapore-s-UOB-to-launch-digital-bank-in-Thailand.

36. Jessica Lin, "UOB Is Going After Asean's Millennials with a Digital Bank Called TMRW—and Its Biggest Draw Could Be a Game That Levels-Up with Savings," Business Insider Singapore, February 14, 2019, https://www.businessinsider.sg/uob-is-going-after-aseans-millennials-with-a-digital-bank-called-tmrw-and-its-biggest-draw-could-be-a-game-that-levels-up-with-savings/.

37. Lin, "UOB Is Going After Asean's Millennials."

38. Lin, "UOB Is Going After Asean's Millennials."

39. Jonathan Wheatley, "Does Investing in Emerging Markets Still Make Sense?" *Financial Times*, July 15, 2019, https://www.ft.com/content/0bd159f2-937b-11e9-aea1-2b1d33ac3271.

40. BCG analysis, relying on data from the Economist Intelligence Unit (EIU) database.

41. BCG analysis, relying on data from the Economist Intelligence Unit (EIU) database.

42. BCG analysis, relying on data from the Economist Intelligence Unit (EIU) database.

43. Bernard Marr, "The Amazing Ways Chinese Face Recognition Company Megvii (Face++) Uses AI and Machine Vision," *Forbes*, May 24, 2019, https://www.forbes.com/sites/bernardmarr/2019/05/24/the-amazing-ways-chinese-face-recognition-company-megvii-face-uses-ai-and-machine-vision/#58e4b7fd12c3.

44. "Ever Better and Cheaper, Face-Recognition Technology Is Spreading," *Economist*, September 9, 2017, https://www.economist.com/business/2017/09/09/ever-better-and-cheaper-face-recognition-technology-is-spreading.

45. Donald R. Lessard and Cate Reavis, "CEMEX: Globalization 'The CEMEX Way,'" MIT Management Sloan School, revised November 16, 2016, https://mitsloan.mit.edu/LearningEdge/CaseDocs/09%20039%20cemex%20%20lessard.pdf.

46. "CEMEX Makes Significant Progress in Asset Disposal Program," Associated Press, March 21, 2019, https://apnews.com/1a037a1fe938441fa389bd5fe6b0cae7.

47. Reeba Zachariah, "Tata Steel to Divest Southeast Operations," *Times of India*, July 21, 2018, https://timesofindia.indiatimes.com/business/india-business/tata-steel-to-divest-southeast-operations/articleshow/65075987.cms; Tata Steel, "Tata Steel Acquires Two Steel Rolling Mills in Vietnam," press release, March 8, 2007, https://www.tatasteel.com/media/newsroom/press-releases/india/2007/tata-steel-acquires-two-steel-rolling-mills-in-vietnam/.

48. Penny Macrae, "At 100, Tata Steel Aims to Double Output," Live Mint, updated August 26, 2007, https://www.livemint.com/Home-Page/eCfuLf5DC4hP0uoHOHvrsM/At-100-Tata-Steel-aims-to-double-output.html.

49. Rosemary Marandi, "China's HBIS Buys Control of Tata Steel's Southeast Asia Business," *Nikkei Asian Review*, January 29, 2019, https://asia.nikkei.com/Business/Business-deals/China-s-HBIS-buys-control-of-Tata-Steel-s-Southeast-Asia-business.

50. Silvia Antonioli, "Steel Firm SSI Hopes New Plant Will Help Bring UK Profit," Reuters, June 13, 2013, https://www.reuters.com/article/ssi-uk-steel/steel-firm-ssi-hopes-new-plant-will-help-bring-uk-profit-idUSL5N0EP20T20130613.

51. Kritika Saxena, "After ThyssenKrupp Fall Out, Tata Steel in Talks with Three Companies to Sell European Operations," CNBC, updated May 28, 2019, https://www.cnbctv18.com/infrastructure/after-thyssenkrupp-fall-out-tata-steel-in-talks-with-three-companies-to-sell-european-operations-3492291.htm; "Tata Steel Cancels Pacts to Sell Southeast Asian Businesses to Hesteel Group," *Economic Times*, August 7, 2019, https://economictimes.indiatimes.com/industry/indl-goods/svs/steel/tata-steel-arm-snaps-pact-with-hbis-group-to-divest-majority-stake-in-se-asia-biz/articleshow/70561112.cms.

52. Rakhi Mazumdar, "Tata Steel Rejigs India, Europe Operations," *Economic Times*, updated August 12, 2019, https://economictimes.indiatimes.com/industry/indl-goods/svs/steel/tata-steel-rejigs-india-europe-operations/articleshow/70636697.cms?from=mdr.

53. Mike Wittman (former vice president of supply chain for Mars Chocolate North America), interview with BCG research team, July 18, 2019; Douglas Yu, "Mars to Bring Maltesers to the US & Canada," Confectioner News, March 13, 2017, https://www.confectionerynews.com/Article/2017/03/13/Mars-to-launch-Maltesers-in-the-US-Canada.

54. Mike Wittman, interview with BCG research team, July 18, 2019.

55. Masaaki Tsuya, interview with BCG research team, November 2, 2019.

56. Dr. Horst Kayser, interview with BCG team, 2019.

57. Dr. Horst Kayser, interview with BCG team, 2019.

58. "Siemens Inks Deal with Alibaba to Launch Digital Products in China," Reuters, July 9, 2018, https://www.reuters.com/article/us-siemens-alibaba/siemens-inks-deal-with-alibaba-to-launch-digital-products-in-china-idUSKBN1JZ22U; "Siemens China : and Wuhan Sign Strategic Cooperation Agreement," Market Screener, November 11, 2019, https://www.marketscreener.com/news/Siemens-China-and-Wuhan-sign-strategic-cooperation-agreement--29563000/.

59. "Siemens in China," Siemens, accessed January 6, 2020, https://new.siemens.com/cn/en/company/about/siemens-in-china.html.

60. Dr. Horst Kayser, interview with BCG team, 2019.

61. Analysis based on data found in Siemens annual reports spanning 2012–2019.

62. For this entire paragraph, we rely on Ouyang Cheng, interview with BCG research team, August 22, 2019.

63. For more on this topic, please see Peter H. Diamandis, "Introducing the Augmented World of 2030," September 6, 2019, https://singularityhub.com/2019/09/06/introducing-the-augmented-world-of-2030/.

Chapter 4: Engineer an Ecosystem

1. These numbers derive from our research benchmarking more than forty ecosystems. For more on the size and scope of ecosystems, please see Nikolaus Lang, Konrad

von Szczepanski, and Charline Wurzer, "The Emerging Art of Ecosystem Management," BCG Henderson Institute, January 16, 2019, https://www.bcg.com/publications /2019/emerging-art-ecosystem-management.aspx.

2. Nicole Jao, "China's Mobile Payment Market Fourth Quarter Growth Dwindled," Technode, March 28, 2019, https://technode.com/2019/03/28/chinas-mobile-payment-market-fourth-quarter-growth-dwindled/.

3. Evelyn Cheng, "How Ant Financial Grew Larger Than Goldman Sachs," CNBC, June 8, 2018, https://www.cnbc.com/2018/06/08/how-ant-financial-grew-larger-than -goldman-sachs.html.

4. BCG research and analysis based on proprietary databases and company websites.

5. "Ant Financial: How a Bug Took on the World," Asia Money, September 26, 2019, https://www.euromoney.com/article/b1h7mtyfd5d8lg/ant-financial-how-a-bug-took-on-the-world.

6. "Ant Financial: How a Bug Took on the World."

7. BCG research and analysis based on proprietary databases and company websites.

8. BCG company research; Rita Liao, "Alibaba's Alternative to the App Store Reaches 230M Daily Users," Techcrunch, January 29, 2019, https://techcrunch.com/2019/01/29 /alibaba-alipay-mini-programs-230m-users/.

9. BCG company research; "Ant Financial: How a Bug Took on the World"; "Ant Financial," Fast Company, January 2020, https://www.fastcompany.com/company/ant -financial.

10. John Detrixhe, "China's Ant Financial, Thwarted in the US, Is Expanding Rapidly in Europe," Quartz, March 15, 2019; "Ant Is Worth 50% More Than Goldman with $150 Billion Valuation," Bloomberg, April 10, 2018, http://www.bloomberg.com/news /articles/2018-04-11/ant-is-worth-50-more-than-goldman-with-150-billion-valuation.

11. Harvey Morris, "China's March to Be the World's First Cashless Society: China Daily Contributor," Straittimes, April 8, 2019, https://www.straitstimes.com/asia/east -asia/chinas-march-to-be-the-worlds-first-cashless-society-china-daily-contributor.

12. Morris, "China's March to Be the World's First Cashless Society."

13. Donna Lu, "China Is Showing the Rest of the World How to Build a Cashless Society," New Scientist, January 9, 2019, https://www.newscientist.com/article /mg24132120-100-china-is-showing-the-rest-of-the-world-how-to-build-a-cashless -society/#ixzz60rB4qQ63. A number of countries around the world as of 2019 were doing away with old-fashioned paper money and embracing digital financial transactions. A study in Malaysia found that a sizable majority of consumers—70 percent— would opt to buy from stores that let them pay digitally rather than with paper money (Harizah Kamel, "Malaysia Is Fast Becoming a Cashless Society," Malaysian Reserve, September 20, 2019, https://themalaysianreserve.com/2019/09/20/malaysia-is-fast -becoming-a-cashless-society/). In Sweden, where only a fifth of people use ATMs to withdraw cash, thousands of people have implanted computer chips into their hands, allowing them access to a whole new kind of convenience. With a casual wave of the hand, they can pay for their groceries or buy tickets on public transportation (Liz Alderman, "Sweden's Push to Get Rid of Cash Has Some Saying, 'Not So Fast,'" New York

Times, November 21, 2018, https://www.nytimes.com/2018/11/21/business/sweden -cashless-society.html; Maddy Savage, "Thousands of Swedes Are Inserting Microchips Under Their Skin," National Public Radio (*All Things Considered*), October 22, 2018, https://www.npr.org/2018/10/22/658808705/thousands-of-swedes-are-inserting -microchips-under-their-skin?t=1541532530852).

14. Michael Lyman, Ron Ref, and Oliver Wright, "Cornerstone of Future Growth: Ecosystems," Accenture, 2018, https://www.accenture.com/_acnmedia/PDF-77/Accenture -Strategy-Ecosystems-Exec-Summary-May2018-POV.pdf#zoom=50.

15. Nikolaus Lang, Konrad von Szczepanski, and Charline Wurzer, "The Emerging Art of Ecosystem Management," BCG Henderson Institute, January 16, 2019, https:// www.bcg.com/publications/2019/emerging-art-ecosystem-management.aspx. The following section of the chapter is a loose adaptation of this article and draws heavily on its argument and illustrations.

16. "Together 2025+," Volkswagen AG, accessed January 14, 2020, https://www .volkswagenag.com/en/group/strategy.html.

17. Andrew Krok, "VW Car-Net's Massive Updates Include 5 Free Years of Remote Access," CNET, September 17, 2019, https://www.cnet.com/roadshow/news/vw-car -net-overhaul-update-connectivity-remote-access/.

18. BCG analysis of the Volkswagen ecosystem based on Volkswagen's website, press reports, and websites of Volkswagen's ecosystem partners.

19. Lang, von Szczepanski, and Wurzer, "The Emerging Art of Ecosystem Management."

20. "[Infographic] Get Smart: The Latest in What SmartThings Can Do for You," Samsung Newsroom, October 30, 2019, https://news.samsung.com/global/infographic -get-smart-the-latest-in-what-smartthings-can-do-for-you.

21. Amazon, "Amazon Introduces an Array of New Devices and Features to Help Make Your Home Simpler, Safer, and Smarter," press release, September 25, 2019, https://press.aboutamazon.com/news-releases/news-release-details/amazon-introduces -array-new-devices-and-features-help-make-your.

22. "AKQA & Dyson Launch a Connected Way to Clean with Dyson Link App," Little Black Boom, September 18, 2014, https://lbbonline.com/news/akqa-dyson -launch-a-connected-way-to-clean-with-dyson-link-app/; Tanya Powley, "Dyson Helps Launch Design Engineering School at Imperial College," *Financial Times*, March 22, 2015, https://www.ft.com/content/73b0b9ac-cf15-11e4-893d-00144feab7de.

23. John Markoff and Laura M. Holson, "Apple's Latest Opens a Developers' Playground," *New York Times*, July 10, 2008, https://www.nytimes.com/2008/07/10 /technology/personaltech/10apps.html. The five-million figure is a projection: Sarah Perez, "App Store to Reach 5 Million Apps by 2020, with Games Leading the Way," Techcrunch, August 10, 2016, https://techcrunch.com/2016/08/10/app-store-to-reach -5-million-apps-by-2020-with-games-leading-the-way/.

24. Kevin Kelleher, "Developer's $34 Billion Earnings from Apple's App Store Rose 28% in 2018," *Fortune*, January 28, 2019, https://fortune.com/2019/01/28/apple -app-store-developer-earnings-2018/; Lauren Goode, "App Store 2.0," Verge, accessed February 9, 2020, https://www.theverge.com/2016/6/8/11880730/apple-app-store

-subscription-update-phil-schiller-interview; "Apple Rings in New Era of Services Following Landmark Year," Apple, updated January 8, 2020, https://www.apple.com /newsroom/2020/01/apple-rings-in-new-era-of-services-following-landmark-year/.

25. BCG company research.

26. Harriet Agnew, "Digital Health Start-Up Doctolib Raises €150m at a €1bn+ Valuation," *Financial Times*, March 19, 2019, https://www.ft.com/content/58ba164e-4a62 -11e9-bbc9-6917dce3dc62; Romain Dillet, "Doctolib Grabs $20 Million for Its Booking Platform for Doctors," Techcrunch, October 12, 2015, https://techcrunch.com/2015 /10/12/doctolib-grabs-20-million-for-its-booking-platform-for-doctors/.

27. Alexa's strategic partners either make devices with Alexa built in or allow Alexa as a route to access their platform.

28. Erika Malzberg, "Caterpillar and the Age of Smart Iron," Zuora, May 22, 2017, https://www.zuora.com/2017/05/22/caterpillar-and-the-age-of-smart-iron/; Bob Woods, "Caterpillar's Autonomous Vehicles May Be Used by NASA to Mine the Moon and Build a Lunar Base," CNBC, October 23, 2019, https://www.cnbc.com/2019/10/23 /caterpillar-and-nasa-developing-autonomous-vehicles-to-mine-the-moon.html.

29. This section of the chapter is a loose adaptation of Michael G. Jacobides, Nikolaus Lang, Nanne Louw, and Konrad von Szczepanski, "What Does a Successful Ecosystem Look Like?" BCG, June 26, 2019, https://www.bcg.com/publications/2019/what-does -successful-digital-ecosystem-look-like.aspx. The section draws heavily on this article's argument and illustrations.

30. It's the world's second-place search engine according to stat counter: "Everything You Need to Know About Baidu: The Largest Search Engine in China," Search Decoder, accessed February 4, 2020, https://www.searchdecoder.com/largest-search-engine-in -china-baidu; "Baidu Announces Project Apollo, Opening Up Its Autonomous Driving Platform," GlobalNewswire, April 18, 2017, https://www.globenewswire.com/news -release/2017/04/19/1018939/0/en/Baidu-Announces-Project-Apollo-Opening-Up -its-Autonomous-Driving-Platform.html.

31. Meng Jing, "Baidu Leads Tesla, Uber and Apple in Developing Self-Driving Cars," *South China Morning Post*, January 18, 2018, https://www.scmp.com/tech/enter prises/article/2129559/baidu-leads-tesla-uber-and-apple-developing-self-driving-cars.

32. Kyle Wiggers, "Baidu's DuerOS Voice Platform Is Now on 400 Million Devices," Venture Beat, July 2, 2019, https://venturebeat.com/2019/07/02/baidus-dueros-voice -platform-is-now-on-400-million-devices/.

33. BCG research and analysis.

34. Kyle Wiggers, "Baidu's Autonomous Cars Have Driven More Than 1 Million Miles Across 13 Cities in China," Venture Beat, July 2, 2019, https://venturebeat.com /2019/07/02/baidus-autonomous-cars-have-driven-more-than-1-million-miles-across -13-cities-in-china/.

35. Ryan Daws, "Shanghai Becomes the First Chinese City to License Self-Driving Cars to Carry Passengers," IoT News, September 19, 2019, https://www.iottechnews.com /news/2019/sep/19/shanghai-first-chinese-city-license-self-driving-cars-passengers/.

36. "Amazon Introduces the Alexa Fund: $100 Million in Investments to Fuel Voice Technology Innovation," Business Wire, June 25, 2015, https://www.businesswire.com

/news/home/20150625005704/en/Amazon-Introduces-Alexa-Fund-100-Million
-Investments.

37. Chris Ziegler, "Nokia CEO Stephen Elop Rallies Troops in Brutally Honest
'Burning Platform' Memo? (Update: It's Real!)," Engadget, February 8, 2011, https://
www.engadget.com/2011/02/08/nokia-ceo-stephen-elop-rallies-troops-in-brutally
-honest-burnin/.

38. These questions draw heavily on the prescriptive advice in Lang, von Szczepanski,
and Wurzer, "The Emerging Art of Ecosystem Management."

Chapter 5: Flex How You Make It

1. BCG analysis based on data extracted from Oxford Economics and OECD.org.

2. N. Chandrasekaran (chairman of Tata Sons), interview with the authors, January
14, 2020.

3. "TCS Hungary Townhall 2019," Tata Consultancy Services, accessed January
20, 2020, https://www.mytcscareer.com/; "TCS Opens Fifth Delivery Centre
in China," *Business Standard*, January 20, 2013, https://www.business-standard.com
/article/technology/tcs-opens-fifth-delivery-centre-in-china-110082200076_1.html;
Tata Consultancy Services, "TCS Opens New Global Delivery Center in Argentina,"
press release, accessed January 1, 2020, https://www.tcs.com/tcs-new-delivery-center
-argentina; "Annual Report 2018–2019: Growth and Transformation with Business 4.0,"
Tata Consultancy Services, https://www.tcs.com/content/dam/tcs/investor-relations
/financial-statements/2018-19/ar/annual-report-2018-2019.pdf.

4. "Tata Consultancy Services," Tata Consultancy Services, accessed January 20,
2020, https://www.ibef.org/download/Tata_Consultancy_Services.pdf.

5. BCG research and analysis based on ValueScience, NASDAQ, and NSE.

6. BCG research and analysis based on BCG ValueScience and annual reports;
N. Chandrasekaran, interview with the authors, January 14, 2020.

7. "Asia with Little Variation in the Share of World Footwear Exports," World
Footwear, September 14, 2016, https://www.worldfootwear.com/news/asia-with-little
-variation-in-the-share-of-world-footwear-exports/1882.html.

8. Mark Abraham et al., "The Next Level of Personalization in Retail," BCG, June
4, 2019, https://www.bcg.com/publications/2019/next-level-personalization-retail.aspx.

9. Catrin Morgan et al., "Use of Three-Dimensional Printing in Preoperative Planning in Orthopaedic Trauma Surgery: A Systematic Review and Meta-analysis," *World
Journal of Orthopedics* 11, no. 1 (January 18, 2020), http://dx.doi.org/10.5312/wjo.v11.
i1.57.

10. "'ECU' Is a Three Letter Answer for All the Innovative Features in Your Car: Know
How the Story Unfolded," Embitel, accessed March 8, 2020, https://www.embitel.com
/blog/embedded-blog/automotive-control-units-development-innovations-mechanical
-to-electronics; Jeff Desjardins, "How Many Millions of Lines of Code Does It Take?"
Visual Capitalist, February 8, 2017, https://www.visualcapitalist.com/millions-lines-of
-code/.

11. Emmanuel Lagarrigue, interview with BCG team, October 30, 2019.

12. Zach Stolzenberg, "Adidas: Racing to Supply Chain 4.0," Harvard Business School Digital Initiative, November 12, 2017, https://digital.hbs.edu/platform-rctom /submission/adidas-racing-to-supply-chain-4-0/; Tansy Hoskins, "Robot Factories Could Threaten Jobs of Millions of Garment Workers," *Guardian*, July 16, 2016, https:// www.theguardian.com/sustainable-business/2016/jul/16/robot-factories-threaten -jobs-millions-garment-workers-south-east-asia-women; "Adidas's High-Tech Factory Brings Production Back to Germany," *Economist*, January 14, 2017, https://www .economist.com/business/2017/01/14/adidass-high-tech-factory-brings-production -back-to-germany.

13. "Adidas' First Speedfactory Lands in Germany," Adidas, accessed February 12, 2020, https://www.adidas-group.com/en/media/news-archive/press-releases/2015/adidas -first-speedfactory-lands-germany/.

14. Sara Germano, "Adidas to Close Sneaker Factory in the U.S., Move Production to Asia," *Wall Street Journal*, November 11, 2019, https://www.wsj.com/articles/adidas -to-close-sneaker-factory-in-the-u-s-move-production-to-asia-11573485445?mod=hp _lista_pos2.

15. Peter Rosenfeld, interview with BCG team, July 19, 2019.

16. Peter Rosenfeld, interview with BCG team, July 19, 2019.

17. Beau Jackson, "3D Bioprinting Center of Excellence Launched by Amber and Johnson & Johnson," 3D Printing Industry, February 22, 2018, https://3dprintingindustry.com /news/3d-bioprinting-center-excellence-launched-amber-johnson-johnson-129373/.

18. Corey Clarke, "Johnson & Johnson Partners with Bioprinters to Create 3D Printed Knee," 3D Printing Industry, January 6, 2017, https://3dprintingindustry.com /news/johnson-johnson-partner-bioprinters-create-3d-printed-knee-102336/.

19. "Partner Up—Building a Global Manufacturing Network," Medical Device, May 8, 2017, https://www.medicaldevice-developments.com/features/featurepartner-up -building-a-global-manufacturing-network-5846594/.

20. Peter Pham, "Vietnam's Trade War Balancing Act," *Forbes*, November 29, 2018, https://www.forbes.com/sites/peterpham/2018/11/29/vietnams-trade-war-balancing -act/#63db28677b36. In the shoe industry, manufacturing sourced in China has declined while that sourced in Vietnam has increased as companies have sought to evade the impact of the China-US trade war and benefit from lower labor costs in Vietnam. Nike, Puma, and adidas are all helping to drive this trend with their sourcing strategies.

21. Company data provided to BCG.

22. Hemani Sheth, "Samsung Invests $500 Million for New Smartphone Display Manufacturing Plant in India," *Hindu Business Line*, updated January 20, 2020, https:// www.thehindubusinessline.com/info-tech/samsung-invests-500-million-for-new -smartphone-display-manufacturing-plant-in-india/article30605865.ece.

23. "Samsung to Expand U.S. Operations, Open $380 Million Home Appliance Manufacturing Plant in South Carolina," Samsung Newsroom, June 28, 2017, https:// news.samsung.com/us/samsung-south-carolina-home-appliance-manufacturing-plant -investment-newberry/.

24. Anil Chaudhry (zone president and MD, India, Schneider Electric), interview with BCG team, July 12, 2019.

25. "MindSphere Application Centers," Siemens, accessed February 19, 2020, https://new.siemens.com/global/en/products/software/mindsphere/application-centers .html; Brian Buntz, "Siemens Exec Dishes on MindSphere Industrial IoT Platform," IOT Today, June 7, 2019, https://www.iotworldtoday.com/2019/06/07/siemens-exec-dishes-on-mindsphere-industrial-iot-platform/.

26. Tomas Kellner, "Wind in the Cloud? How the Digital Wind Farm Will Make Wind Power 20 Percent More Efficient," GE Reports, September 27, 2015, https://www.ge.com/reports/post/119300678660/wind-in-the-cloud-how-the-digital-wind -farm-will-2/.

27. Markets and Markets, "Digital Twin Market Worth $35.8 Billion by 2025," press release, accessed February 19, 2020, https://www.marketsandmarkets.com/PressReleases /digital-twin.asp.

28. "Industrial Digital Twins: Real Products Driving $1B in Loss Avoidance," GE Digital (blog), accessed February 19, 2020, https://www.ge.com/digital/blog/industrial -digital-twins-real-products-driving-1b-loss-avoidance.

Chapter 6: Let the Data Run Through It

1. Rich Miller, "Facebook Accelerates Its Data Center Expansion," Data Center Frontier, March 19, 2018, https://datacenterfrontier.com/facebooks-accelerates-data -center-expansion/.

2. Arindam Bhattacharya, "Digital Globalisation vs Geopolitical Globalisation: A Tale of Two Worlds," *Economic Times*, June 18, 2017, https://economictimes.indiatimes .com/tech/internet/digital-globalisation-vs-geopolitical-globalisation-a-tale-of-two -worlds/articleshow/59173111.cms?from=mdr; Analysis based on data from TeleGeography, April 2019.

3. BCG analysis based on Gartner data.

4. J. Clement, "Global Digital Population as of April 2020," Statista, June 4, 2020, https://www.statista.com/statistics/617136/digital-population-worldwide/.

5. BCG analysis based on data from ITU. For more on what a fixed broadband basket entails, please visit "ICT Price Basket Methodology," ITU, accessed March 12, 2020, https://www.itu.int/en/ITU-D/Statistics/Pages/definitions/pricemethodology.aspx.

6. "Internet of Things Forecast," Ericsson, accessed March 9, 2020, https://www .ericsson.com/en/mobility-report/internet-of-things-forecast.

7. Caroline Donnelly, "Public Cloud Competition Prompts 66% Drop in Prices Since 2013, Research Reveals," Computer Weekly, January 12, 2016, https://www .computerweekly.com/news/4500270463/Public-cloud-competition-results-in-66 -drop-in-prices-since-2013-research-reveals.

8. "Volume of Data/Information Created Worldwide from 2010 to 2025," Statista, February 28, 2020, https://www.statista.com/statistics/871513/worldwide-data -created/.

9. "The 2017 Global CVC Report," CB Insights, 2017, https://relayto.com/cdn /media/files/ZaqycE4xRtyhl7er5GgE_CB-Insights_CVC-Report-2017.pdf; Kathleen Walch, "Is Venture Capital Investment in AI Excessive?" *Forbes*, January 5, 2020, https://

www.forbes.com/sites/cognitiveworld/2020/01/05/is-venture-capital-investment-for-ai
-companies-getting-out-of-control/#7c37438c7e05.

10. Ian Sherr, "Fortnite Reportedly Will Pull in an Epic $3 Billion Profit This Year,"
CNET, December 27, 2018, https://www.cnet.com/news/fortnite-reportedly-will-pull
-in-an-epic-3-billion-profit-this-year/.

For more on Fortnite, please also see Akhilesh Ganti, "How Fortnite Makes Money,"
Investopedia, August 20, 2019, http://www.investopedia.com/tech/how-does-fortnite
-make-money/; Felix Richter, "The Biggest Free-to-Play Cash Cows of 2019," Statista,
January 3, 2020, https://www.statista.com/chart/16687/top-10-free-to-play-games/;
Rupert Neate, "Fortnite Company Epic Games Valued at Nearly $15bn After Cash
Boost," *Guardian*, October 28, 2018, https://www.theguardian.com/games/2018/oct/28
/fortnite-company-epic-games-valued-15bn.

11. Kayla Matthews, "Precision Farming: AI and Automation Are Transforming
Agriculture," Data Center Frontier, October 31, 2019, https://datacenterfrontier.com
/precision-farming-ai-and-automation-are-transforming-agriculture/.

12. Ofir Schlam, "4 Ways Big Data Analytics Are Transforming Agriculture," Future
Farming, July 15, 2019, https://www.futurefarming.com/Tools-data/Articles/2019/7/4
-ways-big-data-analytics-are-transforming-agriculture-450440E/.

13. Bhaskar Chakravorti, "A Game Plan for Technology Companies to Actually Help
Save the World," Conversation, November 6, 2018, https://theconversation.com/a-game
-plan-for-technology-companies-to-actually-help-save-the-world-105007.

14. Cassie Perlman, "From Product to Platform: John Deere Revolutionizes Farming," *Harvard Business Review*, August 25, 2017, https://digital.hbs.edu/data-and
-analysis/product-platform-john-deere-revolutionizes-farming/.

15. Perlman, "From Product to Platform."

16. Alejandro Sayago, interview with BCG team, October 23, 2019.

17. "S-Series Combines," John Deere, accessed March 9, 2020, https://www.deere
.com/en/harvesting/s-series-combines/?panel=harvest.

18. For more, please see John Deere's website, http://www.deere.com.

19. "John Deere Operations Center," John Deere, accessed March 9, 2020, https://
www.deere.com/en/technology-products/precision-ag-technology/data-management
/operations-center/. The company's ExactEmerge technology enables high-precision
seeding while the planter still moves horizontally at record speeds: https://www.deere
.com/assets/publications/index.html?id=6f7a8a69.

20. For more information, please see "S-Series Combines."

21. Adele Peters, "How John Deere's New AI Lab Is Designing Farm Equipment for a
More Sustainable Future," *Fast Company*, September 11, 2017, https://www.fastcompany
.com/40464024/how-john-deeres-new-ai-lab-is-designing-farm-equipment-for-more
-sustainable-future.

22. Bernard Marr, "The Amazing Ways John Deere Uses AI and Machine Vision
to Help Feed 10 Billion People," *Forbes*, March 15, 2019, https://www.forbes.com/sites
/bernardmarr/2019/03/15/the-amazing-ways-john-deere-uses-ai-and-machine-vision
-to-help-feed-10-billion-people/#2fa699232ae9.

23. Peters, "How John Deere's New AI Lab Is Designing Farm Equipment."

24. C. Williams, "Farm to Data Table: John Deere and Data in Precision Agriculture," Harvard Business School Digital Initiative, November 12, 2019, https://digital.hbs.edu/platform-digit/submission/farm-to-data-table-john-deere-and-data-in-precision-agriculture/.

25. Scott Ferguson, "John Deere Bets the Farm on AI, IoT," Light Reading, March 12, 2018, https://www.lightreading.com/enterprise-cloud/machine-learning-and-ai/john-deere-bets-the-farm-on-ai-iot/a/d-id/741284.

26. For more, please see John Deere's website, http://www.deere.com.

27. Sharon O'Keeffe, "FarmConnect Initiated by John Deere, Claas and CNH Industral," *Farm Weekly*, November 19, 2019, https://www.farmweekly.com.au/story/6497351/machinery-companies-collaborate-on-data/.

28. O'Keeffe, "FarmConnect."

29. "Deere & Company Board Elects John May as CEO and Board Member," press release, August 29, 2019, https://www.prnewswire.com/news-releases/deere--company-board-elects-john-may-as-ceo-and-board-member-300909127.html.

30. For this paragraph, I am indebted to "L'Oréal Data-Driven Marketing & Digital Focus Continues to Boost Sales," Digital Media Solutions, December 3, 2019, https://insights.digitalmediasolutions.com/articles/loreal-sees-record-sales-growth.

31. "L'Oréal Data-Driven Marketing & Digital Focus."

32. Rory Butler, "L'Oréal Powers Its R&D by Processing 50 Million Pieces of Data a Day," *Manufacturer*, November 5, 2019, https://www.themanufacturer.com/articles/loreal-powers-its-rd-by-processing-50-million-pieces-of-data-a-day/.

33. Butler, "L'Oréal Powers Its R&D."

34. "L'Oréal Data-Driven Marketing & Digital Focus."

35. "How Open Science and External Innovation Are Transforming Drug Development," Stat, accessed March 10, 2020, https://www.statnews.com/sponsor/2018/08/30/transforming-drug-development-allergan/.

36. "Biotechs Investments Disrupt Big Pharma Business Model," *BNP Paribas*, December 11, 2019, https://group.bnpparibas/en/news/biotechs-investments-disrupt-big-pharma-business-model.

37. "Annual Report," GlaxoSmithKline, 2018, https://www.gsk.com/media/5347/strategic-report.pdf.

38. "GSK and 23andMe Sign Agreement to Leverage Genetic Insights for the Development of Novel Medicines," press release, July 25, 2018, https://www.gsk.com/en-gb/media/press-releases/gsk-and-23andme-sign-agreement-to-leverage-genetic-insights-for-the-development-of-novel-medicines/.

39. "Open Targets," Hyve, accessed March 10, 2020, https://thehyve.nl/solutions/open-targets/.

40. "About UK Biobank," Biobank, accessed March 10, 2020, https://www.ukbiobank.ac.uk/about-biobank-uk/.

41. "Siemens AG," *Encyclopaedia Britannica*, accessed March 10, 2020, https://www.britannica.com/topic/Siemens-AG.

42. "Siemens Sells Mobile Phone Biz to BenQ," *China Daily*, updated June 8, 2005, http://www.chinadaily.com.cn/english/doc/2005-06/08/content_449618.htm.

43. Dr. Horst Kayser, interview with BCG team, March 17, 2018; "History: Wind Power Pioneers," Siemens, accessed March 10, 2020, https://www.siemensgamesa.com /en-int/about-us/company-history.

44. Based on informal conversations with leaders at Siemens. For additional information, please see Eric Johnson, "A Big Brain for Power Plant Diagnostics," *Living Energy* 9 (December 2013): 65, https://assets.new.siemens.com/siemens/assets/api/uuid:dbfd4b 0d225b592bd2e6ded1c4210cfe2e403a8d/version:1533824147/power-plant-diagnostics -rds-living-energy-9.pdf.

45. "Annual Report 2019," Siemens, 2019, https://assets.new.siemens.com/siemens /assets/api/uuid:59a922d1-eca0-4e23-adef-64a05f0a8a61/siemens-ar2019.pdf; Georgina Prodhan, "Siemens Sees Scale, Data Privacy as Winners in Digital Race," Reuters, December 15, 2017, https://www.reuters.com/article/us-siemens-digital/siemens-sees -scale-data-privacy-as-winners-in-digital-race-idUSKBN1E90YY; "Siemens—Business Fact Sheets," Siemens, 2019, https://www.siemens.com/investor/pool/en/investor _relations/equity-story/Siemens-Business-Fact-Sheets.pdf.

46. Dr. Horst Kayser, interview with BCG team, March 17, 2018.

47. Schneider Electric, "Schneider Electric Launches Next Generation of EcoStruxure™, the Architecture and Platform for End-to-End IoT-Enabled Solutions at Scale," PR Newswire, November 29, 2016, https://www.prnewswire.com/news-releases /schneider-electric-launches-next-generation-of-ecostruxure-the-architecture-and -platform-for-end-to-end-iot-enabled-solutions-at-scale-300369412.html.

48. Schneider Electric, "Schneider Electric Launches."

49. "Ambitious Outlook. Positive Action. Full Accountability," Schneider Electric, 2018, https://www.se.com/ww/en/assets/564/document/69032/2018-annual-report.pdf; "Digital Innovations for a Sustainable World," Schneider Electric, 2019, https:// www.se.com/ww/en/assets/564/document/124836/annual-report-2019-en.pdf.

50. Schneider Electric, "Schneider Electric Launches New Digital Ecosystem to Drive Worldwide Economies of Scale for IoT Solutions," PR Newswire, April 1, 2019, https://www.prnewswire.com/news-releases/schneider-electric-launches-new-digital -ecosystem-to-drive-worldwide-economies-of-scale-for-iot-solutions-300821811 .html.

51. Herve Couriel, interview with BCG team, October 25, 2019.

52. Herve Couriel, interview with BCG team, October 25, 2019.

53. Herve Couriel, interview with BCG team, October 25, 2019.

54. "Where Problems Find Solutions," Schneider Electric Exchange, accessed March 11, 2020, https://exchange.se.com/.

55. Emmanuel Lagarrigue, interview with BCG team, October 30, 2019.

56. Herve Couriel, interview with BCG team, October 25, 2019.

57. According to one estimate, the global logistics market was worth estimated 4.7 trillion in 2018: "The Global Logistics Market Reached a Value of US$ 4,730 Billion in 2018 and Will Continue to Rise by 4.9% by 2024," Business Wire, July 3, 2019, https:// www.businesswire.com/news/home/20190703005488/en/Global-Logistics-Market -Reached-4730-Billion-2018.

58. For more, please see the company's website: http://www.flexport.com.

59. "How Gerber Gains End-to-End Supply Chain Visibility and Savings with Flexport," Flexport, accessed March 11, 2020, https://www.flexport.com/customers/gerber/; "How American Metalcraft Serves Up Digital Transformation with Flexport," Flexport, accessed March 11, 2020, https://www.flexport.com/customers/american-metalcraft/; "Leading Smart Travel Brand, Horizn Studios, Breathes New Life into a Centuries-Old Industry and Transforms Operations," Flexport, accessed April 3, 2020, https://www.flexport.com/customers/horizn-studios/.

60. Alex Konrad, "Freight Startup Flexport Hits $3.2 Billion Valuation After $1 Billion Investment Led by SoftBank," *Forbes*, February 21, 2019, https://www.forbes.com/sites/alexkonrad/2019/02/21/flexport-raises-1-billion-softbank/#430462ac5650.

61. "Digitalisation in the Energy Industry: Adapt, or Be Disrupted," Shell, March 5, 2019, https://www.shell.com/business-customers/lubricants-for-business/news-and-media-releases/2019/digitalisation-in-the-energy-industry.html.

62. "Revolutionary Wireless Telematics," Machine Max, accessed March 11, 2020, https://machinemax.com/.

63. Data taken from IDC's Global DataSphere, 2018.

64. Russell Stokes (VP, corporate strategy, Whirlpool), interview with author, June 12, 2019.

65. BCG analysis based on "Total Worldwide Software Revenue Market Share by Market," Gartner Report, April 2019.

66. "Mass Data Fragmentation: The Main Cause of 'Bad Data' and How to Take Control of It," Information Age, May 17, 2019, https://www.information-age.com/mass-data-fragmentation-123482521/.

67. "AI and Data Irony—Ferrari Without Fuel?" Data Quest, November 20, 2019, https://www.dqindia.com/ai-data-irony-ferrari-without-fuel/.

68. Alan Cohen, "The Mass Data Fragmentation Cleanup," *Forbes*, October 24, 2018, https://www.forbes.com/sites/forbestechcouncil/2018/10/24/the-mass-data-fragmentation-cleanup/#55a48cfa67a9.

Chapter 7: Get Focused, Fast, and Flat

1. "ByteDance," generated by PitchBook for Samridhi Agarwal, Boston Consulting Group Global, updated March 4, 2020; "About Us," ByteDance, accessed March 14, 2020, https://job.bytedance.com/en/.

2. Li Mojia (strategy director at ByteDance's Institute of Management Strategy), interview with BCG research team, August 22, 2019.

3. This paragraph is based on internal BCG research.

4. For this entire paragraph, I rely on Li Mojia, interview with BCG research team, August 22, 2019.

5. Material from this paragraph is based on research conducted by BCG's Bruce Henderson Institute.

6. Martin Danoesastro, "Nick Jue on Transforming ING Netherlands and Introducing an Agile Way of Working," BCG, July 17, 2017, https://www.bcg.com/publications/2017/technology-digital-financial-institutions-nick-jue-transforming-ing.aspx.

7. BCG analysis based on data from central banks, corporate websites, and the Economist Intelligence Unit's 2018 Report on Global Retail Banking.

8. Katrina Cuthell, "Many Consumers Trust Technology Companies More Than Banks," Bain, January 9, 2019, https://www.bain.com/insights/many-consumers-trust-technology-companies-more-than-banks-snap-chart/.

9. Erin Lyons, "RBS Takes Inspiration from Amazon and Uber as It Puts Focus on Customer Experience," Phvntom, October 3, 2018, https://phvntom.com/rbs-takes-inspiration-from-amazon-and-uber-as-it-puts-focus-on-customer-experience/.

10. BCG analysis based on data from BCG banking pools, Expand Fintech database, and Fintech Control Tower.

11. ING Investor Day Presentation (2019).

12. "'We Want to Be a Tech Company with a Banking License'—Ralph Hamers," ING, August 8, 2017, https://www.ing.com/Newsroom/News/We-want-to-be-a-tech-company-with-a-banking-license-Ralph-Hamers.htm.

13. Martin Danoesastro, "Nick Jue on Transforming ING Netherlands and Introducing an Agile Way of Working," BCG, July 17, 2017, https://www.bcg.com/publications/2017/technology-digital-financial-institutions-nick-jue-transforming-ing.aspx.

14. For a sober assessment of the matrix structure and its drawbacks dating from the 1990s, please see Stanley M. Davis and Paul R. Lawrence, "Problems of Matrix Organizations," *Harvard Business Review*, May 1978, https://hbr.org/1978/05/problems-of-matrix-organizations; Christopher A. Bartlett and Sumantra Ghoshal, "Matrix Management: Not a Structure, a Frame of Mind," *Harvard Business Review*, July–August 1990, https://hbr.org/1990/07/matrix-management-not-a-structure-a-frame-of-mind.

15. Global corporations today are beset by bureaucracy, or what colleagues of ours at BCG have termed *complicatedness*, defined as "the increase in the number of organizational structures, processes, procedures, decision-rights, metrics, scorecards, and committees that companies impose to manage escalating complexity in their external business environment" (Reinhard Messenböck et al., "Simplify First—Then Digitize," BCG, August 8, 2019, https://www.bcg.com/capabilities/change-management/simplify-first-then-digitize.aspx).

16. Martin Danoesastro (managing director and senior partner in the Boston Consulting Group's Amsterdam office), interview with BCG team, October 16, 2019.

17. See the ING Group's 2014 annual report, 184, downloaded April 19, 2020, at https://www.ing.com/web/file?uuid=9e4a52e6-1746-4a83-b31f-1c5978c8361c&owner=b03bc017-e0db-4b5d-abbf-003b12934429&contentid=33430.

18. Saabira Chaudhuri, "Outfoxed by Small-Batch Upstarts, Unilever Decides to Imitate Them," *Wall Street Journal*, January 2, 2018, https://www.wsj.com/articles/outfoxed-by-small-batch-upstarts-unilever-decides-to-imitate-them-1514910342.

19. "Making Sustainable Living Commonplace," Unilever (Annual Report and Accounts), annual report, 2017, 10, https://www.unilever.com/Images/ara-principle-risk-factors_tcm244-525944_en.pdf.

20. Sanjiv Mehta, interview with BCG team, July 24, 2019; Ajita Shashidhar, "How HUL Got Its Mojo Back," *Business Today*, August 12, 2018, https://www.businesstoday.in/magazine/cover-story/how-hul-got-its-mojo-back/story/280535.html.

21. "Making Sustainable Living Commonplace," Unilever, 2017, 10.

22. Sanjiv Mehta, interview with BCG team, July 24, 2019.

23. "Unilever Investor Event," Hindustan Unilever Limited, December 4, 2018, 23, https://www.hul.co.in/Images/hul-presentation-to-investors_tcm1255-529129_en.pdf.

24. "Unilever Investor Event," Hindustan Unilever Limited, 21.

25. Nitin Paranjpe, interview with BCG research team, July 10, 2019.

26. Nitin Paranjpe, interview with the authors, July 10, 2019.

27. "Making Sustainable Living Commonplace," Unilever, 2017.

28. "Making Sustainable Living Commonplace," Unilever (Annual Report and Accounts), 2016: 27, https://www.unilever.com/Images/unilever-annual-report-and-accounts-2016_tcm244-498880_en.pdf; "Purpose-Led, Future-Fit," Unilever (Annual Report and Accounts), 2019, https://www.unilever.com/Images/unilever-annual-report-and-accounts-2019_tcm244-547893_en.pdf.

29. Grant Freeland, "To Understand the Company of the Future, Head to a Jazz Club," *Forbes*, September 23, 2019, https://www.forbes.com/sites/grantfreeland/2019/09/23/to-understand-the-company-of-the-future-head-to-a-jazz-club/#6e825ab32785.

30. Darrell K. Rigby, Jeff Sutherland, and Hirotaka Takeuchi, "Embracing Agile," *Harvard Business Review*, May 2016, https://hbr.org/2016/05/embracing-agile.

31. For more on agile, see Michael Sherman et al., "Taking Agile Way Beyond Software," BCG, July 19, 2017, https://www.bcg.com/publications/2017/technology-digital-organization-taking-agile-way-beyond-software.aspx.

32. Marco Nink, "To Be Agile, You Need Fewer Processes and Policies," Gallup, January 18, 2019, https://www.gallup.com/workplace/246074/agile-need-fewer-processes-policies.aspx.

33. BCG analysis based on data found in ING annual reports spanning 2014–2019.

34. "Our Organisation," Buurtzorg, accessed March 15, 2020, https://www.buurtzorg.com/about-us/our-organisation/; "Buurtzorg: Revolutionising Home Care in the Netherlands," Center for Public Impact, November 15, 2018, https://www.centreforpublicimpact.org/case-study/buurtzorg-revolutionising-home-care-netherlands/.

35. "Our Organisation"; Sofia Widén, Malin Lidforss, and William A. Haseltine, "Buurtzorg: A Neighborhood Model of Care: Interviews with Jos de Blok and Gertje van Roessel," Access Health International, April 2016; Stevan Ćirković, "Buurtzorg: Revolutionising Home Care in the Netherlands."

36. Jaap van Ede, "The Self-Steering and Care-Driven Teams of Buurtzorg," Business Improvement, 2014, https://www.business-improvement.eu/lead_change/Buurtzorg_autonomous_teams.php; Jef J.J. van den Hout and Orin C. Davis, *Team Flow: The Psychology of Optimal Collaboration* (Cham, Switzerland: Springer: 2019), 80–81.

37. Widén, Lidforss, and Haseltine, "Buurtzorg," 1.

38. "Buurtzorg's Healthcare Revolution: 14,000 Employees, 0 Managers, Sky-High Engagement," Corporate Rebels, accessed March 15, 2020, https://corporate-rebels.com/buurtzorg/.

39. Blake Morgan, "How Fidelity Creates Its Vision for Customer Experience," *Forbes*, April 5, 2016, https://www.forbes.com/sites/blakemorgan/2016/04/05/how-fidelity-creates-amazing-customer-experiences/#3446ae7159c7; Robin Wigglesworth,

"Fidelity's Search for the Technology of Tomorrow," *Financial Times*, October 19, 2019, https://www.ft.com/content/b90cbc8a-ef45-11e9-bfa4-b25f11f42901.

40. "Internal Auditing Around the World, Volume 15: Fidelity Investments," Protiviti, accessed June 11, 2020, https://www.protiviti.com/US-en/insights/iaworld-fidelity-investments.

41. For more on platforms, please see Allison Bailey et al., "Organizing for the Future with Tech, Talent, and Purpose," BCG, September 16, 2019, https://www.bcg.com/publications/2019/organizing-future-tech-talent-purpose.aspx; Rich Hutchinson, Lionel Aré, Justin Rose, and Allison Bailey, "The Bionic Company," BCG, November 7, 2019, https://www.bcg.com/publications/2019/bionic-company.aspx.

42. Robert Marques, interview with BCG research team, March 10, 2020.

43. This paragraph draws from internal BCG research and analysis.

44. Mary Jo Kreitzer et al., "Buurtzorg Nederland: A Global Model of Social Innovation, Change, and Whole-Systems Healing," *Global Advances in Health and Medicine* 4, no. 1 (January 2015).

45. "What Is R² Data Labs?" Rolls-Royce, accessed March 15, 2020, https://www.rolls-royce.com/products-and-services/r2datalabs.aspx.

46. "R² Data Labs Ecosystem," Rolls-Royce, accessed March 20, 2020, https://www.rolls-royce.com/products-and-services/ecosystem.aspx.

47. Rich Hutchinson et al., "The Bionic Company," BCG, November 7, 2019, https://www.bcg.com/publications/2019/bionic-company.aspx.

48. Jim Hemerling et al., "It's Not a Digital Transformation Without a Digital Culture," BCG, April 13, 2018, https://www.bcg.com/publications/2018/not-digital-transformation-without-digital-culture.aspx.

49. Hemerling et al., "It's Not a Digital Transformation."

50. Deborah Lovich et al., "Agile Starts—or Stops—at the Top," BCG, May 17, 2018, https://www.bcg.com/publications/2018/agile-starts-or-stops-at-the-top.aspx.

51. Allison Bailey et al., "Organizing for the Future with Tech, Talent, and Purpose," BCG, September 16, 2019, https://www.bcg.com/publications/2019/organizing-future-tech-talent-purpose.aspx.

52. Bob Black, interview with BCG team, January 13, 2020.

53. Lars Marquardt et al., "Blending Old and New Ways of Working to Drive Digital Value," BCG, October 21, 2019, https://www.bcg.com/publications/2019/blending-old-new-ways-working-drive-digital-value.aspx.

54. Martin Danoesastro, interview with BCG team, October 16, 2019.

Chapter 8: Thrive with Talent

1. "Unilever Opens €50m Leadership Development Facility," Unilever, June 28, 2013, https://www.unilever.com.sg/news/press-releases/2013/leadership-development-facility.html.

2. Stephen Remedios, "What Goes into Building a CEO Factory?" Management Innovation Exchange, July 14, 2013, https://www.managementexchange.com/story/what-goes-building-ceo-factory; Sudhir Sitapati, "How Hindustan Unilever Became a

CEO Factory and a Company with Good Middle-Class Values," Print, January 5, 2020, https://theprint.in/pageturner/excerpt/how-hindustan-unilever-became-a-ceo-factory -and-company-with-middle-class-values/344917/.

3. BCG research and analysis.

4. Angus Loten, "America's Got Talent, Just Not Enough in IT," *Wall Street Journal*, October 15, 2019, https://www.wsj.com/articles/americas-got-talent-just-not-enough -in-it-11571168626.

5. "Future of Work," Korn Ferry, accessed March 17, 2020, https://www.kornferry .com/challenges/future-of-work.

6. J. Puckett et al., "Fixing the Global Skills Mismatch," BCG, January 15, 2020, https://www.bcg.com/publications/2020/fixing-global-skills-mismatch.aspx.

7. "How to Future-Proof Your Workforce," BCG, accessed March 17, 2020, https:// www.bcg.com/featured-insights/how-to/workforce-of-the-future.aspx.

8. J. Puckett et al., "Fixing the Global Skills Mismatch," BCG, January 15, 2020, https://www.bcg.com/publications/2020/fixing-global-skills-mismatch.aspx.

9. Rainer Strack et al., "Decoding Digital Talent," BCG, May 15, 2019, https://www .bcg.com/publications/2019/decoding-digital-talent.aspx.

10. Shawn Achor et al., "9 Out of 10 People Are Willing to Earn Less Money to Do More-Meaningful Work," *Harvard Business Review*, November 6, 2018, https:// hbr.org/2018/11/9-out-of-10-people-are-willing-to-earn-less-money-to-do-more -meaningful-work.

11. For this paragraph, we rely on Leena Nair, interview with BCG team, June 17, 2019.

12. Kathleen Hogan, "When People Are the Priority, Everything Else Falls into Place," LinkedIn, June 4, 2019, https://www.linkedin.com/pulse/when-people-priority -everything-else-falls-place-kathleen-hogan/.

13. Hogan, "When People Are the Priority."

14. Angus Loten, "'Talent War' at Home Prompts U.S. Employers to Take Another Look Abroad," *Wall Street Journal*, May 30, 2019, https://www.wsj.com/articles/talent -war-at-home-prompts-u-s-employers-to-take-another-look-abroad-11559257791.

15. "iCIMS Survey Finds Increased Acceptance of Tech Candidates with Non-Traditional Educations," Globe Newswire, September 17, 2018, https://www.globenews wire.com/news-release/2018/09/17/1571757/0/en/iCIMS-Survey-Finds-Increased -Acceptance-of-Tech-Candidates-with-Non-Traditional-Educations.html.

16. Rainer Strack et al., "How to Gain and Develop Digital Talent and Skills," BCG, July 19, 2017, https://www.bcg.com/publications/2017/people-organization-technology -how-gain-develop-digital-talent-skills.aspx.

17. "Leap: A Modern Apprenticeship," Microsoft, accessed March 17, 2020, https:// www.industryexplorers.com/.

18. Sue Shellenbarger, "Make Your Job Application Robot-Proof," *Wall Street Journal*, December 16, 2019, https://www.wsj.com/articles/make-your-job-application-robot -proof-11576492201; "Balancing the Risks, Rewards of People Analytics," *Wall Street Journal*, May 30, 2018, https://deloitte.wsj.com/cio/2018/05/30/balancing-the-risks -rewards-of-people-analytics/.

19. Ingrid Lunden, "GM Confirms Sidecar Acquisition as Auto Makers Take Tech Ambitions up a Gear," TechCrunch, January 19, 2016, https://techcrunch.com/2016/01/19/whos-driving/.

20. Sandeep Soni, "Acqui-Hiring: The New Normal in Talent Acquisition," *Entrepreneur*, March 20, 2015, https://www.entrepreneur.com/article/248598.

21. "Wipro's Mantra: Acquire to Grow," M&A Critique, accessed March 18, 2020, https://mnacritique.mergersindia.com/wipro-technologies-growth-by-acquisition/.

22. "Wipro to Acquire US-Based ITI for USD 45 Million," *Economic Times*, January 5, 2019, https://economictimes.indiatimes.com/tech/ites/wipro-to-acquire-us-based-iti-for-usd-45-million/articleshow/69664283.cms?from=mdr.

23. Andrew Karpie, "Wipro Acquires Appirio for $500M to Reach for the Cloud, Leverage Power of the Crowd," Spend Matters, October 21, 2016, https://spendmatters.com/2016/10/21/wipro-acquires-appirio-500m-reach-cloud-leverage-power-crowd/; Chris Barbin, "One Year Later: Appirio (A Wipro Company)," Appirio, December 12, 2017, https://hub.appirio.com/cloud-powered-blog/one-year-later-appirio-a-wipro-company.

24. Wipro, "Wipro Digital to Enhance Digital Transformation Capability with Designit," press release, July 9, 2015, https://www.wipro.com/en-IN/newsroom/press-releases/2015/wipro-digital-to-enhance-digital-transformation-capability-with-/.

25. Teressa Iezzi, "Unilever Looks to Forge New Partnerships with Startups with the Launch of the Foundry," *Fast Company*, May 21, 2014, https://www.fastcompany.com/3030940/unilever-looks-to-forge-new-partnerships-with-startups-with-the-launch-of-the-foundry.

26. "Unilever's Platform for Partnering with Start-Ups to Accelerate Innovation on a Global Scale," Unilever Foundry, accessed March 18, 2020, https://www.theunileverfoundry.com/.

27. "What Corporate Incubators and Accelerators Can Mean for Your Business," *Entrepreneur*, February 15, 2017, https://www.entrepreneur.com/article/287495.

28. "Here's How Large Firms Can Innovate by Collaborating with Startups," *Forbes*, May 10, 2018, https://www.forbes.com/sites/iese/2018/05/10/heres-how-large-firms-can-innovate-by-collaborating-with-startups/#30a166de2241.

29. Judith Wallenstein et al., "The New Freelancers: Tapping Talent in the Gig Economy," BCG Henderson Institute, January 2019, http://image-src.bcg.com/Images/BCG-The-New-Freelancers-Jan-2019_tcm9-211593.pdf.

30. Judith Wallenstein et al., "The New Freelancers," 5.

31. For these figures and more information, please see http://www.tongal.com.

32. Tongal.com, accessed January 19, 2020.

33. "Unilever Launches New AI-Powered Talent Marketplace," Unilever, June 24, 2019, https://www.unilever.com/news/press-releases/2019/unilever-launches-ai-powered-talent-marketplace.html.

34. Shaun Sutner, "New Kronos Headquarters Design Mirrors Reinvention Play," Search HR Software, May 29, 2018, https://searchhrsoftware.techtarget.com/feature/New-Kronos-headquarters-design-mirrors-reinvention-play.

35. For coverage of the company's Dublin office, for instance, please see "First Look: From Gyms and Music Rooms to Baristas and Yoga . . . Inside LinkedIn's New €85m EMEA HQ Office in Dublin," *Independent*, September 18, 2017, https://www.independent.ie/business/technology/first-look-from-gyms-and-music-rooms-to-baristas-and-yogainside-linkedins-new-85m-emea-hq-office-in-dublin-36142701.html.

36. Katie Jacobs, "Dogs in the Office: How Nestlé Makes It Work," *HR Magazine*, February 11, 2016, https://www.hrmagazine.co.uk/article-details/dogs-in-the-office-how-nestle-makes-it-work-1; Grace Newton, "Nestle in York Now Lets Staff Take Bring Their Dogs to Work," *Yorkshire Post*, April 4, 2019, https://www.yorkshirepost.co.uk/news/nestle-in-york-now-lets-staff-take-bring-their-dogs-to-work-1-9691747.

37. Alexander Purdy (former John Deere employee), interview with BCG team, October 10, 2019.

38. "No One Reaches More Machines with Smarter Technology Than John Deere," John Deere, accessed March 20, 2020, https://www.deere.com/en/our-company/john-deere-careers/work-here/isg/.

39. Shawn Achor et al., "9 Out of 10 People Are Willing to Earn Less Money to Do More-Meaningful Work," *Harvard Business Review*, November 6, 2018, https://hbr.org/2018/11/9-out-of-10-people-are-willing-to-earn-less-money-to-do-more-meaningful-work.

40. Leena Nair, interview with BCG team, June 17, 2019.

41. "People with Purpose Thrive," Unilever, accessed March 19, 2020, https://careers.unilever.com/global/en/people-with-purpose-thrive.

42. Leena Nair, interview with BCG team, June 17, 2019.

43. "Project #ShowUs: Dove's Disruptive New Partnership to Shatter Stereotypes," Unilever, May 15, 2019, https://www.unilever.com/news/news-and-features/Feature-article/2019/project-showus-doves-disruptive-new-partnership-to-shatter-stereotypes.html.

44. Leena Nair, "Have You Found Your Purpose?" Medium, November 22, 2018, https://medium.com/@leenanairHR/have-you-found-your-purpose-heres-how-4d93f7bccaa9.

45. Leena Nair, interview with BCG team, June 17, 2019.

46. Jörgen Sundberg, "How Unilever Developed a New EVP and Employer Brand," Link Humans, accessed March 20, 2020, https://linkhumans.com/unilever/.

47. "LinkedIn," Tulsa Marketing Online, accessed March 19, 2020, https://www.tulsamarketingonline.com/linkedin-lists-its-10-most-followed-pages/. Their rankings oscillate, but as of March 25, 2020, they counted 9.4 million followers on LinkedIn ("Unilever," LinkedIn, accessed March 26, 2020, https://www.linkedin.com/company/unilever/).

48. Meghan French Dunbar, "How Nature Became the World's Largest B Corp—and How Its Helping," Conscious Company Media, January 5, 2016, https://consciouscompanymedia.com/sustainable-business/how-natura-became-the-worlds-largest-b-corp-and-how-its-helping/; Daniel Azevedo (BCG managing director and partner and CCO for Natura), interview with BCG team, July 11, 2019.

49. Keyvan Macedo, interview with BCG team, December 20, 2019.

50. Keyvan Macedo, interview with BCG team, December 20, 2019.

51. Carol Fulp, *Success Through Diversity: Why the Most Inclusive Companies Will Win* (Boston: Beacon Press, 2018). Research has found a clear connection exists between diversity and engagement levels. In companies with low engagement scores, for instance, a greater gender gap exists ("BCG's Gender Diversity Research: By the Numbers," BCG, accessed March 19, 2020, https://www.bcg.com/en-us/capabilities/diversity-inclusion/gender-diversity-research-by-numbers.aspx).

52. Frances Brooks et al., "Winning the Race for Women in Digital," BCG, November 28, 2018, https://www.bcg.com/en-us/publications/2018/winning-race-women-digital.aspx.

53. Ruth Umoh, "Meet America's Best Employers for Diversity 2020," *Forbes*, January 21, 2020, https://www.forbes.com/sites/ruthumoh/2020/01/21/meet-americas-best-employers-for-diversity-2020/#31144fcd5739.

54. Rainer Strack et al., "Decoding Digital Talent."

55. Orsolya Kovacs-Ondrejkovic et al., "Decoding Global Trends in Upskilling and Reskilling," BCG, November 2019, https://www.bcg.com/publications/2019/decoding-global-trends-upskilling-reskilling.aspx.

56. Bob Black, interview with BCG team, January 13, 2020.

57. Laura Heller, "Walmart Launches Tech Incubator Dubbed Store No. 8," *Forbes*, March 20, 2017, https://www.forbes.com/sites/lauraheller/2017/03/20/walmart-launches-tech-incubator-store-no-8/#13ee844e2dcb.

58. Adam Kearney, "We Digitized Google's Peer Recognition," Medium, May 2, 2016, https://medium.com/@K3ARN3Y/how-google-does-peer-recognition-188446e329dd; John Quinn, "A Look at Google's Peer-to-Peer Bonus System," Bonusly (blog), accessed March 20, 2020, https://blog.bonus.ly/a-look-at-googles-peer-to-peer-bonus-system/.

59. Børge Brende, "We Need a Reskilling Revolution. Here's How to Make It Happen," World Economic Forum, April 15, 2019, https://www.weforum.org/agenda/2019/04/skills-jobs-investing-in-people-inclusive-growth/; "The Future of Jobs Report," Economic Forum, 2018, ix, http://www3.weforum.org/docs/WEF_Future_of_Jobs_2018.pdf.

60. "The Future of Jobs Report," 12.

61. "The Future of Jobs Report," 13.

62. Orsolya Kovacs-Ondrejkovic et al., "Decoding Global Trends."

63. Orsolya Kovacs-Ondrejkovic, "What Would You Do to Stay Relevant at Work?" LinkedIn, November 7, 2019, https://www.linkedin.com/pulse/what-would-you-do-stay-relevant-work-orsolya-kovacs-ondrejkovic/.

64. In fact, approximately two-thirds of employees "will experience significant change in their job profiles in the next five years" (Vikram Bhalla et al., "A CEO's Guide to Talent Management Today," BCG, April 10, 2018, https://www.bcg.com/publications/2018/ceo-guide-talent-management-today.aspx).

65. "What Is FutureSkills?" FutureSkills, accessed March 26, 2020, http://futureskills.nasscom.in/about-futureskill.html#whyFutureSkill. NASSCOM, the industry's trade association, identified ten emerging technologies ("What Is FutureSkills?").

66. "NASSCOM," NASSCOM, July 17, 2019, accessed March 21, 2020, https://www.nasscom.in/sites/default/files/media_pdf/pr_hr_summit%202019.pdf.

67. "What Is FutureSkills," FutureSkills, accessed March 21, 2020, http://futureskills.nasscom.in/about-futureskill.html#whyFutureSkill.

68. "Nasscom," Nasscom, July 17, 2019, accessed March 21, 2020, https://www.nasscom.in/sites/default/files/media_pdf/pr_hr_summit%202019.pdf; Venkatesh Ganesh and KV Kurmanath, "Modi Launches Nasscom's 'Future Skills' Platform," *Hindu Business Line*, February 19, 2018, https://www.thehindubusinessline.com/info-tech/modi-launches-nasscoms-future-skills-platform/article22800117.ece.

69. "How Does It Work," FutureSkills, accessed March 21, 2020, http://futureskills.nasscom.in/how-does-it-work.html.

70. Ganesh and Kurmanath, "Modi Launches Nasscom's 'Future Skills' Platform."

71. "FutureSkills: A NASSCOM Initiative," NASSCOM, accessed March 26, 2020, https://www.nasscom.in/sites/default/files/FutureSkills_An_Industry_Response.pdf; Shilpa Patankar, "Wipro, Nassscom Tie-Up for Future Skills Platform," *Times of India*, December 21, 2019, https://timesofindia.indiatimes.com/business/india-business/wipro-nassscom-tie-up-for-future-skills-platform/articleshow/72914868.cms.

72. Paragraph based on BCG research and analysis.

73. Debbie Weinstein, "How L'Oréal Is Preparing for the Next Evolution of Digital Marketing," Think with Google, June 2018, https://www.thinkwithgoogle.com/intl/en-aunz/advertising-channels/video/how-loreal-preparing-next-evolution-digital-marketing/.

74. "AT&T Invests $1 Billion in Employee Reskilling," Aspen Institute, March 12, 2018, https://www.aspeninstitute.org/of-interest/upskilling-news-att-invests-1-billion-employee-reskilling/.

75. Susan Caminiti, "AT&T's $1 Billion Gambit: Retraining Nearly Half Its Workforce for Jobs of the Future," CNBC, March 13, 2018, https://www.cnbc.com/2018/03/13/atts-1-billion-gambit-retraining-nearly-half-its-workforce.html.

76. Aaron Pressman, "Can AT&T Retrain 100,000 People?" *Fortune*, March 13, 2017, https://fortune.com/longform/att-hr-retrain-employees-jobs-best-companies/.

77. Caminiti, "AT&T's $1 Billion Gambit."

78. Caminiti, "AT&T's $1 Billion Gambit."

79. Kate Rogers, "Manufacturers to Spend $26.2 Billion on 'Upskilling' in 2020 to Attract and Keep Workers," CNBC, January 17, 2020, https://www.cnbc.com/2020/01/17/manufacturers-to-spend-26point2-billion-on-upskilling-workers-in-2020.html.

80. Scott Snyder, "Talent, Not Technology, Is the Key to Success in a Digital Future," World Economic Forum, January 11, 2019, https://www.weforum.org/agenda/2019/01/talent-not-technology-is-the-key-to-success-in-a-digital-future/.

81. Rich Hutchinson et al., "The Bionic Company," BCG, November 7, 2019, https://www.bcg.com/publications/2019/bionic-company.aspx.

82. Bob Desimone, "What High-Performance Workplaces Do Differently," Gallup, December 12, 2019, https://www.gallup.com/workplace/269405/high-performance-workplaces-differently.aspx.

83. Shawn Achor et al., "9 Out of 10 People Are Willing to Earn Less Money to Do More-Meaningful Work," *Harvard Business Review*, November 6, 2018, https://

hbr.org/2018/11/9-out-of-10-people-are-willing-to-earn-less-money-to-do-more
-meaningful-work.

84. Charles Mitchell et al., "The CEO View of Risks and Opportunities in 2020,"
Conference Board, accessed March 21, 2020, https://files.constantcontact.com
/ff18da33701/9f112366-808b-4de4-b342-60b0f843784a.pdf.

85. "Key Skills Needed to Survive the 21st Century," Jobiness (blog), January 14,
2019, http://blog.jobiness.com/key-skills-needed-to-survive-the-21st-century/.

Chapter 9: Embrace Always-On Transformation

1. N. Chandrasekaran, interview with BCG team, January 14, 2020.

2. David Leonard and Claude Coltea, "Most Change Initiatives Fail—but They
Don't Have To," Gallup, May 24, 2013, https://news.gallup.com/businessjournal/162707
/change-initiatives-fail-don.aspx.

3. Data derived from a search on the S&P Capital IQ database.

4. "Microsoft Market Cap 2006–2019," Macrotrends, accessed March 25, 2020,
https://www.macrotrends.net/stocks/charts/MSFT/microsoft/market-cap.

5. Rolf Harms (general manager, strategy and acquisitions, at Microsoft), interview
with BCG team, September 2019.

6. Satya Nadella, *Hit Refresh: The Quest to Rediscover Microsoft's Soul and Imagine a
Better Future for Everyone* (New York: Harper Business, 2017), 66.

7. Eugene Kim, "Microsoft Has a Strange New Mission Statement," Business
Insider, June 25, 2015, https://www.businessinsider.com/microsoft-ceo-satya-nadella
-new-company-mission-internal-email-2015-6.

8. "Annual Report 2017," Microsoft, accessed Mach 25, 2020, https://www.microsoft
.com/investor/reports/ar17/index.html.

9. Krzysztof Majdan and Michał Wasowski, "We Sat Down with Microsoft's
CEO to Discuss the Past, Present and Future of the Company," Business Insider,
April 20, 2017, https://www.businessinsider.com/satya-nadella-microsoft-ceo-qa-2017
-4?IR=T.

10. Jordan Novet, "How Satya Nadella Tripled Microsoft's Stock Price in Just Over
Four Years," CNBC, July 18, 2018, https://www.cnbc.com/2018/07/17/how-microsoft
-has-evolved-under-satya-nadella.html; Matt Asay, "Who Really Contributes to Open
Source," InfoWorld, February 7, 2018, https://www.infoworld.com/article/3253948
/who-really-contributes-to-open-source.html#tk.twt_ifw.

11. Ron Miller, "After 5 Years, Microsoft CEO Satya Nadella Has Transformed
More Than the Stock Price," TechCrunch, February 4, 2019, https://techcrunch.com
/2019/02/04/after-5-years-microsoft-ceo-satya-nadella-has-transformed-more-than
-the-stock-price/.

12. Austin Carr and Dina Bass, "The Most Valuable Company (for Now) Is Having
a Nadellaissance," Bloomberg, May 2, 2019, https://www.bloomberg.com/news/features
/2019-05-02/satya-nadella-remade-microsoft-as-world-s-most-valuable-company.

13. Data derived from the S&P capital IQ database and the BCG ValueScience
Center.

14. This chapter draws heavily on Jim Hemerling, Julie Kilmann, and Dave Matthews, "The Head, Heart, and Hands of Transformation," Boston Consulting Group, November 5, 2018, https://www.bcg.com/publications/2018/head-heart-hands-transformation .aspx. The conceptual framework developed in this chapter originally appeared there, and we've also borrowed terminology where necessary to convey key ideas. This chapter also draws concepts and phrases from an in-person presentation Hemerling has given called "The Head, Heart, and Hands of Transformation."

15. Hemerling, Kilmann, and Matthews, "The Head, Heart, and Hands of Transformation."

16. Patti Sanchez, "The Secret to Leading Organizational Change Is Empathy," *Harvard Business Review*, December 20, 2018, https://hbr.org/2018/12/the-secret-to -leading-organizational-change-is-empathy.

17. Hemerling, Kilmann, and Matthews, "The Head, Heart, and Hands of Transformation."

18. Cathy Carlisi et al., "Purpose with the Power to Transform Your Organization," BCG, May 15, 2017, https://www.bcg.com/en-us/publications/2017/transformation -behavior-culture-purpose-power-transform-organization.aspx.

19. Nadella, *Hit Refresh*, 68.

20. Nadella, *Hit Refresh*, 75.

21. Nadella, *Hit Refresh*, 79.

22. Nadella, *Hit Refresh*, 79–80.

23. Cathy Carlisi et al., "Purpose with the Power to Transform."

24. See Jim Hemerling et al., "It's Not a Digital Transformation Without a Digital Culture," BCG, April 13, 2018, https://www.bcg.com/publications/2018/not-digital -transformation-without-digital-culture.aspx.

25. Nadella, *Hit Refresh*, 100.

26. Nadella, *Hit Refresh*, 102–103.

27. Rolf Harms, interview with BCG team, September 2019.

28. Rolf Harms, interview with BCG team, September 2019.

29. Nadella, *Hit Refresh*, 118–120.

30. Simone Stolzoff, "How Do You Turn Around the Culture of a 130,000-Person Company? Ask Satya Nadella," Quartz, accessed March 25, 2020, https://qz.com/work /1539071/how-microsoft-ceo-satya-nadella-rebuilt-the-company-culture/.

31. Nadella, *Hit Refresh*, 9–10.

32. Sandra J. Sucher and Shalene Gupta, "Layoffs That Don't Break Your Company," *Harvard Business Review*, May–June 2018, https://hbr.org/2018/05/layoffs-that-dont -break-your-company.

33. Sandra Sucher, "There's a Better Way to Do Layoffs: What Nokia Learned, the Hard Way," LinkedIn, May 3, 2019, https://www.linkedin.com/pulse/theres-better-way -do-layoffs-what-nokia-learned-hard-sandra-sucher/.

34. Sucher and Gupta, "Layoffs That Don't Break Your Company."

35. Sucher, "There's a Better Way to Do Layoffs."

36. Sucher, "There's a Better Way to Do Layoffs."

37. Sucher, "There's a Better Way to Do Layoffs."

38. Sucher, "There's a Better Way to Do Layoffs."

39. Sucher, "There's a Better Way to Do Layoffs."

40. BCG analysis based on data from the S&P Capital IQ database.

41. John Callaham, "Microsoft Is Helping Fund Startups Created by Laid Off Smartphone Workers in Finland," Windows Central, August 2, 2016, https://www.windowscentral.com/microsoft-tries-help-laid-smartphone-workers-finland-find-new-jobs.

42. Gerard O'Dwyer, "Finland's IT Sector Recovers After Break-Up of Nokia," Computer Weekly, December 12, 2018, https://www.computerweekly.com/news/252454294/Finlands-IT-sector-recovers-after-break-up-of-Nokia.

43. O'Dwyer, "Finland's IT Sector Recovers."

44. Jay Yarrow, "Microsoft's CEO Sent Out a Giant Manifesto to Employees About the Future of the Company," Business Insider, July 10, 2014, https://www.businessinsider.com/microsofts-ceo-email-2014-7.

45. Samantha McDonald, "Nike to Open Paris Flagship in the Most Expensive Building on the Champs-Élysées," Footwear News, October 8, 2019, https://footwearnews.com/2019/business/retail/nike-champs-elysees-headquarters-house-of-innovation-paris-1202852317/.

46. Hilary Milnes, "In Effort to Grow Direct Sales, Nike Integrated Its App Strategy into Its Stores," Digiday, March 26, 2019, https://digiday.com/retail/nike-integrated-app-strategy-stores/.

47. Khadeeja Safdar, "Nike's Strategy to Get a Lot More Personal with Its Customers," Wall Street Journal, March 13, 2019, https://www.wsj.com/articles/nikes-strategy-to-get-a-lot-more-personal-with-its-customers-11557799501.

48. Morgan Forde, "Company of the Year: Nike," Supply Chain Dive, December 9, 2019, https://www.supplychaindive.com/news/nike-supply-chain-Celect-dive-awards/566234/.

49. Alfonso Segura, "The Fashion Retailer," Fashion Retail Blog, April 16, 2018, https://fashionretail.blog/2018/04/16/5015/.

50. BCG analysis of data from S&P Capital IQ and BCG ValueScience Center.

51. Martin Reeves et al., "Preemptive Transformation: Fix It Before It Breaks," BCG Henderson Institute, August 17, 2018, https://www.bcg.com/publications/2018/preemptive-transformation-fix-it-before-it-breaks.aspx.

52. Reeves et al., "Preemptive Transformation."

53. Polly Mosendz, "Microsoft's CEO Sent a 3,187-Word Memo and We Read It So You Don't Have To," Atlantic, July 10, 2014, https://www.theatlantic.com/technology/archive/2014/07/microsofts-ceo-sent-a-3187-word-memo-and-we-read-it-so-you-dont-have-to/374230/.

54. Steve Denning, "How Microsoft Vanquished Bureaucracy with Agile," Forbes, August 23, 2019, https://www.forbes.com/sites/stevedenning/2019/08/23/how-microsoft-vanquished-bureaucracy-with-agile/#5d26bb3c6f58.

55. Steve Denning, "Surprise: Microsoft Is Agile," Forbes, October 27, 2015, https://www.forbes.com/sites/stevedenning/2015/10/27/surprise-microsoft-is-agile/#45dd014a2867.

56. Mosendz, "Microsoft's CEO Sent a 3,187-Word Memo."

57. Jim Hemerling, Julie Kilmann, and Dave Matthews, "The Head, Heart, and Hands of Transformation," BCG, November 5, 2018, https://www.bcg.com/publications /2018/head-heart-hands-transformation.aspx.

58. We've borrowed these questions, with some adaptation, from a presentation delivered by one of us (Jim Hemerling).

Beyond Great Leadership

1. Roland Busch, interview with BCG team, February 17, 2020.

2. Satya Nadella, interview conducted by BCG, Seattle, Washington, June 4, 2019.

3. Roberto Marques, interview with BCG team, March 10, 2020.

4. Roberto Marques, interview with BCG team, March 10, 2020.

5. N. Chandrasekaran, interview with BCG team, September 17, 2019.

6. Roberto Marques, interview with BCG team, March 10, 2020.

7. Lars Fæste et al., "Transformation: The Imperative to Change," BCG, November 3, 2014, https://www.bcg.com/en-us/publications/2014/people-organization -transformation-imperative-change.aspx.

8. N. Chandrasekaran, interview with BCG team, September 17, 2019.

INDEX

Dr. Arindam Bhattacharya is senior partner at Boston Consulting Group's New Delhi office. He has been the head of BCG India; is the cofounder and fellow of the BCG Henderson Institute, BCG's thought leadership arm; and is a member of leadership team of Global Advantage practice. He has been researching, writing, and consulting on the subject of globalization and global business models and has given a TED talk on the topic. He has coauthored the book *Globality: Competing with Everyone from Everywhere for Everything*, named by the *Economist* to its Best of the Year list.

Dr. Nikolaus Lang is senior partner at Boston Consulting Group's Munich office and global leader of BCG's Global Advantage practice, supporting clients on an array of globalization-related topics, ranging from geopolitics and trade to joint ventures and digital ecosystems. Dr. Lang is BCG's foremost expert on mobility, connectivity, and self-driving vehicles. For the past years, he has led BCG's collaboration with the World Economic Forum on the future of mobility, helping oversee the piloting and launch of autonomous vehicles in the city of Boston.

Jim Hemerling is senior partner at Boston Consulting Group's San Francisco office and a leader in the firm's People & Organization and Transformation Practices. He has been the leader of BCG Greater China and is a fellow of BCG Henderson Institute. His work with clients and his research focus on holistic, human-centric approaches to organizational transformation. He speaks often on the topic and has given a widely viewed TED talk titled, "5 Ways to Lead in an Era of Constant Change."

PublicAffairs is a publishing house founded in 1997. It is a tribute to the standards, values, and flair of three persons who have served as mentors to countless reporters, writers, editors, and book people of all kinds, including me.

I. F. STONE, proprietor of *I. F. Stone's Weekly*, combined a commitment to the First Amendment with entrepreneurial zeal and reporting skill and became one of the great independent journalists in American history. At the age of eighty, Izzy published *The Trial of Socrates*, which was a national bestseller. He wrote the book after he taught himself ancient Greek.

BENJAMIN C. BRADLEE was for nearly thirty years the charismatic editorial leader of *The Washington Post*. It was Ben who gave the *Post* the range and courage to pursue such historic issues as Watergate. He supported his reporters with a tenacity that made them fearless and it is no accident that so many became authors of influential, best-selling books.

ROBERT L. BERNSTEIN, the chief executive of Random House for more than a quarter century, guided one of the nation's premier publishing houses. Bob was personally responsible for many books of political dissent and argument that challenged tyranny around the globe. He is also the founder and longtime chair of Human Rights Watch, one of the most respected human rights organizations in the world.

• • •

For fifty years, the banner of Public Affairs Press was carried by its owner Morris B. Schnapper, who published Gandhi, Nasser, Toynbee, Truman, and about 1,500 other authors. In 1983, Schnapper was described by *The Washington Post* as "a redoubtable gadfly." His legacy will endure in the books to come.

Peter Osnos, *Founder*

Would you like your people to read this book?

If you would like to discuss how you could bring these ideas to your team, we would love to hear from you. Our titles are available at competitive discounts when purchased in bulk across both physical and digital formats. We can offer bespoke editions featuring corporate logos, customized covers, or letters from company directors in the front matter can also be created in line with your special requirements.

We work closely with leading experts and organizations to bring forward-thinking ideas to a global audience. Our books are designed to help you be more successful in work and life.

For further information, or to request a catalogue, please contact: **business@johnmurrays.co.uk**

Nicholas Brealey Publishing is an imprint of John Murray Press.